The Early Transnational Chinese Cinema Industry

Based on extensive original research, including in studio archives, industrial surveys, official records, trade journals, and English and Chinese newspapers, this book explores the role of the American film industry in the development of cinema in China. It examines the Chinese industry's response to the American industry and the consequences of this response. It also considers the attitudes of Chinese film practitioners towards Hollywood and the contribution of those figures who acted as intermediaries between the two industries. Overall, the book casts much new light on the early development of the film industry in China and demonstrates the huge influence Hollywood had on it.

Yongchun Fu is an associate professor in the School of Media and Design, Ningbo Institute of Technology, Zhejiang University, China.

Media, Culture and Social Change in Asia
Series Editor: Stephanie Hemelryk Donald

Editorial Board

Gregory N. Evon, University of New South Wales
Devleena Ghosh, University of Technology, Sydney
Peter Horsfield, RMIT University, Melbourne
Chris Hudson, RMIT University, Melbourne
Michael Keane, Curtin University
Tania Lewis, RMIT University, Melbourne
Vera Mackie, University of Wollongong
Kama Maclean, University of New South Wales
Laikwan Pang, Chinese University of Hong Kong
Gary Rawnsley, Aberystwyth University
Ming-yeh Rawnsley, School of Oriental and African Studies, University of London
Jo Tacchi, Lancaster University
Adrian Vickers, University of Sydney
Jing Wang, MIT
Ying Zhu, City University of New York

The aim of this series is to publish original, high-quality work by both new and established scholars in the West and the East, on all aspects of media, culture and social change in Asia.

60 South Korean Popular Culture and North Korea
Edited by Youna Kim

61 Russian Nationalism
Imaginaries, Doctrines, and Political Battlefields
Marlene Laruelle

62 Digital China's Informal Circuits
Platforms, Labour and Governance
Elaine Jing Zhao

63 The Early Transnational Chinese Cinema Industry
Yongchun Fu

For a full list of available titles please visit: https://www.routledge.com/Media-Culture-and-Social-Change-in-Asia-Series/book-series/SE0797

The Early Transnational Chinese Cinema Industry

Yongchun Fu

LONDON AND NEW YORK

First published 2019
by Routledge
2 Park Square, Milton Park, Abingdon, Oxon OX14 4RN

and by Routledge
52 Vanderbilt Avenue, New York, NY 10017

Routledge is an imprint of the Taylor & Francis Group, an informa business

© 2019 Yongchun Fu

The right of Yongchun Fu to be identified as author of this work has been asserted by him in accordance with sections 77 and 78 of the Copyright, Designs and Patents Act 1988.

All rights reserved. No part of this book may be reprinted or reproduced or utilised in any form or by any electronic, mechanical, or other means, now known or hereafter invented, including photocopying and recording, or in any information storage or retrieval system, without permission in writing from the publishers.

Trademark notice: Product or corporate names may be trademarks or registered trademarks, and are used only for identification and explanation without intent to infringe.

British Library Cataloguing-in-Publication Data
A catalogue record for this book is available from the British Library

Library of Congress Cataloging-in-Publication Data
A catalog record has been requested for this book

ISBN: 978-1-138-59237-7 (hbk)
ISBN: 978-0-429-49006-4 (ebk)

Typeset in Times New Roman
by codeMantra

To Haibo, Joe, and Yoyo

Contents

List of figures		ix
List of tables		xi
Acknowledgements		xiii
1	Introduction	1
2	Technology and the trans/national in China's transition to sound	29
3	Response in distribution systems: from 'parrot' to 'butterfly'	49
4	Capitalism with Chinese characteristics: the mode of production in Chinese cinema	72
5	Movie matchmakers: the intermediaries between the American and the Chinese film industries	89
6	Measuring the outcome of China's response through statistics	109
7	Conclusion	135
	Index	139

List of figures

1.1	Bioscoping in Mingxing Film Company, c.1923	18
4.1	The Corporation Structure of Lianhua	78
5.1	Arthur Israel	93
5.2	Thomas Suffert	94
6.1	United States Exports of Motion-Picture Film to China (in feet)	125
6.2	The Income of Mingxing, 1926–1935 (yuan)	126

List of tables

3.1	The Distribution Schedule of *Helen's Babies* (1924) in Shanghai	54
3.2	The Distribution Schedule of *Foundling* (1924) in Shanghai	54
3.3	The Distribution Schedule of *Grand Hotel* (1932) in China	56
3.4	The Distribution Schedule of *The Spring Dream of the Lute* (1933) in Shanghai	57
3.5	The Distribution Schedule of *Morning in the Metropolis* (1933) in Tianjin	59
3.6	The Distribution Schedule of *Night in the City* (1933) in Shanghai	60
3.7	The Distribution Schedule of *Adventures in the Battlefield* (1933) in Shanghai	62
3.8	The Distribution Schedule of *Torrent* (1933) in China	62
6.1	American Film Company Performance in Shanghai	117
6.2	Chinese Film Company Performance in Shanghai	117
6.3	The Overall Performance in Shanghai in 1934	120
6.4	The Box Office Receipt and POPSTAT Index for Films Distributed by United Artists in 1934	123

Acknowledgements

Writing a book is an adventure, and an academic book is no exception. In retrospect, I feel extremely grateful for the support of colleagues, friends, and family during the writing of this book.

This book originated from my doctoral thesis, undertaken at the University of Auckland, New Zealand, between 2009 and 2014. I would like to thank my two supervisors – Xuelin Zhou 周學麟 and Laurence Simmons – for their invaluable advice and continued support after graduation. Paul Clark, my PhD advisor, encouraged my interest in early Chinese film history and my urge to pursue empirical evidence. I express my thanks to Zheng Han 鄭涵 for his continual academic support over the years. Professor Zheng is the person who introduced me to academia. The late Jin Guanjun 金冠軍, my supervisor at Shanghai University, remains my lifelong mentor and model. Sheldon Lu 魯曉鵬 encouraged me to publish my doctoral thesis. Thanks also to Emilie Yueh-yu Yeh 葉月瑜 for her help on this book and with my academic career. Yoshino Sugawara 菅原慶乃 and Sun Shaoyi 孫紹誼 each reviewed one chapter. Shi Chuan 石川 provided me a copy of Lu Jie's diary, which significantly benefited the writing of my chapter on modes of production. I thank Song Hwee Lim 林松輝 for his insight and honest suggestions on my academic career. Special thanks to Stephanie Hemelryk Donald for her interest in this book and her encouragement and suggestions. Mike Walsh helped me to explain the distribution terms and shared his knowledge on the United Artists Corporation.

I take this opportunity to thank Olivia Macassey, who is way more than a copy editor to me. Her diligent persistence inspired me during a hard time. Peter Sowden and Rebecca McPhee at Routledge have provided enthusiastic editorial support and guidance. I feel grateful to my colleagues and friends in New Zealand and China for discussion and companionship over the years: Jani Wilson, Susan Potter, Cassandra Barnett, Anna Jackson, Echo Zi Fan 樊梓, Zhao Peng 趙鵬, Luo Ting 羅婷, Cao Xiaojie 曹小傑, and Xue Feng 薛峰. At Ningbo Institute of Technology, I am indebted to Shao Peiren 邵培仁 for introducing me to this university. Thanks are due to my colleagues Wang Junwei 王軍偉, Qiu Zitong 邱子桐, and Maria Elena Indelicato.

xiv *Acknowledgements*

This research for this book was funded by The National Social Science Fund of China (國家社科基金藝術學項目 18BC07530). In addition, I am thankful to the following individuals and institutions for permission to reprint the photographs in this book: David Crellin and Historical Photographs of China, University of Bristol. I am grateful to Anthony Jesu, Verna Jesu, and Rigo Jesu for providing information about A. E. Lauro. Chapters 3 and 5 were previously published in the *Journal of Chinese Cinemas*. Chapter 4 appeared in *Sungkyun Journal of East Asian Studies*. I thank these two journals for permission to reprint the material here.

I am indebted to my family in Linqu, Ningbo, Shijiazhuang, and New Zealand. I am deeply grateful to my wife, Haibo Hou 侯海博, and my twin children, Houmuxi Fu 付侯慕熙 and Houqingxi Fu 付侯晴熙, who continue to inspire me in all that I do. I dedicate this book to my family.

1 Introduction

What would the American film industry bring to a domestic film industry outside the United States? This question has often been raised since Hollywood films started to dominate world film markets after the First World War. The reason, in the words of Kristin Thompson, is that "[m]ost national cinemas ... consist not only of domestic tendencies, but also of the influences film-makers and audiences picked up from the presence of American films."[1] Left-wing critics, in particular those who subscribe to theories of cultural imperialism, assert that an aggressive American film industry is a threat to domestic film industries outside of the United States as the hegemony of Hollywood diverts domestic film audiences and oppresses the development of the domestic film industries.[2] Meanwhile, right-wing critics argue that the American film industry benefits a domestic film industry as it provides the latter with a competitive environment and a model.[3] Such debates have become inflamed in the wake of an upsurge of theories of globalisation, particularly those of cultural imperialism. A better understanding of the relations between the American and the domestic film industries, in my view, needs to be based on a more detailed understanding of the past.

I believe that the American film industry has been able to help domestic cinema in some cases and oppress it in other cases, depending on how the domestic film industry has responded to the influence of Hollywood. Focussing on the case of China, this book addresses how the Chinese film industry responded to the American film industry in the 1920s and 1930s. It explores the formation of the Chinese film industry and the role America played in the process of that formation. This book demonstrates that as China commenced and consolidated its own film industry in the early twentieth century, it consciously responded to the American film industry. The expansion of the American industry in China and the emergence of the domestic film industry shows that the latter does not necessarily diminish in the shadow of Hollywood. On contrast, the case of China in the early twentieth century demonstrates that a domestic film industry could emerge and achieve growth along with the expansion of the American film industry in the local market.

Whilst my findings on China's industrial approach to the American film industry seem to echo the claims of right-wing critics, it is not my ambition or intention to build a definite link between the presence of the American film industry and the development of domestic film industries across the board. I agree with some notions of right-wing critics, such as the claim that the American film industry provided a competitive context for the domestic film industry. However, I believe that it is a mistake to state a definite link between the presence of the American film industry and the growth or diminution of the domestic film industry. The growth and decline of a domestic film industry in the shadow of the American film industry is subject to a number of factors and contexts, including the size of the domestic industry, the role played by local government, the extent of cultural proximity to Hollywood, and the domestic film industry's attitude towards its American counterpart.

The relationship between the American and the Chinese film industries is a key topic in Chinese film studies. First, Hollywood was the primary counterpart for the domestic film industry in the first half of the twentieth century. Hollywood films had dominated the Chinese film market since the second half of the 1910s, taking up around 75 per cent of the total market share in terms of box office revenues. Compared with domestic films, Hollywood films were sophisticated in language, performance, financial budget, and commercial promotion. Domestic films were forced to maintain competitive advantages when competing with Hollywood films. Second, the American film industry was the most significant model for the Chinese industry to imitate. When the Chinese film industry commenced in the early 1920s, Hollywood cinema was already present: a giant counterpart and a source of inspiration. To Chinese film practitioners, there were few options but to learn from Hollywood films. There is abundant evidence of how Chinese film practitioners learned from the American film industry in the first half of the twentieth century, from camera movement to montage, from film production to film exhibition.[4]

The aim of my book is threefold. First, the central concern of this book is to articulate the relations between the American and the Chinese film industries in the early stage of cinema, that is, 1897–1937. I illustrate five prominent perspectives with respect to this topic: namely, (1) the role the American film industry played in the formation of the Chinese film industry, (2) the attitudes of Chinese practitioners towards collaboration with the American film industry, (3) the dynamic of China's response to the American film industry, (4) the contribution of intermediaries between Hollywood and China, and (5) the results of China's response to the American film industry. These five perspectives have either been ignored or deserve rethinking due to the problematic methodology of the existing literature on the subject. I hope that my investigation of the relations between the American industry and China from a historical and industrial perspective will contribute to the current debate on cultural globalisation within the broader field of the film industry as well as in transnational cinema studies.

Second, it is my intention to deepen scholarly understanding of the history of the Chinese domestic film industry from 1897 to 1937, in particular, in the 1920s and 1930s. This is a formative period for the Chinese film industry, in which domestic film production began taking shape. There is clear evidence that the number of domestic films released was maintained at over 50 per year in the 1920s and 1930s, while no more than five films in total were produced prior to the 1920s. Watching films became a popular and regular entertainment in urban cities. Chinese film practitioners established and innovated a series of industrial systems during this period, including a studio system, a distribution system, a film star system, and a theatre chain system. Meanwhile, China completed its cinematic transition to talkie pictures. However, in contrast to the fruitful literature on film culture, scholarship on film industry remains extremely poor.[5] This book aims to enrich the study of the Chinese film industry by investigating the film technology, distribution systems, the mode of productions, intermediary figures, and box office reception of the Chinese film industry in the early twentieth century.

The third contribution of this book relies on an understanding of the presence of Hollywood films in China in the early twentieth century. Hollywood dominated the Chinese film market in terms of total market share, including box office income and the number of titles, as I mentioned earlier. In addition, Hollywood cinema was the model for the domestic film industry as well as a constructive force in its making. As Xiao Zhiwei puts it, "no discussion of Chinese film history can be complete without taking into full account the presence of Hollywood."[6] Nevertheless, the picture of the American film industry presence in China is far from clear at this stage due to a lack of fundamental information. In this book, I explore several key issues which contribute to our knowledge of Hollywood films in China, including the introduction of Hollywood talkie pictures into China, the number of Hollywood films which circulated there, and the box office receipts of such films in China in the 1930s. In exploring these issues, I aim to benefit discussions such as those on cultural imperialism by providing empirical support.

Theoretical framework

As the title itself implies, 'transnational' is a keyword of this book. In the following passages, I review and revisit the transnational turn in Chinese film studies. Since the last two decades of the twentieth century, scholarship has witnessed a paradigmatic shift from a "national cinema approach" to a "transnational cinema approach." The national cinema approach locates "films and cinemas within their national contexts and/or treats a country's cinematic output as a distinct object of study."[7] To a large extent, national cinema is "defined against Hollywood," suggesting a clear-cut distinction between Hollywood and the domestic film industry and culture.[8]

Since the late 1980s, the dominant paradigm of the national cinema approach has been increasingly challenged. Two prominent figures who problematise the national cinema approach deserve special notice: Andrew Higson and Stephen Crofts. Andrew Higson remedies the national cinema approach by suggesting a "more inward-looking means, constituting a national cinema ... in terms of its relationship to an already existing national political, economic and cultural identity and set of traditions."[9] In the same vein as Higson, Stephen Crofts addresses the varieties of national cinema. In his taxonomy, he differentiates between eight types of national cinema in a discussion which "takes into account the three main industrial categories of production, distribution and exhibition, and audiences as well as those of textuality and national representation."[10] The work of Higson and Crofts may have remedied 'national cinema' theory, but they still leave many questions unsolved. In an account written in 2000, Higson admits that his earlier formulation is problematic because it "tends to assume that national identity and tradition are already fully formed and fixed in place," and it "takes borders for granted."[11] Higson thus suggests a replacement of the concept of "national cinema" with "transnational cinema." The reason for this shift, according to Higbee and Lim, is that the term "transnational cinema" is "a subtler means of understanding cinema's relationship to the cultural and economic formations that are rarely contained within national boundaries."[12]

"Scholarship on Chinese cinemas," as Higbee and Lim indicate, "has been at the forefront of the theorizing [of] the transnational."[13] Sheldon Lu is one of the first scholars to introduce the "transnational" into Chinese film studies. Writing in 1997, Lu points out that "Chinese *national* cinema can only be understood in its properly transnational context," and "one must speak of Chinese cinemas in the plural and as transnational in the ongoing process of image-making throughout the twentieth century."[14] Lu's edited volume *Transnational Chinese Cinemas* marked a "watershed moment in the study of Chinese cinemas," and the words "transnational Chinese cinemas" now "name the field that we study and are used routinely."[15] It is not an exaggeration to say that exploring Chinese cinemas from a transnational perspective has become intellectually fashionable.

Transnational scholarship, however, has yet to turn its proper attention to historiography. In *Transnational Chinese Cinemas*, Lu proposes four levels on which to examine "transnationalism in the Chinese case." The last level concerns historical studies. Here, Lu calls for an exploration of the prehistory of Chinese cinema, a period ahead of the formation of national cinema which takes the transnational into account. Unfortunately, most works on this topic are contemporary in focus or, in Chris Berry's words, "approach the transnational in a synchronic rather than a diachronic mode."[16] One of the very few exceptions is Jeremy Taylor's account on the Amoy-dialect film industry, *Rethinking Transnational Chinese Cinemas*.[17] Amoy-dialect films were produced in 1950s and 1960s Hong Kong and exported to Hokkien-speaking communities, including Taiwan, the Philippines, and other South-East Asian countries. The significance of studying

Amoy-dialect film lies in "the disconnection between Amoy-dialect film and any given nation-state"; therefore, it does not fit the familiar theoretical notion of transnationalism.[18]

With regard to my project, employing a transnational cinema framework, instead of a conventional national framework, may benefit the study of Chinese film industry history in two ways. First, it may provide a better understanding of issues and debates which the previous national paradigm has found difficult to deal with. The American film industry's contribution to the domestic film industry is a case in point. In taking national boundaries for granted, the previous 'national cinema' approach acknowledges the contribution of the American film industry as an outside force. Therefore, such an approach explores how national cinema imitates Hollywood in modes of production, film style, and industrial system or examines how national cinema differentiates itself from Hollywood in order to define itself. Scholars such as Higson tend to examine the 'inside' function of the American film industry in domains including film exhibition and consumption within the framework of national cinema. However, as John Hill argues in the case of British films, Higson's work could "lead to the conclusion that Hollywood films are in fact a part of the British national cinema because these are the films which are primarily used and consumed by British national audiences."[19] As a matter of fact, Higson's argument could destabilise the concept of national cinema to a considerable extent, given that national cinema is usually defined against that of Hollywood. A transnational framework could largely solve the problems of the conventional national framework with regard to the receipts of foreign films. This is because a transnational approach regards the national as a construct and sees transnational forces as potentially contributing to its construction. In Chapter 2, I will examine the contribution of a transnational force – the American film industry – to the construction of the national in the domain of film technology.

Second, the transnational framework may shed light on the "blind spots in film history that were previously covered or glossed over the national cinema paradigm."[20] Transnational cinema studies may make space for blind spots like "the phenomena that not only cross but straddle and defy borders."[21] Intermediaries between the American and the Chinese film industries are instances of this. These intermediary figures, such as Chinese merchants who distributed Hollywood films, registered their companies overseas, straddling national borders. Their contributions to the Chinese film industry have been forgotten and misunderstood in national cinema accounts, which place the national in a central light. A transnational cinema framework may help to re-evaluate the function of intermediaries, which has been obscured by the former approach.

Literature review

Scholarship on the relations between the American film industry and the Chinese film industry remains nascent so far for political and pragmatic reasons. First, during most of the twentieth century, the American film industry was treated as an aggressor to domestic film industries outside of the United States. Such treatment was worse from the 1950s to the 1980s, when the ideological conflicts between the United States and China were fierce. Therefore, standard Chinese film literature on the period studied here has had little intention of admitting the influence of Hollywood on Chinese films.[22] Second, lack of access to primary material is one major obstacle for the study of the relationship between the American and the Chinese film industries. For research on industry, primary documents pertaining to both sides, that is, China and the United States, are necessary. However, a number of key materials on the Chinese side were lost in the wake of the bombings of Shanghai by Japanese forces in 1932 and 1937.

Nevertheless, there exists a limited amount of literature that provides valuable background information about the American film industry in China, the rise of the Chinese film industry in the 1920s and 1930s, and China's response to Hollywood films. In the following, I will review the existing literature from these three perspectives.

Given China's insignificant position in Hollywood's global market at the time, when studying Hollywood's overseas market, the material on Hollywood films in China remains limited. In her study on the rise of the American film industry's dominance in the world, eminent film historian Kristin Thompson briefly illustrates Hollywood's market in China in the 1910s and 1920s. She shows the dominance of Pathé production in the early 1910s and how Hollywood films gradually replaced the position of French films by virtue of "institut[ing] distribution procedures abroad."[23]

Marie Cambon is a pioneer who examines the American film industry in China. Her master's dissertation examines the "pervasive" role that Hollywood films played in the "consumer and film culture" in the "cultural context of Shanghai."[24] The major research objects of Cambon's dissertation are film audiences and the production of Chinese films. Her dissertation is one of the first accounts of Chinese film audiences. Based on her interviews with film audience and film practitioners of the 1930s, she suggests that film audiences in 1920s and 1930s Shanghai, first, had a stronger preference for Hollywood than Chinese films (in particular among intellectuals) and, second, were more "diverse" than those described in historical texts.[25] Cambon's research on the production of Chinese films unfolds from two perspectives: film genres and film aesthetics.

Xiao Zhiwei is one of the few historians who specialises in Hollywood films in China and the Chinese film industry. His essays "Hollywood in China, 1897–1950: A Preliminary Survey" and the updated version "American Films in China Prior to 1950" are insightful studies on the 'reel relations' between China and the United States from an industrial perspective.[26]

Xiao's two essays provide a chronological survey of Hollywood in China, from the early days of Hollywood's penetration into the Chinese market in the late nineteenth century to the moment the American film industry was banned from Mainland China in the 1950s. Xiao presents a large amount of useful information about the territorial scope of the American film industry's distribution and the profit-sharing system it employed in China. Xiao also points out that the exhibition of Hollywood films in China was subject to variations in territory and length of showing time as well as to the tastes of Chinese audiences.

In addition, Xiao gives an estimate on the number of Hollywood films screened and the income of American corporations in China. By exploring primary materials from China and the United States, Xiao proposes that "the number of American films distributed in China averaged 400 titles annually."[27] These 400 titles were newly released films. In the 1930s, China's cinemas screened numerous old Hollywood films. According to my analysis of the records of commercial screenings, 615 Hollywood films were screened in Shanghai in 1934.[28] In addition to the number of American films circulated in China, Xiao estimates that "Hollywood's average annual earnings from China" ranged from six to seven million U.S. dollars.[29]

A more recent account on the American film industry in China is Zhang Qian's 2009 doctoral dissertation *From Hollywood to Shanghai: American Silent Films in China*.[30] Zhang focusses on "how Hollywood films were consumed" in 1920s Shanghai and "what impact [Hollywood films] might have upon Shanghai culture."[31] Drawing upon primary materials from one of the major Hollywood corporations, the United Artists Corporation, he articulates the function of the distribution agents of Hollywood majors. Zhang details how the distribution of Hollywood films operated in the 1920s, using the case of a United Artists agent in Shanghai, Krisel & Krisel. His account shows how the revenue-sharing and block booking systems operated in China, and how the distribution agent worked closely with American diplomats to beat piracy and promote Hollywood films.

To sum up, the aforementioned accounts provide a well-grounded basis for understanding the American film industry in China and the Chinese film industry in the early twentieth century. Yet several prominent dimensions remain largely under studied. First, little is known about the distribution system of Chinese films, although several essays briefly address the distribution of Hollywood films in China.[32] Second, the field of technology in the Chinese film industry is almost invisible in scholarship in English. For instance, compared to the literature on Hollywood's sound conversion, there exists little scholarship which addresses the history of the conversion to talkies in China in the 1930s.[33] Third, together with audience and exhibition studies in general, scholarship on the box office receipts of Chinese and Hollywood films in China is new to Chinese film studies.[34] In this book, I aim to fill in these research gaps regarding the Chinese film industry.

In the following, I will examine the literature on the relations between the American and the Chinese film industries, and Chinese films in general. The existing scholarship acknowledges the essential influence of the American film industry on the Chinese industry and the latter's imitation of Hollywood film systems, such as the star system and the studio system. In comparison with the scholarship on film industry, the literature on Chinese film culture and film texts realises the complexity of the relations between Hollywood and Chinese films. Some scholars notice that Chinese film-makers went beyond mere imitation and created the unique identities of Chinese films by incorporating other sources.[35]

Cambon, who explores the American film industry's encounters in China in her account, also analyses the relations between the two industries, paying special attention to the exhibition of Hollywood films in Shanghai and the issues it raised. She details the confrontation and compromise between Hollywood's distributors and Chinese practitioners, including exhibitors, authorities, and cultural elites. Specifically, she examines: (1) how the expansion of the American film industry's exhibition business invoked reactions from nationalists, (2) how Chinese authorities censored Hollywood films for "humiliating China," and (3) how the Chinese exhibitors united in the late 1930s to "secure better deals" from Hollywood distributors.[36]

Cambon gives currency to the imitative attitudes of the Chinese film industry towards the American industry. She demonstrates how Chinese film-makers 'modelled' Hollywood in the development of genres such as detective films and melodrama.[37] She also briefly introduces China's film star system, regarding it as an imitation of Hollywood. According to Cambon, China's star system emerged after Mary Pickford's visit to Shanghai.[38] The star-making system, like the American film industry, was associated with, and endorsed by, the commercialism of Shanghai. In addition, the naming and shaping of Chinese film stars apparently showed the strong influence of Hollywood in the 1920s and 1930s.[39] Like Cambon, Xiao mentions that the Chinese film industry imitated Hollywood in the early twentieth century. He proposes that "Hollywood provided an important source of inspiration as well as materials for the Chinese film industry."[40]

This approach suggesting Chinese imitation is striking, but it is inadequate to describe the complicated relations between the Chinese and the American film industries. It is evident that such an approach pays attention to the similarities between the two industries. However, it fails to notice the ways in which they were distinct from one another. The Chinese film industry system was subject to the conditions of industrial development and the specific situation of its Chinese context. It is true that China's distribution system, for instance, was generated by an imitation of that of the United States. However, as the Chinese domestic film industry developed, the configuration of its distribution system was influenced by particular, local conditions. One instance of this influence is that China did not follow the conventional policy in American distribution, that is, allowing only one print to be circulated at a certain run theatre in a given city. On the contrary,

Chinese distributors circulated as many prints as possible at Shanghai theatres in the 1930s. This was due to both the enjoyment of government favour and the pressure of cost-recovery. In this book, I will demonstrate that the relationship between the American and the Chinese film industries involved different stages of response which were more complex than the mere "imitation" or "sinification" suggested by the existing literature.

In comparison with the preliminary study in the field of the film industry, film literature on Chinese film texts and cultures has begun to realise that the complexity of the relations between Hollywood and Chinese films involves more than mere imitation. Scholars in this field have introduced what I call the 'synthesis' approach to describe how the identity of Chinese cinema emerged in the wake of learning from Hollywood films. Ma Ning is one of the first scholars to introduce the 'synthesis' approach when examining China's response to Hollywood. In his 1989 essay "The Textual and Critical Difference of Being Radical: Chinese Leftist Films in the 1930s," Ma examines the mode of film-making of leftist films in the 1930s in terms of their relations to the Hollywood model. He notices that in melodrama, Chinese film-makers "deviated from" the tradition of Hollywood norms, with the purpose of transforming Chinese audiences.[41] The central argument of Ma's essay is that Chinese films built up a "unique Chinese synthesis" of Hollywood continuity editing and Soviet montage.[42] Here, Ma suggests, Chinese cinema imitated Hollywood cinema but differed from this model by drawing on other sources of inspiration (Soviet montage films), thereby creating its own unique style. It is not an overstatement to say that Ma Ning has established a paradigm in the study of the relations between Hollywood and Chinese films.

Following Ma's example, scholars of film culture have pointed out how other sources, together with the Hollywood model, were synthesised in Chinese film texts. In his account of Hollywood's influence on Chinese films in the 1930s, Leo Lee first outlines how Chinese film-makers imitated their Hollywood counterparts. For instance, the establishment of theatre chains is regarded as "a move in direct imitation of the Hollywood distribution system."[43] In addition, Chinese film practitioners "simply imitated the acting styles and lighting design as well as the camera movements of Hollywood pictures."[44] Furthermore, Lee states that Chinese films went beyond mere imitation. Taking film narrative as an example, he argues that "Chinese cinema was a popular hybrid genre consisting of diverse cultural elements – both old and new, drawn from both visual and print sources."[45] For instance, the slow rhythm of early Chinese films, and their combination of the traditions of montage and long take, can be seen as a "stylistic hybridity" due to the limitations of the physical conditions of film-making in the 1930s.[46]

One central issue concerning the construction of the Chinese film industry is nationalism, and it shapes the attitude of China towards Hollywood. In *The World According to Hollywood, 1918–1939*, Ruth Vasey examines how the foreign film market influenced the American film industry's business strategy and shaped the content of Hollywood films. She points out that the "cultivation of diplomatic channels of protest" in and outside China "had a significant impact on the [American film] industry," despite the fact that China's market only accounted for 0.8 per cent of Hollywood's foreign market.[47] For instance, in view of a potential protest from the Chinese authorities, Warner Bros studios had to insert a preface into *West of Shanghai* (dir. John Farrow, 1937) to explain why the uniform worn by the protagonist differs from that of the National Army of China.[48]

A significant account of nationalism in Chinese film is given in Hu Jubin's *Projecting a Nation: Chinese National Cinema before 1949*. In this study, based on national cinema theory, Hu categorises early Chinese films into different types of nationalism and claims that "[t]he issue of nation is the determining principle shaping the Chinese cinema before 1949."[49] The 1920s was a period of industrial nationalism, and the 1930s witnessed the interaction between class nationalism; the ideological discourse of the Communist Party; and traditional nationalism, invested in by the Nationalist Party. Industrial nationalism in the 1920s, in Hu's words, "prioritized the establishment of the film industry as the Chinese nation's domestic industry."[50] The major theme of nationalism in the Chinese film industry of the 1930s conformed to the ideological conflicts between the Communist and Nationalist parties. Class nationalism and traditional nationalism shared an ideological base, that is, an anti-imperialist standpoint because both parties alleged that they were fighting against the aggression of imperialism – particularly from the Japanese. However, the two ideologies of nationalism varied on the issue of class since class struggle was the "central value" of the Communist Party, while the Nationalist Party "advocated the idea of national survival by endorsing Confucian values as 'Chinese tradition' and entirely evading the issue of class."[51] Hu's major concerns in this study are film production and film culture, but he notes the industrial development of Chinese film in the 1920s. He probes how Chinese film practitioners associated the establishment of film corporations with the discourse of "contend[ing] with foreign film companies" and "safeguard[ing] ... the economic and cultural interests of the Chinese nation."[52] Under the light of nationalism, two production tendencies existed in the 1920s: westernisation and sinicisation. Examples of westernisation include the genres of slapstick, family melodrama, and social problem films, while traditional costume films and martial arts films reflect the tendency of sinicisation in 1920s China.

It is probably correct to say that nationalism was not the central concern of the Chinese film industry in the first half of the twentieth century, although it may have served as the central concern of later Chinese film culture. The Chinese film industry prior to 1949 was driven by profits rather than nationalistic sentiment. Nationalistic accounts neglect the industry contributions of prominent figures who held few nationalistic sentiments. One such figure is Lo Kan (盧根, a.k.a. Lu Gen), a significant film exhibitor and distributor in early twentieth-century China. Unlike film-makers who enjoyed the spotlight, exhibitors and distributors like Lo Kan seldom expressed their political viewpoints publicly. In many cases, they deliberately concealed their sentiments and sought to avoid involvement with unpredictable political campaigns. Consequently, their contributions are usually buried under the dust of nationalistic texts. In addition, the nationalist point of view risks simplification as it neglects the complexity of film practitioners in the Chinese film industry. In this book, I look at specific practitioners who stood as intermediaries between the American and the Chinese film industries, and shed light on their contributions to the domestic film industry (rather than to nationalist discourse).

In examining the function of intermediaries, my approach can be seen in a similar light to that of Xiao Zhiwei's essay "Translating Hollywood Film to Chinese Audience."[53] Xiao's is the first account to address the "in-between production" of agencies and intermediaries in relation to the consumption of Hollywood films in the Chinese context. Specifically, Xiao underlines how the intermediaries between Hollywood films and Chinese audiences, encompassing film authorities, critics, distributors, and exhibitors, "shaped audience reception of American films" by injecting their own political, economic, and cultural agendas.[54] In addition, in a number of cases the original texts of Hollywood films were redefined, consciously or unconsciously, in the process of translating film titles into Chinese. Inspired by Xiao's essay, my study will further explore the function of intermediaries between the American and the Chinese film industries, focussing on how they benefited the development of the Chinese film industry in the early twentieth century.

To sum up, the existing literature has carried out pioneering research on the relations between these two film industries in the 1920s and 1930s. Some preliminary study has been done on the rise of the domestic film industry and the American film industry's presence in 1920s and 1930s China from an industrial perspective. However, some issues remain open for study. First, little has been done on several prominent domains of the Chinese film industry, including film technology, the distribution system, and domestic market performance. Second, the Chinese film industry's response to the American film industry deserves further exploration from several perspectives, given the flaws in the existing literature. These perspectives encompass the role that Hollywood has played in the making of the Chinese domestic film industry, the dynamics of that industry's response to Hollywood, and the function of intermediaries between the two industries. These research gaps are the starting points of the current volume.

Research questions

The questions this book seeks to answer are as follows:

1 What is the role that the American film industry played in the Chinese film industry as a global/transnational force? It is known that Hollywood

figures as the Chinese film industry's largest rival and model; however, some other functions of the American film industry with regard to the domestic film industry deserve investigation.
2   What are the dynamics of the Chinese film industry's approach to the American film industry? Is it merely one of imitation? Or did a more complicated dynamic operate in the history of China's response to Hollywood in the early twentieth century?
3   What contribution did intermediary figures make? There is a group of intermediaries who stood between the American film industry and China, responsible for introducing American industrial knowledge and technology into China. How, and to what extent, did they shape China's response to the American film industry?
4   How can we evaluate the results of China's response to the American film industry through reliable empirical evidence? To what extent did the American film industry dominate China's film market in the early twentieth century? A thorough investigation of the Chinese film industry's approach to its American counterpart should include the outcome of this response.

In this book, I will place these research questions in the context of the construction of the Chinese film industry from 1897 to 1937 in order to examine the relations between the American and the Chinese film industries.

An overview of the film industry

Before I proceed further into the Chinese film industry's approach to the American film industry, a brief introduction of the rise of the Chinese film industry will be helpful to readers. In the following section, I trace the history of the emergence of the Chinese film industry along with the development of the American film industry's trade in China. First, I point out two major characteristics of the market structure of Chinese cinema: namely, it is market-driven, and it is a duopoly. Second, this section observes the rise and expansion of the American film business in China, focussing on its domination there. Third, I examine the rise of the Chinese film industry alongside the expansion of American films, addressing the paths of its development and other fundamental information about it.

The Chinese film market in the early twentieth century was basically a capitalist structure. That is to say, commercial orientation was the vital characteristic of the Chinese film market, not only for the American film industry's exploration in China but also for the Chinese film industry itself. The pursuit of profit was the primary aim of film practitioners in the Chinese film industry. Therefore, in this book, I will treat the innovation of film technology and the film system in the Chinese film market as a drive for pursuing profit rather than for "retrieving economic rights"[55] or other grand nationalistic discourses that were employed at the time, although I have little doubt about the patriotic sentiments of Chinese film practitioners. In addition, a dual hegemony, Hollywood and Chinese film in this case, was another major characteristic of the capitalist structure of 1920s and 1930s China. Despite the occasional appearance of European films, Hollywood and domestic production dominated China's screens in the early twentieth century. In 1934, of the 1,026 films shown on Shanghai's screen, only 42 films or 2 per cent were European films, excluding British films. The unfamiliarity of European languages (excluding English) was one major obstacle for the expansion of European film into China.[56] As an American market survey noted, "American distributors in China give no thought to competition from other foreign films. They are concerned with competition from Chinese ... films."[57] The expansion of one industry could possibly have constituted a threat to the other. For instance, American diplomats in China kept a close watch on the production of Chinese sound films since they believed that "any substantial increase in the number of sound films produced by Chinese studios will eventually operate to curtail the demand for foreign pictures as good Chinese pictures will divert a large portion of Chinese patrons from foreign pictures."[58]

The first film screening place in China occurred in Hong Kong in 1897, although Shanghai's Xu Garden was erroneously credited in the literature for a long time. Law Kar and Frank Bren convincingly demonstrate that on 23 April 1897 Maurice Charvet presented films in Hong Kong for the first time.[59] A month later, Harry Welby Cooke screened films at Astor House in Shanghai, an event which at the time was marked as the beginning of the film market in Mainland China.[60] The film machine used in Astor House was an Animatoscope, invented by Edison.[61] French films, in particular Pathé productions, dominated the Chinese film market until the end of the First World War, thanks to Pathé's successful distribution business in China. A report in 1914 showed that American films accounted for merely 25 per cent of the total market share in terms of box office income in China, although audiences in Shanghai enjoyed American films "because of their realism, purposefulness, and strength of plot."[62]

At the end of the First World War, the American film industry established and maintained its domination in China. Evidence of this is that the importation of exposed film stock from the United States to China boomed more than 20 times in less than 20 years. In 1913, the number of feet of exposed film stock imported into China was 170,740. The number amounted to 3,484,265 in 1929. In addition, the American film industry maintained its domination in the arena of film equipment. At least four factors explain the success of the domination of Hollywood films in China. The first factor is the interruption of French film production in China after the First World War. As it was with other European cinemas, the business of French films was largely handicapped by the war: "new production was drastically reduced ... [and] shipping problems ... from Europe to other areas played havoc with what little production remained."[63] This opportunity helped the expansion of American films in China.

Second, the opening of distribution branches worldwide was crucial to the American film industry's success in international markets.[64] In the early 1910s, a large number of American films were distributed in China through their sale agents in London, such as the Motion Pictures Sales Company, the sale supplier for the Arcade Theatre in Tianjin in 1913.[65] This is echoed by America's entire export policy. According to Kristin Thompson, London was "the center of American foreign distribution between 1909 and 1916."[66] After the First World War, American companies shifted their distribution strategy to directly set up distribution branches abroad, instead of using the pre-war agents. In 1917, Universal took the lead in establishing a branch office in China. Fox followed in its footsteps. By 1927, all major Hollywood studios had branch offices or sales agents in China. In addition to direct representatives and sales agents, there were a number of Chinese independent distributors in China who were responsible for the circulation of Hollywood films. They handled older American films as well as European and Chinese films.[67]

Third, Hollywood's sophistication in its utilisation of film language and technology contributed to its dominance. Compared to the Chinese film industry, Hollywood developed a universal film language, not only satisfying domestic film audiences but also catering to international patrons. In addition, English was the most popular foreign language used in China. It was understood by most foreign residents and upper- and middle-class Chinese citizens, who constituted the bulk of the audience for Hollywood films in China.

Fourth, the American government provided strong backup for the expansion of the American film industry. As Kerry Segrave proves, the American film industry obtained massive indirect aid from the American government.[68] When conflict arose between the American film industry and China, American diplomats and consulates spared no effort in facilitating the American industry's interests, for instance by helping Hollywood films to become exempt from censorship and reducing duty and taxation.[69]

The total number of Hollywood films shown on China's screens remains unknown so far. In the 1930s, the number of Hollywood films imported into China exceeded 300 per annum. A number of old American films were also being shown on China's screens. Based on the statistics of the screening records, 666 American films were circulating in China's cinema theatres in 1934, and productions of Hollywood major studios account for 615.

The reception of American films varied, depending on the tastes of Chinese audiences. In the 1920s and 1930s, almost every Hollywood feature film was introduced in China. However, not all films were appreciated. The American market survey suggests that Chinese audiences enjoyed films with "a minimum of dialogue, a maximum of action, good scenic effects and a universal plot."[70] Therefore, comedy, musical, and action were the top three genres in terms of popularity in China.[71] In addition, a market survey noticed that the tastes of Chinese audiences varied as well. For instance, *Tom Sawyer* (dir. John Cromwell, 1930), a picture adapted from Mark Twain's children's book, was appreciated by Chinese students since "Mark Twain's classic has been translated into Chinese and is considered a true portrayal of American life during the middle of the nineteenth century."[72]

In the wake of screening foreign films, China started its own experiments in film production. In 1905, Fengtai Photography Studio is alleged to have produced the "first Chinese film" – *Ding Jun Mountain* (定軍山, 1905) in Beijing, a documentary of popular Peking Opera.[73] Despite the reputation of Beijing as the birthplace of Chinese cinema, Shanghai was the centre of the production, distribution, and exhibition of Chinese films in the first half of the twentieth century. The Asiatic Film Company (亞西亞製造影片公司), set up in 1913 in Shanghai, is one of the earliest – if not the first – enterprises in Chinese film history. It is known for training the "Founders of Chinese Films," including Zhang Shichuan 張石川 and Zheng Zhengqiu 鄭正秋. Early writings identify Benjamin Brodsky as the founder of the Asiatic Film Company in the late 1900s. Recent research, however, suggests that Brodsky's film business appeared to have little connection with the Asiatic.[74] My own research indicates that it is too early to ascertain the relations between Brodsky and the Asiatic. At this stage, it is safe to say that the Asiatic was in the hands of two American merchants: Thomas H. Suffert and Arthur J. Israel.[75] The Asiatic Film Company was likely to be defunct after 1915.

In the late 1910s and early 1920s, several film companies were established in Shanghai. In 1918, the Commercial Press, then the largest private publication house, organised a film department and started to produce scenarios for educational films. In 1921, two other new corporations were established: namely the Shanghai Film Society and the Shanghai Motion Picture Corporation. Nevertheless, the establishment of these film companies did not bring dramatic change to the Chinese film industry in general. For instance, the number of domestic feature films released remained fixed at two or three per year. Limited as it is, reference to annual figures for the imported feet of negative film and unexposed film for production may offer a way to document the development of the industry. By 1922, the negative film stock used annually for film production was less than 120,000 feet. By contrast, the figure for 1924 was 2,165,005 feet, twenty times that of 1922.

The scenario of the Chinese film industry underwent a dramatic change after 1923, when Mingxing (a.k.a. the Star Motion Pictures Producing Corporation 明星) released *Orphan Rescuing Grandfather* (孤兒救祖記). The success of *Orphan* attracted many Chinese speculators, in the middle of the 1920s, to the film field, eager for quick turnovers. In 1925, the number of registered film companies amounted to over 100. One source described such so-called "mushroom" corporations: "[t]hree or four optimists would scrape together a few thousand dollars, secure a play, rig up or hire a studio and equipment of sorts, engage the necessary actors, and set to work."[76] Most of them did not survive their first year. One exception that deserves special note is Tianyi (a.k.a. the Unique Film Company 天一). By virtue of producing traditional costume films (in which the background to the stories was ancient China, and protagonists wore traditional Chinese costumes), Tianyi became a major studio in the Chinese film industry, parallel to Mingxing. Tianyi was also a pioneer in producing sound pictures. After a volcanic eruption of development in 1925, the Chinese film industry had been steadily developing. The annual quantity of motion picture film for domestic productions was maintained at a level of over 1,000,000 feet from 1925 onwards.

By 1931, the capacity of the Chinese film industry had been strengthened due to the organisation of Lianhua (a.k.a. The United Photoplay Service 聯華). Luo Mingyou 羅明佑, a powerful figure in the film exhibition business, organised Lianhua by merging several midsize studios. Lianhua transformed the direction of production, making films which displayed "an uncompromising attitude to social problems and in a sense connected film-making to the May Fourth spirit" in the early 1930s.[77] More importantly, the establishment of Lianhua reinforced the power of the Chinese film industry in the 1930s. American official market reports regarded Lianhua as "the most important producing corporation" in terms of financial backing and possible development.[78] It was capitalised with 1,000,000 yuan, the largest investment in the film production business at that time.[79] By contrast, the registered capital of Mingxing was only 100,000 yuan, 10 per cent of that of Lianhua. In addition, the pictures released by Lianhua were all well received and made a profit of 45,000 yuan in 1931, an outstanding record for the domestic film studios.[80]

In the 1920 and 1930s, the Chinese film industry basically maintained an oligopoly structure. In the 1920s, large studios, including Mingxing, Tianyi, and Great China Lilium (大中華百合) were loosely seen as the 'Big Three.' Lianhua became one of the "Big Three" after it merged Great China Lilium in the 1930s. These three studios dominated the production of the Chinese film industry in the 1930s. China released 1,169 films from 1922 to 1937, while the total number of films released by Mingxing, Tianyi, and Lianhua amounted to 413, accounting for 35 per cent of the total.[81] From 1935, newly organised studios, such as Xinhua (新華) and Yihua (a.k.a. Yihwa 藝華), challenged the positions of the 'Big Three.' Both Xinhua and Yihua had strong capital backgrounds. In the wake of China's transition to talkie pictures, both were supplied with sound machines and released nothing but sound pictures. Their films were well received in the Chinese film market. By contrast, the 'Big Three' either suffered from deficits or the shortage of working capital. In 1936, Lianhua declared bankruptcy, and Mingxing was on the edge of bankruptcy. After the outbreak of the Second Sino-Japanese War in 1937, the economic structure of the Chinese film industry changed dramatically. Mingxing suspended its production, while Tianyi shifted its business to Hong Kong and Nanyang. Yihua and Xinhua continued to release films and replaced Mingxing and Tianyi in the Chinese film market.

The increasing number of Chinese pictures released suggests the growing scale of the Chinese film industry. A close look at Figure 1.1 finds that there was a general increase in the number of Chinese pictures in the 1920s and 1930s. In the three years from 1921 to 1923, only 13 pictures of feature length were produced in China. In 1924, 16 productions were released, which was more than the numbers produced in the previous three years combined; in 1925, the number was 66. The industry continued to grow until 1931, a year in which approximately 100 pictures were produced. Despite the fact that the number of pictures released declined after 1931, it appears that the Chinese film industry had "passed through the period of ... stabilization."[82] Companies with robust financial backing had competitively survived the pressure of China's conversion to sound in the period between 1926 and 1931, while those "firms with little or no capital ha[d] nearly all been eliminated."[83]

No film historian has even questioned that the Chinese film industry was unable to compete with its Hollywood counterpart, whether in terms of production costs or industry scale. The production costs for a silent Chinese picture were roughly 30,000 yuan, while the cost of a sound picture amounted to 50,000 yuan.[84] The scale of the production end of the Chinese film industry can be seen in the number of its employees and the total amount of investment. In 1932, the Chinese film industry employed approximately 2,000 persons and invested 1,429,000 yuan in property and equipment.[85]

The growth of the American film industry's trade and China's own internal trade contributed to the prosperity of the exhibition sector. China's film exhibition started in 1897. The alleged first standard cinema in Shanghai was established by a Spaniard named Antonio Ramos in 1907.[86] Ramos subsequently established several other theatres in Shanghai and Hong Kong, and became a film mogul. Up to 1931, there were 273 theatres in China, and the total seating capacity accounted for 195,000, giving 716 programmes daily.[87] The scale of investments in the exhibition sector, including land, buildings, and equipment, exceeded seven million yuan.[88] A market survey estimated that "the total daily attendance in China's theaters amounted to 292,500" in 1931.[89] A 1936 source estimates the gross receipts of Chinese theatres "roughly at about 10,000,000 yuan, or just about one-third of one percent of the gross receipts of American movie houses for the same year."[90]

For any part of the film business, Shanghai was the most significant centre in China. For the American film industry, Shanghai was the centre of the distribution of Hollywood films in China, along with Hong Kong. In the 1930s, nearly all distribution representatives of major American studios

Figure 1.1 Bioscoping in Mingxing Film Company, c.1923. Image courtesy of David Crellin and Historical Photographs of China, University of Bristol.

in China situated their head offices in Shanghai. To the domestic film industry, Shanghai was the principal locus of motion picture production. "In 1934, out of 55 concerns engaged in film production, 48 were in Shanghai."[91] Shanghai was also the principal centre of film exhibition. In 1931, 44 out of a total 273 cinemas were located in Shanghai, and the revenue from these theatres "amounted to about one-third of the entire revenue" for China.[92] In addition, Shanghai was the site of importation for motion pictures and film production and reproduction equipment. Considering the significance of Shanghai, the major concern of my book focusses on this city.

The organisation

This book constitutes five chapters. Following the Introduction, Chapter 2 explores the role that the American film industry played in the Chinese film industry in the 1930s, paying particular attention to Chinese cinematic conversion to sound. This chapter shows that Hollywood not only served as a model for the Chinese film industry but also was directly integrated into its construction.

Chapter 3 examines the dynamic relations between the Chinese film industry and the American film industry. This chapter focusses on the emergence and optimisation of the Chinese distribution system. It shows that China first imitated America's distribution system in the 1920s and innovated its own based on the American industry in the 1930s. This chapter suggests that a power-relation analysis is the key to understanding the relations between the American and the Chinese film industries.

Chapter 4 investigates China's mode of production prior to 1937 in comparison with its Hollywood counterpart. In contrast to the distribution system, the traits in China's production system – the powerful position of director – proved to be rather negative in terms of its film economy. The traits developed in China's mode of production, I suggest, contributed to a vulnerable film industry in the 1930s.

Chapter 5 highlights the function of intermediaries in China's response to the American film industry. Intermediary figures can be defined as those merchants and practitioners who stood between the American and the Chinese film industries. Three groups of intermediaries are specified in this chapter, that is, American film practitioners in China, Chinese merchants distributing Hollywood films, and Chinese film practitioners who had studied in the United States. Standard historical literature, fuelled by nationalism, has failed to value them, consequently neglecting their contribution to the domestic film industry. This chapter shows that intermediary figures bridged the gap between the American and the Chinese film industries, and facilitated the development of the domestic film industry. The chapter suggests that patriotic sentiment should not be the only criterion in the evaluation of the history of the Chinese film industry.

Chapter 6 explores the market performance of the Chinese film industry by comparing it with that of Hollywood in China. This chapter explores the outcome of the Chinese film industry's approach to the American film industry and shows that Hollywood's dominance of this industry was not monolithic. From some perspectives, the domestic film industry outranked Hollywood.

This book advocates the positive influence of the American film industry in the making and development of a domestic film industry outside of the United States in the early twentieth century. However, I have no intention of producing a definitive answer to the question of the influence of the American film industry on domestic cinema industries as a whole. A case-by-case study with a nuanced analysis of the economic and social situation of each national cinema market is suggested for further exploration of the relations between the American film industry and other national cinemas.

Methodology

As a historical study, this book relies heavily on primary materials on the film industry, which are located in China, the United States, Australia, and New Zealand. Four categories of primary materials are used in this book: studio and industrial archives, English and Chinese newspapers in the early twentieth century, trade journals and market reports, and unpublished diaries written by producers.

The United Artists Corporation Records, held by the Wisconsin Historical Society, provides exclusive primary records on the American film industry's business in China. The black book, correspondence, and reports between the New York headquarters of United Artists and its agents in China have been of significant benefit to my study of Hollywood's distribution in China and of the Chinese film market in general.

Another prominent source on the American film industry's film business in China and the industrial background of Chinese cinema is found in "Records of the U.S. Department of State Relating to the Internal Affairs of China," released by the U.S. National Archives and Records Administration (NARA). Two specific market reports were particularly helpful: namely "Motion Pictures in China" (1931) and "The Motion Picture Industry in China" (1932). These reports were conducted by various American consular officers throughout China and provided thorough investigations of the Chinese film market concerning Hollywood films as well as the domestic film industry in the early 1930s. They examine the American film industry's distribution and exhibition practices in China, along with the taxation and censorship of Hollywood films there. The surveys supply reliable information about the production modes and the reception of Chinese films in the domestic film industry. In addition, a general introduction to the history of China's transition to talkie pictures is attached to these surveys.

The Shanghai Municipal Archive contains invaluable archives concerning the operation of Chinese production studios. Three items proved extremely helpful to the present project. The first is the records of the minutes of the meetings of Mingxing shareholders (1927, 1931, and 1933). The records of the minutes provide reliable records of the business operation of a Chinese film company. The second item is the surveys concerning film business in Shanghai (mainly on production and exhibition) collected by the Shanghai Commercial & Saving Bank.[93] Most of the surveys were conducted through the China Mercantile Agency. The companies investigated include Mingxing, Lianhua, Tianyi, and Huawei (華威, a.k.a., Wha Whei Trading Co., hereafter Huawei). The contents include their authorised capital, corporate structures, and financial situations as well as short introductions to executives and shareholders. The third item of interest here is the memos of the Shanghai Jiaotong Bank on Mingxing. The memos detail the sound machinery that Mingxing was granted from the United States by Hong Shen and the value of that machinery. In addition, they document the economic situation of Mingxing from 1935 until its bankruptcy.

The National Library of Australia contains a rich array of newspapers from China, published in Chinese and English. The Chinese newspapers used in this book include the *Xinwen Bao* (新聞報, Shanghai), the *Shen bao* (申報, Shanghai), the *Shang Bao* (商報, Tianjin), and the *Qingdao Shi Bao* (青島時報, Qingdao). English newspapers related to my study, in particular the *North China Daily News* and the *China Press,* were accessed from the National Library of Australia through the inter-loan service of The University of Auckland Library. The *North China Herald* and the *China Weekly Review* were accessed via the database *ProQuest Historical Newspapers: Chinese Newspapers Collection.*

Apart from these primary materials, Chinese film journals and periodicals published in the early twentieth century were accessed at 民國時期電影雜誌彙編 (Selection of Film Journals and Magazines in the Republic of China) and the database titled 全國報刊索引 (National Index to Chinese Newspapers & Periodicals).

In the interest of accuracy, this book employs traditional Chinese characters instead of *pinyin*, and these are followed by an English name, if applicable. The reader will find that the English translations of film titles in this book are slightly different from those which are widely accepted. The English titles I use here originate from the previews of commercial Chinese titles published in English newspapers and periodicals in 1920s and 1930s China, in particular in the *North China Herald* and the *China Press*. Such English titles were translated and promoted by Chinese studios at that time. For instance, China's first sound picture, *Genv hong mudan* (歌女紅牡丹, dir. Zhang Shichuan, 1931), is translated here as *The Singing Peony* rather than *The Sing Song Girl Peony*, which is popular in literature in English. I have used the accepted translations with respect to those films without published English titles. The filmography attached at the end of this book gives Chinese titles, English titles used in this volume, and their corresponding conventionally accepted English titles. With regard to the currencies employed in this book, 1 yuan equals 0.715 Shanghai dollar, or roughly 0.3 US dollar in the 1930s.

Notes

1 Kristin Thompson, *Exporting Entertainment: America in the World Film Market, 1907–1934* (London: BFI, 1985), ix.
2 Herbert Schiller, *Mass Communication and American Empire* (Boulder: Westview, 1992); Francis Shor, *Dying Empire: U.S. Imperialism and Global Resistance* (London: Routledge, 2010); James Petras, "Cultural Imperialism in the Late 20th Century," *Journal of Contemporary Asia* 23, 2 (1993). Theorists of cultural imperialism contend that the domination of the Hollywood film industry in the global film market has a tendency to create cultural homogenisation by devouring small national industries. See Christophe Germann, "Content Industries and Cultural Diversity: The Case of Motion Pictures," in *Cultural Imperialism: Essays on the Political Economy of Cultural Domination*, ed. Bernd Hamm and Russell Smandych (Ontario: The Broadview Press, 2005), 93–113.
3 One example of such "right-wing" accounts is A. Sreberny-Mohammadi, "The Many Faces of Imperialism," in *Beyond Cultural Imperialism: Globalization, Communication, and the New International Order*, ed. P. Golding and P. Harris (London: Sage, 1997), 49–68. In this sense, the notions of right-wing critics echo those of cultural globalists who do not take American domination for granted. Oft-cited examples include such cases as the "export of Brazilian television program to Portugal and the Mexicization of southern California" [James Curran and Myung-Jin Park, "Introduction," in *De-Westernizing Media Studies*, eds. James Curran and Myung-Jin Park (London: Routledge, 2000), 4]. With regard to the case of China, scholars such as Michael Curtin have given close attention to its active response to Hollywood, arguing that the blossoming of Chinese cinema, along with China's rise as a superpower in the globalisation era, has undermined Hollywood's hegemony. See Michael Curtin, *Playing the Biggest Audience in the World: The Globalization of Chinese Film and Television* (Berkeley: University of California Press, 2007), 3.
4 Andrew Higson, "The Limiting Imagination of National Cinema," in *Cinema and Nation*, ed. Mette Hjort and Scott Mackenzie (London: Routledge, 2002), 104.
5 Recent studies on film culture in 1920s and 1930s China include Leo Ou-fan Lee, *Shanghai Modern: The Flowering of a New Urban Culture in China, 1930–1945* (Cambridge: Harvard University Press, 1999); Laikwan Pang, *Building a New China in Cinema, the Left-Wing Cinema Movement, 1932–1937* (Lanham: Rowman & Littlefield Publishers, 2002); Zhen Zhang, *An Amorous History of the Silver Screen: Shanghai Cinema* (Chicago: The University of Chicago Press, 2005); Yiman Wang, "Moving the Image between Shanghai, Hong Kong and Hollywood from 1920s to 1990s" (PhD, Duke University, 2003).
6 Zhiwei Xiao, "Hollywood in China, 1897–1950: A Preliminary Survey," *Chinese Historical Review* 12, 1 (2005): 72.
7 Annette Kuhn and Guy Westwell, *A Dictionary of Film Studies* (Oxford: Oxford University Press, 2012), 277.
8 Stephen Crofts, "Reconceptualizing National Cinema/S," in *Film and Nationalism*, ed. Alan Williams (New Brunswick: Rutgers University Press, 2002), 49.
9 Andrew Higson, "The Concept of National Cinema," ibid., 60.

10 Stephen Crofts, "Concepts of National Cinema," in *The Oxford Guide to Film Studies*, ed. John Hill and Pamela Gibson (Oxford: Oxford University Press, 1998), 389.
11 Higson, "The Limiting Imagination of National Cinema," 67.
12 Will Higbee and Song Hwee Lim, "Concepts of Transnational Cinema: Towards a Critical Transnationalism in Film Studies," *Transnational Cinema* 1, 1 (2010), 9.
13 Ibid., 14.
14 Sheldon Hsiao-peng Lu, "Historical Introduction, Chinese Cinemas (1896–1996) and Transnational Film Studies," in *Transnational Chinese Cinemas: Identity, Nationhood, Gender*, ed. Sheldon Hsiao-peng Lu (Honolulu: University of Hawaii Press, 1997), 3.
15 Chris Berry and Laikwan Pang, "Introduction, or, What Is an 'S,'" *Journal of Chinese Cinemas* 2, 1 (2008), 3.
16 Chris Berry, "Sino-Korean Screen Connections: Towards a History in Fragments," ibid. 10, 3 (2016), 247–264.
17 Jeremy Taylor, *Rethinking Transnational Chinese Cinemas, the Amoy-Dialect Film Industry in Cold War Asia* (London: Routledge, 2011).
18 Ibid., 124.
19 John Hill, "The Issues of National Cinema and British Film Production," in *New Questions of British Cinema*, ed. Duncan Petrie (London: BFI, 1992), 14.
20 Yingjin Zhang, *Cinema, Space and Polylocality in a Globalizing China* (Honolulu: Hawaii University Press, 2010), 16.
21 Chris Berry, "Transnational Chinese Cinema Studies," in *Chinese Cinema Book*, ed. Song Hwee Lim and Julian Ward (London: BFI, 2010), 11.
22 One exception is Zheng Junli's 鄭君里, *A Short History of Modern Chinese Film*/現代中國電影史略 (Shanghai: Shanghai Liangyou Book Company, 1936). Zheng acknowledges here that the development of Chinese films was a consequence of learning from Hollywood.
23 Thompson, *Exporting Entertainment: America in the World Film Market, 1907–1934*, x.
24 Marie Cambon, "The Dream Palace of Shanghai: American Films in China's Largest Metropolis 1920–1950," (MA, Simon Fraser University, 1993), 6.
25 Ibid., 50.
26 Xiao, "Hollywood in China, 1897–1950: A Preliminary Survey," 72; "American Films in China Prior to 1950," in *Art, Politics, and Commerce in Chinese Cinema*, ed. Ying Zhu and Stanley Rosen (Hong Kong: Hong Kong University Press, 2010), 55–69.
27 Xiao, "Hollywood in China, 1897–1950: A Preliminary Survey," 82.
28 This is my statistic based on the screening commercials published in *Xinwen Bao*, a Shanghai-based daily newspaper, from 1 January to 31 December 31, 1934.
29 Xiao, "Hollywood in China, 1897–1950: A Preliminary Survey," 87.
30 Qian Zhang, "From Hollywood to Shanghai: American Silent Films in China" (PhD, University of Pittsburgh, 2009).
31 Ibid., 10.
32 Xiao, "Hollywood in China, 1897–1950: A Preliminary Survey," 74; Quan Xie and Ying Shen, *The Development of the Early Chinese Film Industry*/中國早期電影產業發展歷程 (Beijing: China Film Press, 2011); Li Yu, *The Research of Chinese Film History: Production, Distribution, and Exhibition*/中國電影專業史：電影製片、發行、放映卷(Beijing: China Film Press, 2006).
33 Douglas Gomery, *The Coming of Sound* (New York: Routledge, 2005).
34 Apart from Xiao Zhiwei's efforts at estimating the box office receipts of Hollywood in China, some recent publications on the exhibition and film reception of Chinese cinema have appeared in the *Journal of Chinese Cinemas*. One

related study is Matthew Johnson, "Journey to the Seat of War: The International Exhibition of China in Early Cinema," *Journal of Chinese Cinemas* 3, 2 (2009): 109–122. It discusses the use of early filmic depictions of China by Western travel lecturers and missionaries. Johnson argues that the colonialism of the West, mirrored in the racist pictures which were also exhibited in China itself, "stimulated" Chinese nationalists to produce the first Chinese films.

35 See details later in this chapter.
36 Cambon, "The Dream Palace of Shanghai: American Films in China's Largest Metropolis 1920–1950," 123.
37 Ibid., 66–67.
38 Ibid., 136. Zhang Zhen argues that the emergence of China's film star system dates back to the early 1920s. At that time, the first generation of film actresses, including Wang Hanlun 王漢倫, Zhang Zhiyun 張織雲, and Yin Mingzhu 殷明珠, emerged in public discourse. See Zhang, *An Amorous History of the Silver Screen: Shanghai Cinema*, xxv.
39 Two examples in hand are Han Langen 韓蘭根 and Liu Jiqun 劉繼群, and Tan Ying 談瑛. Han and Liu were modelled on Laurel and Hardy, while Tan Ying was promoted as a "mysterious lady," echoing Greta Garbo. See "Camera News," *Camera*/开麦拉 1932, 2; Jiazhen, "Tan Ying: Garbo in Yellow Face/黃種嘉寶：談瑛," *Young Movie*/青青電影 3, 1 (1934), 1.
40 Xiao, "American Films in China Prior to 1950," 65.
41 Ning Ma, "The Textual and Critical Difference of Being Radical: Reconstructing Chinese Leftist Films in the 1930s," in *Celluloid China: Cinematic Encounters with Culture and Society*, ed. Harry Kuoshu (Carbondale: Southern Illinois University Press, 2002), 101.
42 Ibid.
43 Lee, *Shanghai Modern: The Flowering of a New Urban Culture in China, 1930–1945*, 85.
44 Ibid., 104.
45 Ibid., 114–115.
46 Ibid., 112.
47 Ruth Vasey, *The World According to Hollywood, 1918–1939* (Devon: University of Exeter Press, 1997), 85, 154–155.
48 Ibid., 175–179.
49 Jubin Hu, *Projecting a Nation: Chinese National Cinema before 1949* (Hong Kong: Hong Kong University Press, 2003), 4.
50 Ibid., 48.
51 Lawrence R. Sullivan, *Historical Dictionary of the Chinese Communist Party* (Lanham: Scarecrow Press, 2012). 61; Hu, *Projecting a Nation: Chinese National Cinema before 1949*, 48.
52 Ibid., 48.
53 Zhiwei Xiao, "Translating Hollywood Film to Chinese Audience: The Role of Agency and Appropriation in Transnational Cultural Encounters," in *Transnational Asian Identities in Pan-Pacific Cinemas*, ed. Philippa Gates and Lisa Funnell (New York: Routledge, 2012), 88–100.
54 Ibid., 94.
55 Wenzhi Huo, "My Hope to the Chinese Film Industry/我對於中國影片事業之希望," *Film Magazine*/電影雜誌 (1924), 1–3.
56 Richard P. Butrick, "The Motion Picture Industry in China, 893.4061, Motion Pictures/69." (4 October 1932), 47–48.
57 "Motion Pictures in China," *Records of the U.S. Department of State relating to the Internal Affairs of China, 1930–1939, 893.4061 Motion Pictures/41* (10 July 1931), 29.

58 "The Motion Picture Industry in China, 893.4061, Motion Pictures/69," 50.
59 Kar Law and Frank Bren, *Hong Kong Cinema: A Cross-Cultural View* (Lanham: Scarecrow, 2005), 6.
60 Ibid., 11.
61 Ibid., 12.
62 "Motion Picture Trade Abroad," *The Moving Picture World*, October–December 1914, 79.
63 Kerry Segrave, *American Films Abroad: Hollywood's Domination of the World's Movie Screens* (London: McFarland, 1997), 12.
64 Thompson, *Exporting Entertainment: America in the World Film Market, 1907–1934*, x.
65 "A Chat from China," *Moving Picture World*, 15, 2 (1913), 150.
66 Thompson, *Exporting Entertainment: America in the World Film Market, 1907–1934*, 29.
67 Letter from American Consulate General, Shanghai, China to Modern Film Sales, New York, 840.6 Motion Pictures, National Archives and Records Administration (NARA), 17 December 1934.
68 Segrave, *American Films Abroad: Hollywood's Domination of the World's Movie Screens*.
69 "Motion Pictures in China," 41.
70 Butrick, "The Motion Picture Industry in China, 893.4061, Motion Pictures/69," 40.
71 "China-Box Office Value," 7 June 1934, China Competitors, *Series 1F: Black books: Foreign Statistics*, United Artists Corporation Records, Box 4, Folder 4–6, Madison: Wisconsin Historical Society.
72 "Motion Pictures in China," 28.
73 Huang Dequan challenges the statement that *Ding Jun Mountain* is the first Chinese film. Huang argues that Fengtai Photo Company had no capacity to produce films at that time. Nevertheless, I maintain that Huang's argument is not very convincing due to a lack of primary and 'hard' evidence. See Dequan Huang, *A Textual Survey of Early Chinese Film History*/中國早期電影史事考證 (Beijing: China Film Press, 2012), 30–45.
74 Law and Bren, *Hong Kong Cinema: A Cross-Cultural View*; Huang, *A Textual Survey of Early Chinese Film History*/中國早期電影史事考證, 46–81.
75 A detailed analysis of the two organisers and the company is available in Chapter 5.
76 "The Chinese Film Industry," *People's Tribune* IX, 1 (1935), 26.
77 Yingjin Zhang, *Chinese National Cinema* (London: Routledge, 2004), 60.
78 "Motion Pictures in China," 19.
79 Ibid. According to another resource, the capital of Lianhua is said to be one million Mexican dollars; however, the report states that only half of them "has been paid up." See "Letter from Bank of China," Shanghai Municipal Archives, "The Industry of Film Production, a Survey Conducted by the Shanghai Commercial and Saving Bank/上海商業儲蓄銀行有關影片業調查資料," (Q275-1-1949).
80 Ibid.
81 A survey of the number of Chinese films prior to 1937 is conducted by Long Jin based on the commercials published in *Shen Bao*. I am grateful to Long Jin 龍锦 for his permission to cite these unpublished statistics.
82 "Motion Pictures in China," 18.
83 Ibid.
84 Butrick, "The Motion Picture Industry in China, 893.4061, Motion Pictures/69," 65–66.
85 Ibid., 23. The conversion is at the rate on 1 October 1932.

86 The well-received theory to date has been that China's first cinema was the Hongkew cinema, which Ramos established in 1908 in Shanghai. However, I have found that, as early as August 1907, the exhibition advertisement for the Colon Cinematograph appeared in *North China Daily News*. The address of the Colon Cinematograph is the same as the later Hongkew Cinema: 112A Chapoo Road, and the published property owner of the Colon Cinematograph is Antonio Ramos (*North China Desk Hong List*, January 1908, p. 48).
87 "Motion Pictures in China," 8.
88 Butrick, "The Motion Picture Industry in China, 893.4061, Motion Pictures/69," 22.
89 Ibid., 9.
90 P. Y Chien, "China's Film Magnete, T.J. Holt, to Seek Ideas Abroad for Development of Moving Picture Industry," *The China Weekly Review* (1937).
91 Lowenthal Rudolf, *The Present Status of the Film in China* (Peiping: The Collectanea Synodalis, 1936), 89.
92 Butrick, "The Motion Picture Industry in China, 893.4061, Motion Pictures/69," 107.
93 Shanghai Municipal Archives, "The Industry of Film Production, a Survey Conducted by the Shanghai Commercial and Saving Bank/上海商業儲蓄銀行有關影片業調查資料"; "The Theatre Houses Industries, a Survey Conducted by the Shanghai Commercial and Saving Bank/上海商业储蓄银行有关影戏院调查资料, Q275-1-2041."

References

Berry, Chris. "Sino-Korean Screen Connections: Towards a History in Fragments." *Journal of Chinese Cinemas* 10, no. 3 (2016): 247–263.

———."Transnational Chinese Cinema Studies." In *Chinese Cinema Book*, edited by Song Hwee Lim and Julian Ward, 11. London: BFI, 2010. 11.

Berry, Chris, and Laikwan Pang. "Introduction, or, What Is an 'S.'" *Journal of Chinese Cinemas* 2, no. 1 (2008): 3.

Butrick, Richard P. "The Motion Picture Industry in China, 893.4061, Motion Pictures/69." (4 October 1932), 74–75.

Cambon, Marie. "The Dream Palace of Shanghai: American Films in China's Largest Metropolis 1920–1950." Simon Fraser University, 1993.

"Camera News." *Camera*/开麦拉, 1932, 2.

"A Chat from China." *Moving Picture World*, 15, no. 2 (11 January 1913): 150.

Chien, P. Y. "China's Film Magnet, T.J. Holt, to Seek Ideas Abroad for Development of Moving Picture Industry." *The China Weekly Review*, 27 February 1937.

"The Chinese Film Industry." *People's Tribune* IX, no. 1 (1 April 1935): 26.

Crofts, Stephen. "Concepts of National Cinema." In *The Oxford Guide to Film Studies*, edited by John Hill and Pamela Gibson, 389. Oxford: Oxford University Press, 1998.

———. "Reconceptualizing National Cinema/S." In *Film and Nationalism*, edited by Alan Williams, 49. New Brunswick: Rutgers University Press, 2002.

Curran, James, and Myung-Jin Park. "Introduction." In *De-Westernizing Media Studies*, edited by James Curran and Myung-Jin Park, 4. London: Routledge, 2000.

Curtin, Michael. *Playing the Biggest Audience in the World: The Globalization of Chinese Film and Television*. Berkeley: University of California Press, 2007.

Germann, Christophe. "Content Industries and Cultural Diversity: The Case of Motion Pictures." In *Cultural Imperialism: Essays on the Political Economy of Cultural Domination*, edited by Bernd Hamm and Russell Smandych, 93–113. Ontario: The Broadview Press, 2005.
Gomery, Douglas. *The Coming of Sound*. New York: Routledge, 2005.
Higbee, Will, and Song Hwee Lim. "Concepts of Transnational Cinema: Towards a Critical Transnationalism in Film Studies." *Transnational Cinema* 1, no. 1 (2010): 9.
Higson, Andrew. "The Concept of National Cinema." In *Film and Nationalism*, edited by Alan Williams, 52–67. New Brunswick, NJ: Rutgers University Press, 2002.
———. "The Limiting Imagination of National Cinema." In *Cinema and Nation*, edited by Mette Hjort and Scott Mackenzie, 67. London: Routledge, 2002.
Hill, John. "The Issues of National Cinema and British Film Production." In *New Questions of British Cinema*, edited by Duncan Petrie, 10–21. London: BFI, 1992.
Hu, Jubin. *Projecting a Nation: Chinese National Cinema before 1949*. Hong Kong: Hong Kong University Press, 2003.
Huang, Dequan. *A Textual Survey of Early Chinese Film History*/中國早期電影史事考證. Beijing: China Film Press, 2012.
Huo, Wenzhi. "My Hope to the Chinese Film Industry/我對於中國影片事業之希望." *Film Magazine*/電影雜誌 (1924): 1–3.
Jiazhen. "Tan Ying: Garbo in Yellow Face/黃種嘉寶：談瑛." *Young Movie*/青青電影 3, no. 1 (1934).
Johnson, Matthew. "Journey to the Seat of War: The International Exhibition of China in Early Cinema." *Journal of Chinese Cinemas* 3, no. 2 (2009): 109–122.
Kuhn, Annette, and Guy Westwell. *A Dictionary of Film Studies*. Oxford: Oxford University Press, 2012.
Law, Kar, and Frank Bren. *Hong Kong Cinema: A Cross-Cultural View*. Lanham: Scarecrow, 2005.
Lee, Leo Ou-fan. *Shanghai Modern: The Flowering of a New Urban Culture in China, 1930–1945*. Cambridge: Harvard University Press, 1999.
Lu, Sheldon Hsiao-peng. "Historical Introduction, Chinese Cinemas (1896–1996) and Transnational Film Studies." In *Transnational Chinese Cinemas: Identity, Nationhood, Gender*, edited by Sheldon Hsiao-peng Lu, 3. Honolulu: University of Hawaii Press, 1997.
Ma, Ning. "The Textual and Critical Difference of Being Radical: Reconstructing Chinese Leftist Films in the 1930s." In *Celluloid China: Cinematic Encounters with Culture and Society*, edited by Harry Kuoshu, 97–109. Carbondale: Southern Illinois University Press, 2002.
"Motion Picture Trade Abroad." *The Moving Picture World*, October–December 1914, 79.
"Motion Pictures in China." Records of the U.S. Department of State relating to the Internal Affairs of China, 1930–1939, 893.4061 Motion Pictures/41 (10 July 1931).
Pang, Laikwan. *Building a New China in Cinema, the Left-Wing Cinema Movement, 1932–1937*. Lanham: Rowman & Littlefield Publishers, 2002.
Petras, James. "Cultural Imperialism in the Late 20th Century." *Journal of Contemporary Asia* 23, no. 2 (1993): 139–148.
Rudolf, Lowenthal. *The Present Status of the Film in China*. Peiping: The Collectanea Synodalis, 1936.

Schiller, Herbert. *Mass Communication and American Empire.* Boulder: Westview, 1992.
Segrave, Kerry. *American Films Abroad: Hollywood's Domination of the World's Movie Screens.* London: McFarland, 1997.
Shanghai Municipal Archives. "The Industry of Film Production, a Survey Conducted by the Shanghai Commercial and Saving Bank/上海商業儲蓄銀行有關影片業調查資料." Q275-1-1949.
———. "The Theatre Houses Industries, a Survey Conducted by the Shanghai Commercial and Saving Bank/上海商业储蓄银行有关影戏院调查资料, Q275-1-2041."
Shor, Francis. *Dying Empire: U.S. Imperialism and Global Resistance.* London: Routledge, 2010.
Sreberny-Mohammadi, A. "The Many Faces of Imperialism." Chap. 49–68. In *Beyond Cultural Imperialism: Globalization, Communication, and the New International Order*, edited by P. Golding and P. Harris, 48–68. London: Sage, 1997.
Sullivan, Lawrence R. *Historical Dictionary of the Chinese Communist Party.* Lanham: Scarecrow Press, 2012.
Taylor, Jeremy. *Rethinking Transnational Chinese Cinemas, the Amoy-Dialect Film Industry in Cold War Asia.* London: Routledge, 2011.
Thompson, Kristin. *Exporting Entertainment: America in the World Film Market, 1907–1934.* London: BFI, 1985.
Vasey, Ruth. *The World According to Hollywood, 1918–1939.* Devon: University of Exeter Press, 1997.
Wang, Yiman. "Moving the Image between Shanghai, Hong Kong and Hollywood from 1920s to 1990s." Duke University, 2003.
Xiao, Zhiwei. "American Films in China Prior to 1950." In *Art, Politics, and Commerce in Chinese Cinema*, edited by Ying Zhu and Stanley Rosen, 55–69. Hong Kong: Hong Kong University Press, 2010.
———. "Hollywood in China, 1897–1950: A Preliminary Survey." *Chinese Historical Review* 12, no. 1 (2005): 72–100.
———. "Translating Hollywood Film to Chinese Audience: The Role of Agency and Appropriation in Transnational Cultural Encounters." In *Transnational Asian Identities in Pan-Pacific Cinemas*, edited by Philippa Gates and Lisa Funnell, 88–100. New York: Routledge, 2012.
Xie, Quan, and Ying Shen. *The Development of the Early Chinese Film Industry/中國早期電影產業發展歷程.* Beijing: China Film Press, 2011.
Yu, Li. *The Research of Chinese Film History: Production, Distribution, and Exhibition/中國電影專業史研究: 電影製片、發行、放映卷.* Beijing: China Film Press, 2006.
Zhang, Qian. "From Hollywood to Shanghai: American Silent Films in China." University of Pittsburgh, 2009.
Zhang, Yingjin. *Chinese National Cinema.* London: Routledge, 2004.
———. *Cinema, Space and Polylocality in a Globalizing China.* Honolulu: Hawaii University Press, 2010.
Zhang, Zhen. *An Amorous History of the Silver Screen: Shanghai Cinema.* Chicago: The University of Chicago Press, 2005.

2 Technology and the trans/national in China's transition to sound

This chapter is a study of the American film industry's contribution to Chinese cinema's conversion to sound from 1931 to 1936. While Hollywood's transition to sound in the late 1920s has drawn enormous attention, little is known about the history of cinema's sound transition in other countries such as China.[1] In addition, the scholarly literature dealing with the relations between the American and the Chinese film industries concentrates on the American film industry's function as a model for the domestic film industry but fails to examine the American film industry's other significant functions.[2] Through an examination of the evolution of China's transition to sound in the 1930s, I argue that the American film industry serves as a constructive force in the formation of the domestic film industry. This chapter suggests that the existing literature advocating the concept of a "national cinema" fails to explain adequately the function of the American film industry in the making of the Chinese national film industry.

To provide a background to China's transition to sound films, I begin this chapter with a brief discussion of the introduction of Hollywood talkies into China in the late 1920s and early 1930s. I then provide an analysis of the American film industry's impact on the coming of sound in Chinese films, focussing on economy and technology. This chapter initially investigates the American film industry's economic influence by showing how it impacted the earliest Chinese talkies and simultaneously encouraged the continued production of silent films. I then explore the function of the American film industry in the field of technology. Three specific issues are stressed: (1) why the American film industry, at the beginning, failed to play a vital role in China's sound conversion; (2) how the American film industry benefited the upsurge of the first wave of competition on sound; and (3) the role American film industry played when China manufactured its own sound machines. The chapter concludes by linking the analysis of the American film industry's contribution to China with the current development of trans/national cinema studies.

The coming of Hollywood talkies

Like its American equivalents, silent films in China had been viewed with live musical accompaniment.[3] Quality theatres employed orchestras to attract patrons during the silent period. In some theatres, film explainers offered live accounts of the narrative.

Shanghai, as the principal centre of film production, distribution, and exhibition in China, was known to be aware of new sound film experiments in the United States from the 1910s to the 1930s. *North China Herald* pointed out that "Shanghai had the reputation of always being up-to-date, getting the latest and newest of everything, especially in regard to entertainment for the public," thanks to the close communication between Shanghai and the outside world.[4] One year after Edison invented the acoustic kinetophone in 1913, Shanghai audiences could experience it at the Victoria Theatre 維多利亞.[5] The preview commercial mentions that audiences could see and hear programmes including "the latest musical comedies, dramas, operas and well known STARS from the Vaudeville Stage faithfully reproduced by this wonderful invention."[6] At the end of 1926, Lee De Forest's Phonofilm was brought to the Pantheon Theatre 百星 by Y. Minagawa, a Japanese exhibitor who had obtained sole rights for the Far East.[7] The Phonofilm presented several programmes including music by Roy Smeck and a speech delivered by President Coolidge in the White House.[8] The Phonofilm had another showing in Shanghai two years later, through the Young Men's Christian Association (YMCA), an important conduit for introducing new technology into modern China. Dr C. H. Roberson, the general secretary of the YMCA in Shanghai, brought another film made by De Forest and exhibited its ability at the Martyrs Memorial Hall in Shanghai in November 1928.[9]

The first fully equipped sound apparatus theatre in China was the Embassy Theatre 夏令配克 in 1929. The sound reproduction equipment was the Photophone brand, made by the Radio Corporation of America (RCA).[10] In January 1929, *Captain Swagger* (dir. Edward H Griffith, 1928) premiered at the Embassy. The expert from the United States credited with installing the equipment and training the operators and mechanics at the Embassy is J. P. Koehler. After his job at the Embassy, Koehler travelled to Perth in July 1929 where he introduced the Photophone machine to Australia for the first time.[11]

The initial responses to talkie pictures from the public were mixed. A comment in the *North China Herald* complained that "[t]he talking completely killed the film. Interest and illusion vanished in a flash. Action slowed down and the actors became utterly wooden and amateurish."[12] In addition, the quality of synchronised sound was far from perfect. The author complained, "[c]onsonants vanished ... and half the words were guesswork ... [T]here was little or nothing to connect the speakers and with their words."[13] The author opined that "[the Embassy] should ship the apparatus back to America and stick to the silent drama."[14] But there were positive responses. A letter from one S.C. Kingsbury suggested it was important to exercise patience until sound film technology improved. Kingsbury stated, "[t]he equipment which Mr Hertzberg had installed undoubtedly represented a tidy sum."[15] Although there were controversial responses and discussions, the talkie box office at the Embassy was promising due to the scarcity of talkie pictures in China. The Embassy opened to packed performances three times a day, and it was reported that the box office receipts broke records.[16]

Attracted by the Embassy's promising business and encouraged by the rapid development in sound technology, the owners of first-class cinemas in Shanghai rushed to install sound machines. By the end of 1930, at least 12 out of 53 theatres installed sound projectors and most first-class theatres showed sound films exclusively.[17] Outside of Shanghai, cities including Hong Kong, Canton, Tianjin, Hankou, Beijing, and Harbin had also installed sound equipment.[18]

Generally speaking, in terms of function, there are two types of sound apparatus. One is a sound reproduction machine or sound projector designed for theatres and the other is a sound recording machine designed for producing films in studios. Both sound reproduction and sound recording machines have two formats, sound-on-disc and sound-on-film. In the beginning, the sound reproduction apparatus installed at Shanghai theatres, such as the Embassy, employed sound-on-disc technology. This technology was soon replaced by a more sophisticated and reliable sound-on-film technology. American products dominated the sound reproduction equipment market. Eleven out of 29 sound reproduction machines installed in Shanghai theatres were West Electric products, while eight theatres equipped with RCA machines, according to 1932 statistics.[19]

The gap in the market and inspiration: two economic contributions of the American film industry in the early 1930s

I now focus on the economic role the American film industry played in the history of China's transition to talkies. Hollywood's move to sound immobilised its own production of silent films. By the end of 1932, Hollywood's absence in the silent film market created a gaping hole in the Chinese film industry, while China itself continued to produce silent films until 1936. Along with the continued development of technology, Hollywood talkies demonstrated to Chinese film-makers that sound film would be an inevitable move in the future. Chinese film producers realised that a transition to sound films was coming, and under these circumstances, Chinese film practitioners commenced experimenting with sound-on-disc technology from 1931.

In the earliest days of the transition to sound, Hollywood films decreased in popularity in China in general, because Hollywood cut the number of silent films to increase the gross of talkie productions. However, Hollywood's talkies did not enjoy the same reception as its silent films. Language was a fundamental barrier. Although a proportion of student audiences would watch Hollywood films as a way of learning English, the number of English-speaking Chinese residents remained few. Even some intellectuals could not understand English. An editor from a leading newspaper claimed that he had seldom gone to cinemas after the arrival of sound film in Shanghai because he had not yet reached the required level of English language comprehension.[20] Another barrier for Hollywood talkies in China was the slow process of installing sound machines in theatres outside of Shanghai. It is noted that over 66 per cent of talking picture theatres in 1932 were located in five principal cities (Shanghai, Hong Kong, Canton, Hankou, and Tianjin).[21] "The original expense of installation, the lack of facilities for servicing and the dangers and difficulties of transportation to interior places" were barriers to installing sound equipment for the cinemas in interior cities.[22] With regard to the cost of installation, the sound equipment alone at the Eastern Theatre 東海 in Shanghai, for instance, cost 11,285.11 yuan, a major expense for any cinema.[23] Given that the price of admission was between 20–30 cents, cinemas in cities like Fuzhou (Foochow) and Yantai did not have enough capital to install sound equipment.[24]

Hollywood's executives, however, paid little attention to the situation of small film markets such as China. The Chinese film market was considered a minor one for the American film industry in the first half of the twentieth century, only accounting for around 1 per cent of Hollywood's foreign revenues.[25] Because of this, the success of talkies in North America and Europe persuaded Hollywood's moguls to shift production to talkie pictures from 1928.[26] Consequently, in early 1933, of the 121 Hollywood films imported to China, only three were silent. That is to say, cinemas without sound capabilities would face serious film shortages. Meanwhile, some of the Chinese audiences became increasingly indifferent to Hollywood's sound films due to the language barrier. This demand in the local market for silent films generated an opportunity for the Chinese silent film industry.

Chinese film-makers soon realised the opportunity for development and continued producing silent films to meet market demand. This is one key reason for which Lianhua was set up in 1930 to produce silent films. Luo Mingyou, the executive of Lianhua, and his employees, produced several silent films between 1930 and 1931, such as *The Reminiscence of Peking* (故都春夢, dir. Sun Yu, 1930), *Love and Duty* (戀愛與義務, dir. Bu Wancang, 1931), and *When a Brother Sacrifices* (義雁情鴛, dir. Wang Cilong, 1930). These silent films not only changed the direction of Chinese film production, but also brought Lianhua considerable profit. It was logical for Lianhua to retain its profitable silent film production, rather than taking the risk of moving to sound. This proved to be a wise decision in the initial stages of the transition to sound. From July 1932 to June 1933, the net profit of Lianhua amounted to 15,911.44 yuan, while several other studios such as Mingxing were in serious deficit.[27]

Apart from taking advantage of the gap in the market left by Hollywood talkies, other key factors contributed to the choice of Chinese film-makers to stay with silent films. First, Chinese films also had a problem of language engagement in talkie production. In contrast to a relatively unified written language, China has numerous dialects. The legitimate national language, Mandarin, did not spread markedly in the 1930s despite the central government's efforts at enforcement. Local governments in autonomy such as Canton authorities strongly resisted government attempts at enforcing the homogenisation of a national language. They regarded Canton dialect as a cornerstone for maintaining local independence.[28] The Chinese film authorities, however, allowed no film to be produced in any language other than Mandarin. Therefore, government pressure to use Mandarin as the national language represented a high risk for Chinese film-makers. Employing Mandarin effectively meant a loss of the Canton market, the second largest in China. But in employing Cantonese, film-makers would face punishment from the government. This dilemma to some extent prevented the development of Chinese sound pictures. As Luo Mingyou declared in 1932, "[o]wing to the existence of many local dialects in China, it is difficult for a Chinese film company to make a talking picture with a popular appeal."[29] The second reason for remaining with silent films was that the cost of producing talkie pictures was higher. The price of a regular sound recording machine amounted to 10,000 yuan in the 1930s. This was a considerable burden for Chinese studios. In addition, while the cost for producing a Chinese silent film ranged from 2,000 to 8,000 yuan, a sound film would cost 8,000 yuan to 17,000 yuan, a significant difference in comparison with the silent films.[30]

Accordingly, China consolidated its silent film business in the late 1920s and early 1930s. When the American film industry introduced sound films to China in 1929, 127 silent films were produced in China, peaking in the first half of the twentieth century. The number of silent productions remained over 100 in both 1930 and 1931. In addition, studio earnings increased dramatically from 1929 to 1931. Taking Mingxing Company for instance, the gross earnings in 1929 accounted for 356,562.58 yuan, and the gross earnings doubled over the next years.[31]

The prosperity of silent films, however, was short-lived, and the arrival of the sound picture was inevitable for the Chinese film industry. The quality of talkie pictures had improved remarkably after the first talkie was shown in China, thanks to the fact that the apparatus had been perfected mechanically. The tastes of Chinese audiences evolved to include sound pictures. The talking picture, therefore, was permanently established, and this was evidenced by the thriving business of Hollywood talkies in China after its decline in the initial stages. But the dialogue still annoyed Chinese audiences, who barely understood English. All these factors suggested that the time for producing Chinese-speaking talkies was coming. A number of studios wanted to earn the credit for producing the first talkies in China, for the sake of honour as well as predictable profit. The credit went to one of the most powerful companies.

The Singing Peony was the first Chinese talkie picture, released by the Mass Paminphone Co. Ltd, a joint company created by Mingxing, a leading film studio, and the Pathé Orient Corporation, a leading recording company and a branch of Pathé in China. Mingxing took responsibility for filming and editing; Pathé was in charge of recording and other sound technology. As early as August 1930, Mingxing announced its plan for producing talkies. On a 100,000 yuan budget, Mingxing assigned its most reputable director, Zhang Shichuan; scriptwriter Hong Shen 洪深; and its most recognisable actors, Butterfly Wu 胡蝶 and Gong Jianong 龔稼農, to ensure that *The Singing Peony* drew a large audience. After eight months of work, *The Singing Peony* was released in March 1931 with its premiere at the Strand Theatre 新光. It was advertised as "a talkie blockbuster that has never been seen before" and "the benchmark film in the Chinese film industry."[32] Indeed, *The Singing Peony* was "an attraction because of its novelty and the fact that it [was] a timely attempt to make a Chinese sound picture."[33] Distributor Huawei sold its copies to the Philippines for 18,000 yuan and Indonesia for 16,000 yuan, a much higher price than that of regular productions.[34] After releasing *The Singing Peony*, Mingxing and Pathé Orient released another synchronised feature, *So, This is Paradise* (如此天堂, dir. Zhang Shichuan), later in 1931.

Small and midsize studios also partook in experimentation with sound film production. Youlian (a.k.a. U Luien Film Co. 友聯) released *The Singing Beauty* (虞美人, dir. Chen Kengran) on 24 May 1931, two months after *The Singing Peony*. This was the second synchronised feature in the history of Chinese cinema. By the end of 1931, Lianhua presented its first synchronised feature *Two Stars* (銀漢雙星, dir. Shi Dongshan, 1931), despite most of its energy being diverted to silent film production. In order to prepare its talkie production, Lianhua established a 'folly' school by incorporating the renowned Bright Moon Follies to train film actors in voice and articulation. In addition, Luo signed performing artists Mei Lanfang 梅蘭芳, Li Minghui 黎明暉, and Zi Luolan 紫羅蘭 to join the cast. Zi Luolan was cast as the heroine in *Two Stars*, which debuted at the Nanking Theatre 南京 on 13 December 1931. Unfortunately, the response to *Two Stars* was unsatisfactory because the film was not properly synchronised in places. More importantly, the tastes of audiences at that time had already shifted to more reliable sound technology.

Supplier and model: Hollywood's contribution to technology in the mid-1930s

The technology utilised in *Two Stars* was the same as that used in *The Singing Peony*, that is, sound-on-disc, a technology that had already been abandoned by Hollywood. In this section, I examine the technological contribution of the American film industry to China's transition to sound. I investigate the various stages of this transition and explore Hollywood's contribution in these phases. More specifically, I focus on three aspects: (1) Hollywood's role in the beginning of China's transition to sound, particularly when China engaged in the sound-on-disc technology; (2) how the first wave of Chinese talkies benefited from Hollywood; and (3) how Hollywood served as a successful model for Chinese engineers during the development phase of Chinese technology.

When China first engaged in sound-on-disc technology during the earliest stage of China's transition to talkies, Hollywood did not have much influence on this technology, as the sound-on-disc technology had dissipated in the United States. The focus of American producers had already shifted to the sound-on-film technology when China started to engage in sound film experiments in 1931. However, Chinese studios could not afford the expense of installing sound-on-film machines in the very early 1930s. For instance, in its initial effort to produce sound films, Mingxing contacted the representatives of West Electric and RCA in Shanghai, seeking out keys to profitability. Both corporations employed similar policies: namely, studios producing sound films needed to pay bonds and royalty fees accounting for around 8 per cent of box office returns. However, due to the low profits at that time, Mingxing could not afford the same costs as its Hollywood counterparts.[35] Chinese film-makers, therefore, were forced to seek support from other sources, and the recording industry became their target. The decision to choose the recording industry was made on the basis of technology since the technology of sound-on-disc films maintained similarities with that of record production. During the production of *The Singing Peony*, sound engineers in the Pathé Corporation made considerable efforts to resolve this issue. Youlian, the producer of China's second sound-on-disc film, could not afford the new technology, whereas Mingxing could. Thus, Youlian used common sound recording technology which recorded discs with an audio track first and then linked it to the image track.

The results of this sound-on-disc technology, however, were unsatisfactory, and synchronisation was an evident problem. During the production of *The Singing Peony*, sound distortion occurred due to a slow rotating speed, which caused the actors' voices to sound sharp.[36] Due to the post-recording process, a slight mistake in an actor's performance could easily ruin synchronicity.[37] This was a long and expensive process. Mingxing's financial reports showed production budgets increased by 33 per cent in 1930 due to sound-on-disc film production.[38] Therefore, after these sound-on-disc trials, Chinese film practitioners opted to pursue a more sophisticated form of technology, that is, sound-on-film technology. Luckily, it did not take long.

In contrast to sound-on-disc, Chinese film-makers had few options for sound-on-film, apart from employing Hollywood's model. The complexity of the sound-on-film technology prevented Chinese film-makers from finding alternative machines. China's first sound-on-film movie, *Peace after Storm*

(雨過天青, dir. Xia Chifeng, 1931), was recorded by an American machine. It was released by Huaguang Sound-on-film Motion Picture Corporation (華光) on 1 July 1931, which was slightly later than the release of *The Singing Beauty*, the second sound-on-disc talkie in China. Huaguang's publicity claimed that the sound machines employed in *Peace after Storm* belonged to K. Henry, an American news cameraman for Paramount studio who was then in Japan. With the intention of reducing costs and ensuring equipment quality, Huaguang dispatched actors and crews to Japan, instead of shipping the equipment to Shanghai.[39] Fuelled by nationalism, film critics attacked *Peace after Storm* as a Japanese production and called for its prohibition. The date of its premiere was just two months before the Manchurian Incident, in which Japanese troops occupied North-East China and caused a national upsurge of hostility towards Japan. A riot occurred during the screening due to nationalists letting off fireworks, despite the fact that no official prohibition had been issued concerning *Peace after Storm*. However, Huaguang did not continue producing talkie pictures, possibly due to the high cost of sound equipment.

The first wave of producing talkie pictures in China benefited from Hollywood after two leading studios, Tianyi and Mingxing, secured sound-on-film equipment from the United States in 1931. In June 1931, Tianyi announced it had secured Fox's Movietone, a relatively sophisticated sound-on-film device, by virtue of the intervention of Leon Britton, a veteran American producer who was known as a fight promoter. Apart from Britton, the experts who were invited to assist in producing Tianyi's talkie picture included Charles Hugo, associate, Bert Cann, chief cameraman, Bryan Guerin, sound engineer, and Joseph Smith, laboratory chief.[40] To perfect synchronicity in their first talkie, Tianyi was reported to have "completely remodelled" their former studio and "built a complete new laboratory in accordance with the most recent developments in the industry."[41] Tianyi also sacrificed its production speed, despite the fact that it was known for its production efficiency. For instance, for Tianyi's first talkie, *Romance of Opera* (歌場春色, dir. Li Pingqian, 1931), the studio could only shoot four or five scenes per day in comparison to ten scenes per day in the silent film era.[42] After a three-month promotional newspaper campaign, *Romance of Opera* finally debuted at the Strand Theatre on 29 October 1931. It was a tremendous box office hit in South-East Asian countries.

Tianyi's acquisition of sound-on-film technology was a massive blow to its main rival, Mingxing. Mingxing executives were clear that the future of talkie pictures was the sound-on-film technology, because of the exceptional sound synchronisation.[43] They were aware of the potential threat to their leading position in the Chinese film industry if they did not evolve their sound technology. Like Tianyi, the executives of Mingxing contacted an American middleman, Harry Garson, a Hollywood producer, who was in Shanghai "arranging for the filming of a local color picture of China" and leading Universal's expedition to film *Ourang* at the time.[44] Through the mediation of Garson, in July 1931 Hong Shen, the scriptwriter of *The Singing Peony*, was dispatched to the United States on behalf of Mingxing to select suitable talkie machines. On 22 August, Hong and Garson returned to Shanghai with sound equipment and a technical crew of 14, which included Sidney Lund, Jack Smith, and Jimmy O. Williamson.[45]

The history of Hong Shen's American journey deserves detailed commentary since fundamental information is lacking about the apparatus, such as the brand, quantity, and cost. In this investigation my assessment must be for the most part based on historical archives. For instance, a financial archive records documents pertaining to the Shanghai Jiaotong Bank loan to Mingxing in 1936, including 59 letters between Mingxing, the Shanghai Jiaotong Bank, and their lawyers.[46] According to this archive, Mingxing borrowed 160,000 yuan from the Shanghai Jiaotong Bank. To convince the bank of its repayment ability, Mingxing vouched for all its productions, business property, and immovable property, and provided a detailed list of its business properties. According to the documents from Shanghai Jiaotong Bank, Mingxing had purchased at least five items of machinery in 1932, and it listed two sound recorders and colour cameras, 84 mercury vapour lamps, two editing machines, one film bulk printer for sound films, and one film splicer. These purchase lists indicate the costs of each machine and the miscellaneous effects. Mingxing paid between 186,766 yuan and 194,298 yuan for purchasing the apparatuses including sound recorders and colour cameras. The real costs would have been higher since the costs listed in the documents did not include the expense of Hong's journey fee and the wages for foreign technicians. The brand of the sound-on-film apparatus is not included in the original documents. On 9 March 1932, a company titled Hollywood Camera Exchange Ltd (HOCAMEX) wrote a letter to Julean Arnold, officer of the Commercial Attaché, with regard to Garson denying liability for unpaid sound equipment.[47] As the only sound equipment developed by this company is called Audio-Camex machine, I confirm that the brand of the sound-on-film apparatus purchased by Mingxing was Audio-Camex. In addition, a Chinese film history journal supports my speculation.[48] It is evident that the colour machine purchased by Mingxing was the Multicolor.[49]

To fully utilise these machines, Mingxing and Garson entered an agreement "forming a closed company which would be titled the Orient Pacific Picture Corporation."[50] This company would have "direct contact with the R.K.O. (Radio-Keith-Orpheum) Distributing Corporation, which would market the films made in China, in the United States and in other countries."[51] The plan to establish the Orient Pacific Picture Corporation, however, was aborted due to Garson breaking the agreement for reasons which are unclear.[52] In hindsight, the enormous expense of the apparatus, naturally consolidated Mingxing's leading position in the Chinese film industry, while it also resulted in a considerable deficit for the company. In 1931, Mingxing's net profit was 19,986.83 yuan. After purchasing the apparatuses in 1932, Mingxing had a sizeable deficit of 47,320.62 yuan.[53]

The lease of sound-on-film apparatuses from the United States by Mingxing and Tianyi caused them to complete as many productions as possible to take full advantage of the lease period. Mingxing and Tianyi fully understood that Chinese talkies were scarce products and that they should capitalise on the market by all means possible. Consequently, synchronised feature production reached its first peak in 1932. Each studio produced eight sound films. To take advantage of sound films, both studios applied for more exhibition permits. The average number of per annum licence applications for talkie pictures underwent a noticeable increase in comparison with silent films in 1930s China. Tianyi applied for 1.9 licences for its silent films, in contrast to 4.43 licences for sound films, and Mingxing averaged 3.96 screening permits for silent films, while sound production permits were 7.55, around double those of silent films.

Hollywood's sound-on-film recording equipment also spawned Chinese imitators. In the 1930s, there were at least seven imitators whose products included sound reproduction and recording apparatus in the Chinese film market. China's attempts to produce its own sound equipment date back to 1930. Huawei distributed and manufactured sound reproduction equipment named Huawei feng/Whaweiphone.[54] Strictly speaking, Whaweiphone was allegedly copied from Movietone, instead of being an original product of Huawei.[55] Whaweiphone, according to a market survey, "had met with a limited acceptance in China," and only 11 Whaweiphones were in operation nationwide.[56] As well as Whaweiphone, another reproduction machine named Orthola circulated in China's film market in the 1930s. Orthola was assembled by the Electric Service Corporation, using both American and Chinese manufactured components. The Electric Service Corporation was registered as an American film company under the provision of the China Trade Act, with its base in Shanghai. As with Whaweiphone, there were 11 theatres equipped with Orthola.

Aisitong/Sinophone, produced by Shi Shipan 石世磐, is the first experimental sound recording equipment designed for film production in China. Shi had previously been educated in the United States and worked in a Hollywood company producing arc lights. His American education and experience provided him with sound knowledge of the available technologies in Hollywood. After returning to China, Shi worked as a producer and cameraman for Mingxing.[57] He was inspired to produce sound machinery after seeing R.C. Robertson's Phonofilm device in 1928.[58] In 1932, Sinophone was finally invented. However few studios were willing to engage with it, and Sinophone dissipated, despite its being used to produce several short documentary films.

After Mingxing and Tianyi secured sound machines from the United States in 1931, Chinese sound engineers began attempts at duplicating these sound-on-film machines, winning support from the executives of the Chinese studios, who wished to avoid the considerable expense of leasing American sound machines. Shao Zuiweng 邵醉翁, the owner and executive of Tianyi, next invited several Chinese engineers to confidentially observe Movietone. The observers included Wu Weiyun 吳蔚雲, Situ Huimin 司徒慧敏, and Tao Shengbai 陶勝百. Situ Huimin and Tao Shengbai later contributed to the outcome of two Chinese sound machines in 1933: Sanyou shi/Sanyou Record and Zhonghua tong/Chinatone, respectively.[59]

Having been educated in the United States, Gong Yuke 龔玉珂, Situ Yimin 司徒逸民, and Ma Dejian 馬德建 formed Diantong (a.k.a. Denton Sound Studio 電通) to market Sanyou Record in 1933. Situ Huimin, who was present at the Movietone demonstration at the Tianyi Studio, was the main promoter of Sanyou Record. In its short life, Sanyou Record was used in several prominent films in Chinese film history. One such film was *Children of the Clouds* (風雲兒女, dir. Xu Xingzhi, 1935). The theme song of the film, *March of the Volunteers*, was later adopted as the national anthem of the People's Republic of China from 1949. Sanyou Record had also been used in two Lianhua productions, *Big Road* (大路, dir. Sun Yu, 1934) and *The Song of the Fishermen* (漁光曲, dir. Cai Chusheng, 1934). The latter obtained one of the first international awards – "an honorary prize at the 1935 Moscow Film Festival" – and achieved the record for the longest continuous run of any film displayed in China.[60]

In 1933 Tao Shengbai, another observer of the Movietone, invented Chinatone, the most widely used sound device up until 1949. At least seven large and midsize studios utilised Chinatone in 1934, and it was even exported to South-East Asia for producing sound films in 1941.[61] The first film which employed Chinatone was *The Legend of Taiping Heavenly Kingdom* (紅羊豪俠傳, dir. Yang Xiaozhong, 1935), which was premiered at the best theatre in Shanghai. Encouraged by the success of this sound film experiment, Zhang Shankun, the producer/investor of the film, formed Xinhua Studio in 1936 and grew to be a recognisable film baron in the 1940s. Not surprisingly, Chinatone continued to record Xinhua's productions, including *New Peach Blossom Fan* (新桃花扇, dir. Ouyang Yuqian, 1935), *Song at Midnight* (夜半歌聲, dir. Maxu Weibang, 1937), and *Sable Cicada* (貂蟬, dir. Bu Wancang, 1938).[62]

It is evident that most Chinese sound machines were duplications of American models. A market survey conducted by the American consul in China indicated that, by virtue of little protection for foreign patents and copyrights in China, Chinese manufacturers could easily duplicate American sound projectors.[63] The market survey pointed out two versions of Chinese sound equipment as examples where copying had taken place, that is, Sinophone and Heming tong/Hemingtone (another Chinese sound machine manufactured by Yan Heming 顏鶴鳴 in 1933). The survey was probably correct on this. Shi Shipan, the founder of Sinophone, claimed that the structure of Sinophone was the same as that of RCA's Photophone machine, despite Sinophone's copyright licence.[64] By contrast, Hemingtone failed to even patent an application. The authorities declared that Hemingtone was nothing but a sound machine "firstly used in China by employing the latest foreign method."[65] In addition, the quality of these duplicated machines was not on par with the American models. A case in point is Chinatone, which was supposedly a more reliable device than others. A director recalled that Chinatone was only equipped with a microphone which weighed five pounds, connected to the recording machine by a fishing pole. The polar pattern of the microphone was so poor that only one direction could be recorded, requiring ongoing adjustment for distance or angle, or it would collapse the sound recording completely.[66]

Regardless of copyright and quality, a major advantage of Chinese sound machines was their cost in comparison to that of the American equipment. According to a market survey conducted in 1932, "of the three American [recording] makes being marketed [in China], the cheapest model sells for approximately 11,900 yuan, [h]owever, the same type of Chinese equipment sold at 8,000 yuan, around 3,900 yuan cheaper."[67] The low price was evidently a key reason why some Chinese production studios preferred to employ Chinese sound machines instead of American machines, despite risks to the quality of their products.

American sound experts provided technical support and training for Chinese engineers. As I mentioned earlier, the sound machines of Mingxing and Tianyi were obtained through the mediation of American film-makers Harry Garson and Leon Britton, respectively. In addition, a number of technicians were invited to assist the talkie production in the initial stage of China's transition to sound. These experts were highly criticised in the literature of the time due to their lofty attitudes, personalities, and high wages.[68] However, these technicians are recognised as those who trained the first generation of Chinese sound engineers. As mentioned, Tianyi's executive secretly invited Chinese engineers to observe an imported sound machine to enable them to conceptualise their own devices for China. Studio executives such as Zhang Shichuan also arranged Chinese assistants for these foreign experts with the intention of 'stealing' their knowledge of sound machines. As soon as the Chinese assistants grasped how to operate the machinery, the executives could dismiss these experts in order to avoid paying high wages. It is documented that the first generation of sound recordists, such as He Zhaozhang, He Zhaohuang, and Zhao Maosheng, received their professional knowledge through instruction from the American technicians.[69]

Thinking "trans/national" in the domain of technology

China's transition to sound provides a case for examining the function of Hollywood within the Chinese film industry in the first half of the twentieth century. During China's transition to talkie pictures, the American film industry played a crucial role in the development of both economic and technological perspectives, suggesting that the American film industry was a constructive force in the formation of the Chinese film industry.

A study of the sector of film technology, particularly cinema's conversion to sound in China, can be seen as a response to the academic transition from the national cinema approach to the transnational cinema approach. As Chris Berry points out, "[t]he national cinema as a theoretical model ... cannot accommodate the movement of films across borders, reception of foreign films and so forth."[70] However, a shift in terminology from the national cinema approach to the transnational cinema approach does not mean that one ignores the significance of the relations between cinema and the national, since "the national continues to exert the force of its presence even within transnational film-making practice."[71] The sector of film technology in China is a case in point. The cinematic conversion to sound can be seen as an effort to construct the national within technology. First, in contrast to other products, which relied almost entirely on importation, sound equipment is one of the very few sectors where China released its own national products. Second, Chinese film critics clearly associated technology with national identity. Zhou Jianyun 周劍雲, for instance, denies the 'Chineseness' of Chinese films since the film equipment and raw material were imported from Europe and American, rather than originating in China.[72] Similarly, some Chinese film critics refused to regard *Peace after Storm* as a Chinese film, since it used American sound apparatus and was produced in Japan.[73] Additionally, Chinese engineers resorted to a nationalistic rhetoric to promote their own sound machines, praising the latter as "glories of the Chinese nation." Therefore, Berry and Farquhar suggest the need for putting "the problem of what the national is – how it is constructed, maintained, and challenged" in Chinese film studies.[74]

In the process of constructing the national, the contribution of the transnational, the American film industry, in this case, should be taken into account. This stands as a major distinction between the conventional national cinema approach and the transnational cinema approach. Under the influence of "national cinema," the methodological approach in the existing literature polarises the function of the American film industry with respect to the Chinese film industry. As one account of national cinema points out, "[t]he American cinema looms large as a term of reference for every national cinema in the West and many beyond."[75] China is no exception. The existing literature claims that Hollywood was largely a model for the domestic film industry in domains such as the film star system and the film studio system.[76] One assumption in these writings is a clear-cut boundary between Hollywood and the domestic film industry. Literally speaking, the concept of a 'model' suggests an *outside position* to the domestic film industry. One can imitate the model or incorporate the model's style but the model itself still stands strictly outside of the subject. An assumption of a clear-cut boundary between the American film industry and the domestic film industry is closely linked with the conventional cinema approach, which argues that a national cinema asserts "its difference from" others and proclaims "its sense of otherness."[77]

As a matter of fact, the American film industry functioned as far more than merely a model for the domestic film industry. The American film industry crossed the national boundary and served as an "inside" force, integrating itself into the making of the Chinese film industry, as this chapter has demonstrated. Economically, Hollywood was a competitor, inspiring and encouraging the Chinese film industry. When Hollywood talkies came into the Chinese film market, the imported sound pictures created market space for Chinese silent films. Many Chinese film practitioners took advantage of the gap in the market, by continuing to produce silent films until 1936. Meanwhile, the continued development of sound synchronisation technologies in Hollywood caused Chinese practitioners to realise that talkies were the future of their film industry. China commenced its own sound experiments from 1931, stimulated by Hollywood's sound film dominance.

Turning to technology, the American film industry was the supplier of technology and master of sound techniques. Big Chinese studios leased sound equipment from the United States directly. American sound technicians were required to train the first Chinese sound engineers. Furthermore, Hollywood's professional sound equipment became the object that Chinese engineers aimed to imitate, if not duplicate. Copycat devices, together with the imported American equipment, contributed to the final stage of the conversion to sound in 1936.

Conclusion

China completed its conversion to talkies in 1936. Thanks to American sound recording machines and cheap copycats, more and more Chinese studios began to release talkies. In 1935, Lianhua became the last major studio to release talkie pictures exclusively after purchasing a second-hand recorder from the United States. In this year, 16 out of 55 Chinese films were silent films. The number had dropped to two by 1936. In the first half of 1937, no silent films were released, five years after China had released its first sound film.

For a long time, the American film industry has been regarded as an invader of the domestic Chinese film industry. Taking this approach, emphasis has been placed on the American film industry's threat to the domestic film industry, and it has been suggested that little conceivable approach could be found for the Chinese film industry apart from resisting the American film industry. Seeing the latter as a constructive force for the Chinese film industry helps us to move beyond the bipolar model of repression versus resistance. It enlightens us to notice the multiple functions of the American film industry in Chinese film studies. From this point of view, an open attitude towards the American industry is crucial for the prosperity of the domestic industry: not only that of a rival but also that of a productive force.

Notes

1 Douglas Gomery, *The Coming of Sound* (New York: Routledge, 2005); Crafton Donald, *The Talkies: American Cinema's Transition to Sound 1926–1931* (Berkeley: University of California Press, 1999). An exception is Zhang Zhen's *An Amorous History of the Silver Screen*. She traces the development of China's transition to sound films by focussing on the transformation of film style as a consequence of the introduction of sound into films.
2 Marie Cambon, "The Dream Palace of Shanghai: American Films in China's Largest Metropolis 1920–1950" (Simon Fraser University, 1993); Zhiwei Xiao, "Hollywood in China, 1897–1950: A Preliminary Survey," *Chinese Historical Review* 12, no. 1 (2005): 72–100.; Ying Zhu and Nakajima Seio, "The Evolution of Chinese Cinema as Industry," in *Art, Politics, and Commerce in Chinese Cinema*, ed. Ying Zhu and Stanley Rosen (Hong Kong: Hong Kong University Press, 2010), 308.
3 Andre Millard, *America on Record: A History of Recorded Sound* (Cambridge: Cambridge University Press, 1995); Daojing Hu, "The Development of Shanghai Film Theatres/上海電影院的發展," in *Continuation of the Research of Shanghai/上海研究資料續編*, ed. Shanghai Tongshe (Shanghai: Shanghai Bookstore Press, 1984), 532–555.
4 "Sound Pictures," *North China Herald*, 2 February 1929.
5 *North China Daily News*, 10 November 1914; Jihua Cheng, Shaobai Li, and Zuwen Xing, *A History of the Development of Chinese Cinema/中國電影發展史* (Beijing: China Film Press, 1980); Hu, "The Development of Shanghai Film Theatres/上海電影院的發展."
6 *North China Daily News*, 10 November 1914.
7 "Talking Film in Shanghai," *North China Herald*, 18 December 1926.
8 Ibid.
9 "Talking Motion Pictures to Be Demonstrated to the Shanghai Public," *China Press*, 11 November 1928.
10 "Pre-View of Talking Picture at Embassy Delights Hearers," *China Press*, 7 February 1929.
11 "Capitol Talkies Are Now Being Installed," *Sunday Times*, 21 July 1929.
12 O.M.G., "Talking Pictures," *North China Herald*, 2 March 1929.
13 Ibid.
14 Ibid.
15 S.C. Kingsbury, "Talking Pictures," *North China Herald*, 2 March 1929.
16 "Talkies," *China Press*, 22 September 1929.
17 Eugene Irving Way, "Motion Pictures in China," (Washington United States Government Printing Office, 1930).
18 Richard P Butrick, "The Motion Picture Industry in China, 893.4061, Motion Pictures/69." (4 October 1932), 160–162.
19 Ibid., 160.
20 Shuluan Feng, "To the Star Motion Pictures Corporation/寫給明星," *Star*/明星 (1936), no page numbers.
21 Butrick, "The Motion Picture Industry in China, 893.4061, Motion Pictures/69," 72.
22 Way, "Motion Pictures in China," 5.
23 Shanghai Municipal Archives, "The Theatre Houses Industries, a Survey Conducted by the Shanghai Commercial and Saving Bank/上海商业储蓄银行有关影戲院调查资料, Q275-1-2041."
24 Way, "Motion Pictures in China," 9.
25 Ruth Vasey, *The World According to Hollywood, 1918–1939* (Devon: University of Exter Press, 1997), 85.
26 Gomery, *The Coming of Sound*.

27 Shanghai Municipal Archives, "The Industry of Film Production, a Survey Conducted by the Shanghai Commercial and Saving Bank/上海商業儲蓄銀行有關影片業調查資料, Q275-1-1949."
28 Zhiwei Xiao, "Constructing a New National Cinema Culture: Film Censorship and the Issues of Cantonese Dialect, Superstition, and Sex in Nanjing Decade," in *Cinema and Urban Culture in Shanghai, 1922–1943*, ed. Yingjin Zhang (Stanford: Stanford University Press, 1999), 184.
29 "Numerous Dialects Make Chinese Talkies Difficult, Says Lo," *China Press*, 29 November 1932.
30 "The Chinese Film Industry," *People's Tribune* IX, no. 1 (1935): 28.
31 Association, China Educational Film. *1934 China Film Yearbook*/中國電影年鑑 (Beijing: China Broadcasting and TV Press, 1934; repr., 2008), 917.
32 *Shen Bao*, 10 March 1931.
33 "Motion Pictures in China," *Records of the U.S. Department of State relating to the Internal Affairs of China, 1930–1939, 893.4061 Motion Pictures/41* (10 July 1931), 21.
34 Bibo Xu, "The Prospect of the Chinese Talkie Pictures/中國有聲電影的展望," *Coral*/珊瑚 (1932): 3.
35 "The Beginning of the Chinese Sound Films/中國有聲電影的開端," *Chinese Film*/中國電影 4 (1957): 59.
36 Ibid., 59.
37 Jianong Gong, *The Memoirs of Gong Jianong*/龔稼農從影回憶錄 (Taipei: Biographical Literature Press, 1980), 201.
38 Shanghai Municipal Archives, "The Seventh Accounts Report of the Star Motion Picture Corporation/明星影片股份有限公司第一屆決算報告, Y9-1-460."
39 "Advertisement," *Shen Bao*, 9 June 1931.
40 By virtue of allying themselves with Tianyi, Leon Britton and Charles Hugo produced a two-reel documentary named *War in China*, presenting actual war scenes between China and Japan. The film was screened at the Roosevelt, Chicago in 1932. See "Educational Releasing Leon Britton War Film," *Film Daily*, 4 March 1932; "Wall Film Booked," *Film Daily*, 21 March 1932.
41 "Man Who Interested King in Movies to Start Talkies Here," *China Press*, 21 July 1931.
42 *Shen Bao*, 4 September 1931.
43 Shanghai Municipal Archives, "The Eighth Accounts Report of the Star Motion Picture Corporation/明星影片股份有限公司第八屆決算報告, Y9-1-461."
44 "Perplexities Surrounding Famed Garbo Redoubled by Shanghai's Nadia Astrova," *China Press*, 21 June 1931.; "'Ourang' Expedition on Last Lap of Journey to Borneo," *Hollywood Filmograph*, 5 July 1930.
45 "Cameramen Off to China," *International Photographer*, August 1931, 38; "Pierce Due in City August 21," *China Press*, 12 August 1931; "Moving Picture Party Arrives on S.S. Pierce," 22 August 1931; "Moving Picture Party Arrives on S.S. Pierce," *China Press*, 22 August 1931.
46 "Correspondences between the Shanghai Commercial and Saving Bank and the Star Motion Picture Corporations on Loan Issues/交通銀行總行業務部及本行承做明星電影片公司押款的往來文書, Q55-2-1371."
47 "Motion Picture, China, 1926–1932," "281 Motion Pictures, Canada 1928 to Cuba 1939," Box number "1306," General Records, 1914–1958, The Bureau of Foreign and Domestic Commerce, RG151, The National Archives II, Maryland. I thank Yoshino Sugawara for providing me a copy of this document.
48 Xu, "The Prospect of the Chinese Talkie Pictures/中國有聲電影的展望," 4.
49 *Shen Bao*, 20 September 1931; "Our Company's Cameras/本公司之攝影機," *Star*/明星 1, no. 4 (1933): 34; Yanqiao Fan, "A Chronological Table of the Star

Motion Picture Corporation/明星影片公司年表," *Star*/明星 7, no. 1 (1936): no page number.
50 "New Film Firm Is Formed Here," *China Press*, 2 July 1931.
51 Ibid.
52 "A Chronological Table of the Star Motion Picture Corporation/明星影片公司年表."
53 Ibid.
54 In some cases, Whaweiphone was called Sidatong/Startone. This can easily cause confusion, because the sound recording machine that Hong Shen imported from the United States was also named Startone.
55 Xu, "The Prospect of the Chinese Talkie Pictures/中國有聲電影的展望," 3.
56 Butrick, "The Motion Picture Industry in China, 893.4061, Motion Pictures/69," 74.
57 Shuren Cheng, *China Film Yearbook*/中國電影年鑒 (Shanghai: China Film Industry Pressing House, 1927).
58 Xu, "The Prospect of the Chinese Talkie Pictures/中國有聲電影的展望," 1–5.
59 Leshan Zhao, "A Preliminary Study on the Development of Film Recording Technology in Shanghai/上海電影錄音技術發展史稿," in *The Historical Collection of Shanghai Cinema*/上海電影史料 (Shanghai: Shanghai Film Bureau, 1995), 208.
60 Yingjin Zhang and Zhiwei Xiao, *Encyclopedia of Chinese Film* (London: Routledge, 1998), 105.
61 These seven film studios include Mingxing, Lianhua, Yihua, Xinhua, Kuaihuolin (快活林), Jinan (暨南), and Meihua (梅花), according to its advertisement. Association, *1934 China Film Yearbook*/中国电影年鉴., 102; A'dan, "The Honourable Record of Chinatone Sound Machine/中華通錄音機出國榮譽," 1941, 4.
62 Guifang Zuo and Liqun Yao, *Tong Yuejuan Huiyilu Ji Tuwen Ziliao Huibian/the Memories of Tong Yuejuan*/童月娟回憶錄暨圖文資料彙編 (Taipei: Cultural Construction Committee, 2002), 42.
63 "Motion Pictures in China," 15.
64 *Shen Bao*, 1 December 1932; "The Survey of Our Country's Talkie Picture Business/我國有聲電影事業之調查," *Commerical and Industrial Semimonthly*/工商半月刊 1931, 29–32.
65 *Shen Bao*, 16 May 1934.
66 Yuqian Ouyang, *The Film Career of Mine*/電影半路出家記 (Beijing: China Film Press, 1961), 58.
67 Butrick, "The Motion Picture Industry in China, 893.4061, Motion Pictures/69," 74–75.
68 Gong, *The Memoirs of Gong Jianong*/龔稼農從影回憶錄, 208.
69 Zhao, "A Preliminary Study on the Development of Film Recording Technology in Shanghai/上海電影錄音技術發展史稿," 201.
70 Chris Berry, "Transnational Chinese Cinema Studies," in *Chinese Cinema Book*, ed. Song Hwee Lim and Julian Ward (London: BFI, 2010), 9.
71 Will Higbee and Song Hwee Lim, "Concepts of Transnational Cinema: Towards a Critical Transnationalism in Film Studies," *Transnational Cinema* 1, no. 1 (2010): 10.
72 Quotes from Jubin Hu, *Projecting a Nation: Chinese National Cinema before 1949* (Hong Kong: Hong Kong University Press, 2003), 16.
73 Xu, "The Prospect of the Chinese Talkie Pictures/中國有聲電影的展望," 3.
74 Chris Berry and Mary Farquhar, *China on Screen* (New York: Columbia University Press, 2006), 3.
75 Tom O'Regan, *Australian National Cinema* (London: Routledge, 2002), 90.
76 Cambon, "The Dream Palace of Shanghai: American Films in China's Largest Metropolis 1920–1950"; Xiao, "Hollywood in China, 1897–1950: A Preliminary

Survey," 71–96; Zhu and Seio, "The Evolution of Chinese Cinema as Industry," 17–34.
77 Andrew Higson, "The Limiting Imagination of National Cinema," in *Cinema and Nation*, ed. Mette Hjort and Scott Mackenzie (London: Routledge, 2002), 18.

References

A'dan. "The Honourable Record of Chinatone Sound Machine/中華通錄音機出國榮譽." 1941, 4.
Association, China Educational Film. *1934 China Film Yearbook*/中國電影年鑑. Beijing: China Broadcasting and TV Press, 1934. 2008.
Berry, Chris. "Transnational Chinese Cinema Studies." In *Chinese Cinema Book*, edited by Song Hwee Lim and Julian Ward, 11. London: BFI, 2010.
Berry, Chris, and Mary Farquhar. *China on Screen*. New York: Columbia University Press, 2006.
Butrick, Richard P. "The Motion Picture Industry in China, 893.4061, Motion Pictures/69." (4 October 1932), 74–75.
Cambon, Marie. "The Dream Palace of Shanghai: American Films in China's Largest Metropolis 1920–1950." Simon Fraser University, 1993.
"Cameramen Off to China." *International Photographer*, August 1931, 38.
"Capitol Talkies Are Now Being Installed." *Sunday Times*, 21 July 1929.
Cheng, Jihua, Shaobai Li, and Zuwen Xing. *A History of the Development of Chinese Cinema*/中國電影發展史. Beijing: China Film Press, 1980.
Cheng, Shuren. *China Film Yearbook*/中國電影年鑑. Shanghai: China Film Industry Pressing House, 1927.
"The Chinese Film Industry." *People's Tribune* IX, no. 1 (1 April 1935): 26.
"Detroit Keeps on Making Records." *The Moving Picture World* 39, no. 12 (22 March 1919).
Donald, Crafton. *The Talkies: American Cinema's Transition to Sound 1926–1931*. Berkeley: University of California Press, 1999.
"Educational Releasing Leon Britton War Film." *Film Daily*, 4 March 1932.
Fan, Yanqiao. "A Chronological Table of the Star Motion Picture Corporation/明星影片公司年表." *Star*/明星 7, no. 1 (October 1936).
Feng, Shuluan. "To the Star Motion Pictures Corporation/寫給明星." *Star*/明星 7, no 1 (1936).
Gomery, Douglas. *The Coming of Sound*. New York: Routledge, 2005.
Gong, Jianong. *The Memoirs of Gong Jianong*/龔稼農從影回憶錄. Taipei: Biographical Literature Press, 1980.
Higbee, Will, and Song Hwee Lim. "Concepts of Transnational Cinema: Towards a Critical Transnationalism in Film Studies." *Transnational Cinema* 1, no. 1 (2010): 9.
Higson, Andrew. "The Limiting Imagination of National Cinema." In *Cinema and Nation*, edited by Mette Hjort and Scott Mackenzie, 67. London: Routledge, 2002.
Hu, Daojing. "The Development of Shanghai Film Theatres/上海電影院的發展." In *Continuation of the Research of Shanghai*/上海研究資料續編, edited by Shanghai Tongshe, 532–555. Shanghai: Shanghai Bookstore Press, 1984.
Hu, Jubin. *Projecting a Nation: Chinese National Cinema before 1949*. Hong Kong: Hong Kong University Press, 2003.
"Man Who Interested King in Movies to Start Talkies Here." *China Press*, 21 July 1931.

Millard, Andre. *America on Record: A History of Recorded Sound*. Cambridge: Cambridge University Press, 1995.
"Motion Pictures in China." *Records of the U.S. Department of State Relating to the Internal Affairs of China, 1930–1939, 893.4061 Motion Pictures/41* (10 July 1931).
"Motion Picture, China, 1926–1932," "281 Motion Pictures, Canada 1928 to Cuba 1939," Box number "1306," General Records, 1914–58, The Bureau of Foreign and Domestic Commerce, RG151, The National Archives II, Maryland.
"Moving Picture Party Arrives on S.S. Pierce." 22 August 1931.
"New Film Firm Is Formed Here." *China Press*, 2 July 1931.
"Numerous Dialects Make Chinese Talkies Difficult, Says Lo." *China Press*, 29 November 1932.
O.M.G. "Talking Pictures." *North China Herald*, 2 March 1929.
O'Regan, Tom. *Australian National Cinema*. London: Routledge, 2002.
"Our Company's Cameras/本公司之攝影機." *Star*/明星 1, no. 4 (1933): 34.
"'Ourang' Expedition on Last Lap of Journey to Borneo." *Hollywood Filmograph*, 5 July 1930.
Ouyang, Yuqian. *The Film Career of Mine*/電影半路出家記. Beijing: China Film Press, 1961.
"Perplexities Surrounding Famed Garbo Redoubled by Shanghai's Nadia Astrova." *China Press*, 21 June 1931.
"Pierce Due in City August 21." *China Press*, 12 August 1931.
"Pre-View of Talking Picture at Embassy Delights Hearers." *China Press*, 7 February 1929.
S.C. Kingsbury. "Talking Pictures." *North China Herald*, 2 March 1929.
Shanghai Municipal Archives. "Correspondences between the Shanghai Commercial and Saving Bank and the Star Motion Picture Corporations on Loan Issues 交通銀行總行業務部及本行承做明星電影片公司押款的往來文書, Q55-2-1371."
———. "The Eighth Accounts Report of the Star Motion Picture Corporation/明星影片股份有限公司第八屆決算報告, Y9-1-461."
———. "The Industry of Film Production, a Survey Conducted by the Shanghai Commercial and Saving Bank/上海商業儲蓄銀行有關影片業調查資料, Q275-1-1949."
———. "The Seventh Accounts Report of the Star Motion Picture Corporation/明星影片股份有限公司第一屆決算報告, Y9-1-460."
———. "The Theatre Houses Industries, a Survey Conducted by the Shanghai Commercial and Saving Bank/上海商业储蓄银行有关影戲院调查资料, Q275-1-2041."
"Sound Pictures." *North China Herald*, 2 February 1929.
"The Survey of Our Country's Talkie Picture Business/我國有聲電影事業之調查." *Commercial and Industrial Semimonthly*/工商半月刊, 1931, 29–32.
"Talkies." *China Press*, 22 September 1929.
"Talking Film in Shanghai." *North China Herald*, 18 December 1926.
"Talking Motion Pictures to Be Demonstrated to the Shanghai Public." *China Press*, 11 November 1928.
Vasey, Ruth. *The World According to Hollywood, 1918–1939*. Devon: University of Exter Press, 1997.
"Wall Film Booked." *Film Daily*, 21 March 1932.
Way, Eugene Irving. "Motion Pictures in China." Washington United States Government Printing Office, 1930.

Xiao, Zhiwei. "Constructing a New National Cinema Culture: Film Censorship and the Issues of Cantonese Dialect, Superstition, and Sex in Nanjing Decade." In *Cinema and Urban Culture in Shanghai, 1922–1943*, edited by Yingjin Zhang, 184. Stanford: Stanford University Press, 1999.

———. "Hollywood in China, 1897–1950: A Preliminary Survey." *Chinese Historical Review* 12, no. 1 (2005): 72–100.

Xu, Bibo. "The Beginning of the Chinese Sound Films/中國有聲電影的開端." *Chinese Film*/中國電影 4 (1957): 59.

———. "The Prospect of the Chinese Talkie Pictures/中國有聲電影的展望." *Corall* 珊瑚 3 (1932).

Zhang, Yingjin, and Zhiwei Xiao. *Encyclopedia of Chinese Film*. London: Routledge, 1998.

Zhao, Leshan. "A Preliminary Study on the Development of Film Recording Technology in Shanghai/上海電影錄音技術發展史稿." In *The Historical Collection of Shanghai Cinema*/上海電影史料, edited by Anonymous, 208. Shanghai: Shanghai Film Bureau, 1995.

Zhu, Ying, and Nakajima Seio. "The Evolution of Chinese Cinema as Industry." In *Art, Politics, and Commerce in Chinese Cinema*, edited by Ying Zhu and Stanley Rosen, 308. Hong Kong: Hong Kong University Press, 2010.

Zuo, Guifang, and Liqun Yao. *Tong Yuejuan Huiyilu Ji Tuwen Ziliao Huibian/the Memories of Tong Yuejuan*/童月娟回憶錄暨圖文資料彙編. Taipei: Cultural Construction Committee, 2002.

3 Response in distribution systems
From 'parrot' to 'butterfly'

This chapter explores the dynamic relations between the American and the Chinese film industries by examining the evolution of China's distribution system in the 1920s and 1930s. The Chinese cinema of these two decades has attracted intense attention from scholars, especially the cinema of the 1930s, the period regarded as "the Golden Age of the Chinese film."[1] However, to date, there has been no serious study of distribution systems. The literature has only focussed on some aspects and details of the distribution of Hollywood and Chinese films. This chapter will examine China's distribution system in the 1920s and 1930s. Employing various primary sources, including studio archives and newspaper commercials, I will explore relations between the American and the Chinese film industries in the distribution domain. I will examine the influence of those relations on China's response, within its own distribution system, to the American film industry. My argument is that the analysis of power relations is a key to understanding this response.

With regard to the response of national culture to foreign cultures, Paul Lee has suggested four patterns of response based on the transformation of form and content, namely, "Parrot, Amoeba, Carol and Butterfly."[2] The 'parrot' pattern refers to a given culture imitating a foreign culture in form and content, like a parrot's mimicry. The 'amoeba' pattern names a condition in which form is changed while substantial content remains. Conversely, the 'carol' pattern is a modified form in which substantial content is changed while the form remains. The 'butterfly' pattern describes a cultural product whose form and content are both changed.[3] In this chapter, the object of classification is the growth of the film distribution system, rather than form and content. The development of China's distribution system can be regarded as undertaking a shift from the 'parrot' pattern to the 'butterfly' pattern in the way that it responded to the American film distribution system. In the early 1920s, China's distribution system could be viewed as a naive parrot, mimicking America's system. A decade later, the distribution system had grown up into a unique 'butterfly.'

This chapter starts with a brief introduction to the emergence of the Chinese distribution business in early Chinese film history, from its beginnings to the early decades of the twentieth century. To examine the response process in the distribution system, I first analyse how the Chinese film industry learned from, and imitated, the American film industry distribution system in the 1920s. Specifically, to characterise this system, I highlight a 'run-clearance-zone' system. In the wake of the evolution of a distribution business in China, local film practitioners gradually developed their own distribution system by responding to the American model within the Chinese context. Next, this chapter traces the development of the distribution system in 1930s China. Through a comparison of the distribution systems of Hollywood cinema in China and Chinese film itself, my conclusion is that the Chinese distribution system, by the 1930s, had grown into a sophisticated and flexible institution, which was more appropriate in the context of the Chinese film market. This chapter concludes with an analysis of power relations in the process of the formation of the Chinese distribution system. Power relations are the foundation for identifying different patterns, stages, and types of mixing, in the process of response. Therefore, I suggest power relations are key to understanding the response process of the Chinese film industry.

The rise of the distribution business in China

Film distribution in China began with the business of screening foreign films in treaty ports such as Shanghai and Hong Kong. Prior to the emergence of professional distribution corporations, exhibitors screening foreign films functioned, in some ways, as distributors. In the wake of an upsurge of film screenings, personal and private importation could not satisfy exhibition demand; as a result, professional distribution corporations emerged. In the 1900s and early 1910s, French films dominated China's screens by virtue of the distribution of Pathé-Phono-Cinema-Chine. American films were obtained "mostly through European exchanges."[4] For instance, a British corporation, the Motion Pictures Sales Company of London, was responsible for distributing American films to the Arcade Theatre in Tianjin.[5] Gradually, professional American exchange corporations emerged in 1910s China. One instance is Benjamin Brodsky's Variety Film Exchange. It set up branches in Hong Kong and Shanghai, responsible for distributing American films to China. In addition, major Hollywood studios invaded the Chinese film market through corporations in China and Singapore. For instance, Lo Kan's Hong Kong Amusements Corporation reportedly monopolised the distribution of Hollywood films in China in 1922–1923.[6] In addition, Fox Pictures films in the early 1920s in China were distributed by a Singapore film exchange named Middle East Films Ltd.[7] Apart from official film distribution, pirated films were rampant in the early 1920s. Two major criminals circulating illegal American film prints in China were Ramos Amusement Company and the Oriental Film Company.[8] Along with the growth of the Chinese film market, the

Response in distribution systems 51

American film industry, spearheaded by Universal in 1921, started to set up branch offices in China to "coordinate the distribution of their films in the country."[9] By the early 1930s, all major Hollywood studios had set up branch offices or exclusive agencies in China, with their head offices in Shanghai and branch offices in the larger cities such as Tianjin.[10] "In cities where the distributors ha[d] no branches or representatives, checkers [were] usually maintained to oversee arrivals and return shipments of films to verify box office receipts."[11] Additionally, in some cases Hollywood distributors entrusted their silent films to Chinese film exchanges to "supply distant interior cities," a distribution method somewhat like the modern "farming out" of distribution.[12]

China's own distribution business emerged with the film production business. Regular film production in China dates from the early 1920s. In the early days, film production corporations were responsible for their own distribution businesses. At that time, communication and connection were very rare between the distribution branches of the studios of China.[13] Large studios like Mingxing and the Commercial Press gradually became involved in the business of distributing other productions alongside their own films. For instance, most of the Chinese films shown in Xiamen in 1927 were distributed by Mingxing.[14] Additionally, another source shows that in 1925 Mingxing obtained the distribution rights to *Shanghai of Victory* (戰功, dir. Xu Xinfu, 1925), a Great China Lilium production.[15] By the 1920s, professional corporations which were responsible for distributing Chinese films had emerged as well. The first cartel formed by Chinese distributors, the United Film Exchange Corporation, commenced in 1926. However, it was dissolved a short time later. In the 1930s, two film exchanges, Huawei and Lianhua, dominated the distribution market of the Chinese film industry. Each signed a long-term contract with studios and with theatres exhibiting Chinese pictures. One source shows that at least 65 theatres across China signed distribution contracts with Huawei in 1931.[16] Like their American counterparts, Chinese distributors usually employed a revenue-sharing system. Large distributors like Huawei divided the country into districts, "each district being under the control of an agent."[17] The distributors charged "a commission of ten per cent" on the net revenue producers obtained and "allot[ed] five per cent to district agents."[18] In its most prosperous period, the total sales of Huawei amounted to 700,000 yuan, with a net profit of 30,000 yuan in 1934.[19]

Many characteristics of distribution operations in China were shared by the American and the Chinese film industries. Both engaged in two methods of distribution. A film was "either leased to the theatre at a certain sum for a definite number of showings or it [was] released on a profit-sharing basis."[20] The profit-sharing basis was more popular for both Hollywood and Chinese films. Writing in 1930, E.I. Way documents the detailed operation of the profit-sharing system in 1930s China:

First and second run theaters usually exhibit film on a percentage basis of approximately 35 per cent of the box-office receipts, with deductions for advertising and minor expenses. All subsequent-run theatres pay anything from $40 to $150 Mex. ($14 to $50 U.S.) per program of nine reels. No legitimate distributor sells outright, since films are usually the perpetual property of the producer.[21]

Geographically speaking, the circuit of distribution for Hollywood and Chinese film was similar in the 1920s: a broken line, with a starting point of Shanghai or Hong Kong, along which films went one by one, from city to city. Shanghai and Hong Kong were the "real distributing centres for China" in the 1920s and 1930s.[22] Hong Kong was the centre for distributing foreign films in South China, while most Hollywood films and Chinese films screened in China were obtained from Shanghai. It is understood that Hollywood and Chinese films usually premiered at the first-run theatres in Shanghai. Distributors then sent film prints in parcels by means of freight or shipment to other big cities including Fuzhou, Hankou, Tianjin, and Nanjing. After showing in these big cities, films were distributed in midsize cities nearby, such as Beijing, Qingdao, Hangzhou, Wuxi, and Xiamen. The film prints were finally shipped back to Shanghai for the third- and subsequent-run showings. Therefore, in the 1920s, to watch new Chinese or Hollywood films alike, patrons in midsize cities such as Qingdao had to wait for rather long periods.

China's distribution system in the 1920s: a 'parrot' pattern

It is fair to say that the establishment of China's distribution system was mainly based on learning from, and imitating, the American film industry. In fact, Chinese film distributors did not conceal their attitude towards the American industry. In 1926, when the United Film Exchange Corporation, the first cartel created by Chinese distributors, was organised, the advertisement in its opening ceremony admitted, "the united distribution of our American counterparts is our example."[23] This attitude of imitating and learning is also discernible through a close examination of the institution of the distribution system. This section looks at the film market in 1925 in Shanghai as a means of investigating the distribution systems for Hollywood and Chinese films. One can find similarities between the two systems in 1925. The Chinese attitude of imitation was attributed to the condition of the Chinese film industry, and in its very initial stages, the rationale of this industry was to seek to learn from the sophisticated American industry and to imitate its distribution system. Both Hollywood and Chinese film followed the rule of the 'run-clearance-zone.'

The 'run-clearance-zone' was seen as a regular and basic distribution system in the classical Hollywood period. It was invented and first used in the American film industry. According to Richard Abel, American film companies in the 1910s such as the General Film Company "innovated a number of distribution practices: a pricing strategy based on each film's age, an early form of block booking, and a run-clearance-zone system."[24] In the 1920s, the run-clearance-zone distribution system was generally employed by other industries. 'Run' refers to "the successive exhibitions of a motion picture in a given area, first-run being the first exhibition in that area, second-run being the next subsequent and so on."[25] The criteria for division into a 'run' for a given theatre include its location, decoration, equipment, and other facilities. 'Clearance' meant "a period of time, usually stipulated in license contracts, which must elapse between runs of the same feature within a particular area or in specified theaters."[26] A major aim for setting a clearance was to channel audiences to watch films from early run theatres. Therefore, this method was able to guarantee the optimisation of the box office since the major studios owned 80 per cent of the first-run houses and the most profitable subsequent-run houses in the United States.[27] The 'zones' were "the areas into which a city is divided for purposes of granting exclusive rights to runs."[28]

Generally speaking, both Hollywood and Chinese film basically followed the rule of a 'run-clearance-zone' mode of distribution in 1925. I have analysed the screening records published in the newspaper X*inwen Bao* (Shanghai) from 1 January to 1 July 1925. In this 172-day period, Shanghai had 1,935 screenings of 256 films, 219 of which were foreign films and 37 of which were Chinese. The first aspect of the system is the 'run,' and theatre runs for screening foreign films were clearly visible in 1925. The Carlton 卡爾登, Embassy, and Isis 上海 theatres were the first-run houses. The Empire 恩派亞, Republic 共和, Universal 萬國, Hongkew 虹口, Victoria, New Allen 新愛倫, and French Concession 法租界 theatres were the second-run houses. Other cinemas, including the Chapei 閘北, the British 大英, and the Freedom 自由, were seen as third-run theatres. Theatres screening Chinese films also showed some characteristics of having 'runs,' although the theatre chain system for Chinese film was in general far from mature. The Palace Theatre 中央 can be seen as the first-run house for Chinese films. However, other subsequent runs remain ambiguous. In addition, it is hard to find a fixed sequence for the showing of Chinese films. To take the film *Awareness* (覺悟, dir. Ling Lianying, 1925) as an example, its showing at the Empire (17 April–18 April) was earlier than that at the Olympia (the predecessor of the Embassy) (23 April–25 April). However, in the screening of *After Separation* (別後, dir. Qin Zhengru, 1925), the Embassy showing (4 January–7 January) was earlier than that at the Empire (16 January–18 January).

A similarity can also be found in terms of 'clearance.' Out of 219 foreign films, 49 had been shown at multiple theatres, and one can observe the presence of 'clearance' in the distribution of all 49.[29] Forty-four of them (90 per cent) have the character of 'clearance.' *Helen's Babies* (dir. William A. Seiter, 1924) is a case in point. As Table 3.1 illustrates, this film was released at the

54 *Response in distribution systems*

Table 3.1 The Distribution Schedule of *Helen's Babies* (1924) in Shanghai

Cinema	Olympia	Empire	Carter
Run	1	2	3
Time	8–11 February	23–24 February	26 February–1 March

Source: Xinwen Bao (Shanghai), 1925.

Table 3.2 The Distribution Schedule of *Foundling* (1924) in Shanghai

Cinema	China	French Concession	New Allen	Popular	Republic
Time	8–11 February	23–24 February	26 February–1 March	9–12 April	26–29 April

Source: Xinwen Bao (Shanghai), 1925.

Olympia from 8 February; twelve days of 'clearance' had been set until it reappeared in the second-run house, the Empire. Moreover, this film had another two days clearance from 24 February to 26 February.

Out of a total of 37 Chinese films, one can observe the characteristic of 'clearance' in 27 films.[30] In the later grouping, 20 (or 74 per cent) show this characteristic. For instance, Table 3.2 shows the exhibition schedule of *Foundling* (棄兒, dir. Dan Duyu, 1924) in 1925. The runs of the listed houses are hard to identify, but the characteristics of 'clearance' can be found through its exhibition schedule. As one can see, 12 days of 'clearance' were set after showing *Foundling* at the China Cinema. Similarly, the film was cleared for 38 days after screening at the New Allen Theatre.

To sum up, in 1920s China, the American film industry had set up a 'run-clearance-zone' system for film distribution, a sophisticated system derived from its American base. For the Chinese film industry in its nascent stage, there were few options apart from following in the footsteps of the American film industry. The 'run-clearance-zone' system therefore became a major distribution method for Chinese films in the 1920s.

The distribution system in 1930s China

The film market of China leapt forward from 1925 onwards. First, in the exhibition market, the number of cinema houses significantly increased. China had 106 cinemas in 1927.[31] By 1930, the number had increased to 233, more than double in three years' time.[32] The theatre chain system had also been well established in large cities like Shanghai, Tianjin, Hankou, and Guangzhou. Each cinema had a set run. By comparison with the situation in 1925, in 1930 a theatre chain system for Chinese films had also been set up. Second, in the field of studio finance, the domestic Chinese film industry had reached growth from 1925 onwards, so film studios could invest more money in expenses for expansion, including purchasing more prints for each film. In addition, it is reasonable to argue that in broad terms the political and military environment in China at the time had an influence on the prosperity of the film market. Compared with the riots and instability of the domestic wars of 1925, a national and unified government had emerged after 1927. A relatively peaceful environment was contributing to the rapid development of the economy.

In this section, I will use 1933 as a sample year through which to examine distribution practices in China in the 1930s. The year 1933 is named "the year of Chinese films."[33] Several prominent Chinese films were released during this year, such as *Night in the City* (城市之夜, dir. Fei Mu) and *Toys* (小玩意, dir. Sun Yu). In addition, it was a box office heyday for the Chinese film industry. Moreover, Hollywood also reached its "golden age" in China in 1933. For instance, the box office of Paramount in China reached 340,000 yuan in 1933, a peak for this major Hollywood studio; after this, its income dropped annually. In 1934, the box office of Paramount in China was 320,000 yuan. The number dropped to 19,200 yuan by 1935, 40 per cent down in comparison with 1934.[34] In this section, I trace the exhibition records from 1 January 1933 to 15 May 1933, through the cinema commercials published in *Xinwen Bao* (Shanghai), *Shang Bao* (Tianjin), and *Qingdao Shibao* (Qingdao). These advertisements document the situation of distribution practices in six cities, namely, Shanghai, Tianjin, Qingdao, Nanjing, Wuxi, and Changzhou. As the centre of film production, distribution, and exhibition, Shanghai showed 567 films for 3,422 times from January to May 1933. Four hundred and ninety-six of them were foreign films, which showed 2,220 times, while 71 were Chinese films, showing 1,202 times. On average, each foreign film was shown 4.48 times, while Chinese films were shown 16.93 times, 3.37 times more than foreign films.

The distribution of Hollywood films in 1933 shows little difference from the situation in 1925. It still basically followed the rule of the 'run-clearance-zone.' In all 496 films analysed in this investigation, there are less than ten exceptions to the rule for foreign films. A close observation of the showing of *Grand Hotel* (dir. Edmund Goulding, 1932) in Shanghai shows that it reflects the 'run-clearance-zone' structure. As indicated in Table 3.3, the Cathay Theatre 國泰 premiered this film from 2 February to 11 February. After 12 days of 'clearance and zone,' it had shown at the second-run theatre, the Carlton theatre. After another 60 days of 'clearance and zone,' this film then had a third chance to be shown on Shanghai's screens. During this 60-day period, Hollywood distributors delivered this picture to Tianjin, where it was screened at the Peace Theatre 平安. After finishing its Shanghai journey, this film travelled to Qingdao for screening in June 1933. As a matter of fact, advertisement for subsequent-run theatres is clearly monitored

56 *Response in distribution systems*

Table 3.3 The Distribution Schedule of *Grand Hotel* (1932) in China

Cinema	Run	Location	Time
Cathay	1	Shanghai	2–11 February
Carlton	2	Shanghai	23–27 February
Carlton*	2	Shanghai	8–11 March
Empire	1	Tianjin	17–23 March
Ritz	3	Shanghai	30 April–6 May
Star	—	Qingdao	30 June–4 July

Sources: Xinwen Bao (1933), Shang Bao (1933) and Qingdao Shibao (1933).

* The Carlton Theatre had a repeated run for showing *Grand Hotel*. This was an exceptional case in 1930s China. A possible explanation is that the box office at the Carlton Theatre performed so well that the distributor licensed Carlton to show this film for a second time.

to protect the income of the first-run theatres. A document from the Film of Trade (China) reported that

> no production shall be advertised specifically and by name for exhibition in any subsequent run theatres in Hongkong and Kowloon until 42 days shall have elapsed after the conclusion of the first run in a recognized first run theatre, and no exhibition of subsequent run shall commence until after a like period shall have elapsed.[35]

The case of Shanghai is likely to be the same as that of Hong Kong.

With respect to the distribution system of Chinese films, there are enormous distinctions to be uncovered when comparing the situation in 1933 with that of 1925. In the following section, 31 Chinese films which premiered between December 1932 and April 1933 serve as a sample for the study of the distribution system of Chinese films. Three major differences have been found by comparing Hollywood and Chinese films of 1933 with those of 1925, namely the 'run and clearance' system, the 'same-run-multipoint-exhibition' system, and the 'zone without clearance' system.

'Run and clearance'

The distribution of Chinese films still obeyed the rule of the 'run' operation in 1933. On this point, there had seldom been any difference in practices between American and Chinese cinema since 1925. However, the run for Chinese film was differently configured and fixed in 1933. In Shanghai, the first run for Chinese films included cinemas such as the Strand, Peking 北京, Guanghua 光華, and Palace Theatres. The second-run houses were the Victoria, Star, Western 西海, Eastern, South-East 東南, Crystal Palace 黃金, Chekiang 浙江, and Venus 榮金 Theatres. The third-run houses included the Empire, Carter 卡德, Boon Lay 蓬萊, Ward 華德, Republic, and Universal Theatres. In terms of 'clearance,' Chinese films in 1933 generally followed a 'clearance' pattern at the first-run and second-run houses, not following it after the second run.

Table 3.4 The Distribution Schedule of *The Spring Dream of the Lute* (1933) in Shanghai

Cinema	Run	Time
Isis	1	16–18 March
Palace	1	16–19 March
Victoria	2	20–22 March
South-East	3	1–4 April
Eastern	3	6–10 April
Star	3	12–14 April
Carter	3	16–19 April
Universal	4	25–27 April
Empire	4	30 April–3 May
Paradise天堂	4	8–10 May

Source: Xinwen Bao (Shanghai), 1933.

The 'clearance' between the first run and the second run is relatively visible in the distribution of Chinese films. Sixteen films from a total of 31 observed samples followed this pattern. For example, *Morning in the Metropolis* (都會的早晨, dir. Cai Chusheng, 1933), produced by Lianhua, premiered in Shanghai at the Peking Theatre from 22 March to 8 April 1933. After 11 days of 'clearance,' it started its secondary showing at the Guanghua, Western, Eastern, Shanse 山西, and South-East Theaters. The production situation of another major studio named Tianyi was similar to that of Lianhua. *Pursuit* (追求, dir. Qiu Qixiang, 1933) – one of Tianyi's productions – was released at the Strand from 22 March to 25 March 1933. After 18 days of clearance, it appeared at the Peking Theatre as a second-run showing. So did productions from small studios such as the China Star 華星. Its production *The Stone of Life* (三生石, dir. Wang Chunyuan, 1932) made its debut at the Guanghua from 1 March to 4 March. Then it was pulled and cleared for 11 days until reappearing at the South-East Theatre.

However, after the second-run showing, Chinese films abandoned the pattern of 'clearance' and engaged in a method I term 'clearancefree.' By 'clearancefree' I mean a distribution system which sets a time interval of less than five days between two given shows. In the Chinese films examined in this section, 25 out of 31 (81 per cent) employed 'clearancefree' distribution after their second-run showing. Table 3.4 shows an example of 'clearancefree.' *The Spring Dream of the Lute* (琵琶春怨, dir. Li Pingqian, 1933) premiered at two houses (the Isis and the Palace) on 16 March and had a second-round show at the Victoria from 20 to 22 March 1933. After eight days of clearance, it entered a 'clearancefree' period. On average, there were only 2.7 days of 'clearance' for each show.

A reasonable explanation for the Chinese distribution engagement of 'clearance' periods between first and second runs is that it was due to considerations of profit, while the employment of 'clearancefree' was motivated by considerations of cost-recovery. Despite the lack of data in the 1930s, a survey of Chinese studios in 1946 reveals that sales in the first-run theatres accounted for 60 per cent of film rentals for Chinese films, and 30 per cent of the gross income comes from the second-run theatres, while the others only took 10 per cent.[36] In addition, producers could access the income from first-run theatres after two months, while it usually took six months to obtain the revenue share from the third- and fourth-run theatres.[37] Therefore, the income from first-run houses was paramount to Chinese film producers, just as it was with Hollywood producers. This was probably the major reason why Chinese film distributors employed the 'clearance' system between first- and second-run theatres to protect sales for the first-run theatres. It would not be fair to say that Chinese film distributors paid no attention to their box office income after the third run, but the pressure from cost-recovery was more important than this smaller income stream. One needs to bear in mind that a shortage of capital was a long-term condition in the Chinese film industry. In 1927, around 75 per cent of Chinese studios were inadequately financed.[38] This situation did not change significantly in the 1930s. For small studios, if a film's cost could not be recovered, it would mean a high risk of bankruptcy for the studio.

Zone: 'same-run-multipoint-exhibition'

One may notice that much of the emphasis of 'run' and 'clearance' methods for Chinese distribution system was focussed on Shanghai. The reason is clear. Shanghai was one of the few cities that had theatre chains at that time. Many cities, such as Hangzhou and Wuxi, only had one regular venue for screening Chinese films. 'Run' and 'clearance' methods could not be adequately employed in cities without theatre chains. Nevertheless, Shanghai failed to take a lead in employing a 'zone' method in the distribution system. A close look at the exhibition market in 1933 shows that the 'zone' system had been well enforced in Tianjin, Changzhou, Nanjing, Wuxi, and Qingdao. However, Shanghai, the largest film market in China, had not made good use of the 'zone' strategy.

It is easy to understand the engagement of 'zones' in cities like Changzhou, Wuxi, and Qingdao. Only one cinema in these cities regularly screened Chinese films and it consequently became a natural 'zone' restriction. For example, in Qingdao, three cinemas were operating in 1933, namely, the Folozu 福祿壽, Star, and Shantung Theatres 山東. The Star concentrated on foreign films, especially Hollywood films. The Folozu occasionally showed Chinese films, but it was closed after April 1934. Therefore, the only venue that showed Chinese film regularly was the Shantung Theatre. Tianjin and Nanjing had more theatres than Qingdao. Nanjing, the capital of the National government, had nine cinemas in 1933. Two theatres were the base for Chinese films, the World Theatre 世界 and the Capital Theatre 首都. However, these two cinemas had their own preferences. The World Theatre had more interest in productions from Tianyi, while the Capital Theatre

Table 3.5 The Distribution Schedule of *Morning in the Metropolis* (1933) in Tianjin

Cinema	Grand	Hopei	Hopei	Tiangong
Run	1	2	2	3
Time	20–21 April	18 May	30 June–1 July	4–8 October

Source: Shang Bao (Tianjin), 1933.

focussed on the films of Lianhua and Mingxing. As a treaty port, Tianjin had ten picture houses, three of which showed Chinese films exclusively: the Guangming 光明, Tiangong 天宫, and Hopei Theatres 河北. In addition, cinemas in Tianjin had reached a relative fixed run system. For Chinese film exhibition, the Grand Theatre was the first-run cinema, while the Hopei and Tiangong Theatres belonged to the category of second-run cinemas. The screen records indicate that all three cinemas had different schedules of exhibition in 1933. Table 3.5 shows one example of the 'zone' set in Tianjin. The premier showing of *Morning in the Metropolis* in Tianjin was at the Grand Theatre from 20 to 21 April 1933. After 27 days of 'clearance and zone,' this film was shown at the Hopei Theatre on 18 May 1933. On June 30, the Hopei Theatre exhibited this film again for two days. In October, the Tiangong Theatre screened this film for the fourth time. One can see that the showing of *Morning in the Metropolis* in Tianjin followed the rule of 'run-clearance and zone' quite firmly.

As the most important venue for film production, distribution, and exhibition in China, Shanghai did not employ the 'zone' system. The reason can be traced to the situation of the theatres of the time. In the 1930s, Shanghai had the most cinemas in China. One source shows that Shanghai had 53 cinemas with a combined 37,000 seats in 1930.[39] Analysis of the newspaper *Xinwen Bao* shows that there were 38 cinemas in 1934, together with another ten vaudeville houses, part of whose business involved showing films. Ten of these 38 cinemas specialised in foreign films, while another 26 cinemas exhibited both foreign and domestic films. Most of the theatres screening Chinese films are identified as second- and third-run houses. Among these 26 cinemas, at least eight houses were second-run, while seven were third-run, based on their aforementioned location, equipment, decoration, and ticket prices. That is to say, if one distributor wished to employ a 'zone' in a second-run house in Shanghai, it could not show in the other seven second-run houses simultaneously. This had two consequences: on the one hand, it would largely extend the screening period, which would definitely increase the burden of cost-recovery; on the other hand, it would risk losing huge audiences, resulting in a great loss for producers and distributors. One needs to bear in mind that Shanghai was the largest city in China in the 1930s, with 3.6 million people. Apparently, the market for Chinese films could not be satisfied by showings in just one theatre at one time.

Table 3.6 The Distribution Schedule of *Night in the City* (1933) in Shanghai

Cinemas	Run	Time
Guanghua	1	8–15 March
Peking	1	8–21 March
Western	2	24–31 March
Eastern	2	24–31 March
South-East	2	24–31 March
Shanse	2	1–6 April
Chekiang	2	1–6 April
Foh On	3	8–10 April
Ward	3	9–11 April
Guanghua	1	12–15 April
Venus	3	13–14 April
Boon Lay	3	22–26 April
Republic	3	23–29 April
Paradise	3	28–30 April
China	3	27–29 April
Orpheum 奧飛姆	3	7–9 May

Source: Xinwen Bao (Shanghai), 1933.

Chinese film distributors clearly noticed the character of the film market in Shanghai and a 'same-run-multipoint-exhibition' system was employed. Literally speaking, the term 'same-run-multipoint-exhibition' refers to a distribution system showing films simultaneously in as many cinemas as possible under a given run. If the American film industry's 'zone' system was a strategy of hunger marketing, 'same-run-multipoint-exhibition' focussed on saturation management. It stressed occupying a market as large as possible to avoid a loss of audience and therefore maximise sales at a given period. In addition, this system could avoid competition between cinemas within the same run. An example is *Night in the City*, one of Lianhua's productions (as shown in Table 3.6). This picture was released at two theatres, the Guanghua and the Peking, in Shanghai on 8 March 1933. On 24 March, three cinemas – the Western, Eastern, and South-East Theaters – started the second-round showing of this film. From 1 April, another two houses (the Shanse and the Chekiang) joined the showing for the third round. The fourth round commenced on 8 April at the Foh On 福安 and Ward Theatres. The record for employing 'same-run-multipoint-exhibition' is held by *Morning in the Metropolis* (1933). Five theatres screened this film in Shanghai (the Guanghua, Western, Shanse, Eastern, and South-East) concurrently from 24 to 29 April.

In summary, the Chinese distribution system in the 1930s matured and moved beyond mimicking the American film industry's 'run-clearance-zone' system. In cities outside of Shanghai, the 'run-clearance-zone' system was inherited. But in Shanghai, the home of film production, distribution, and exhibition in China, Chinese distributors developed a unique 'same-run-multipoint-exhibition' system. This system was based on the context of the Shanghai film market.

A special case: Mingxing's 'zone without clearance'

As the biggest production studio in 1930s China, Mingxing engaged in a unique distribution method in Shanghai, namely the 'zone without clearance' system. The 'zone without clearance' was a distribution system which employed a 'clearancefree' method in the theatre runs in Shanghai while simultaneously using 'zones.' This 'clearancefree' system was enforced in almost every theatre, including the first- and second-run houses. I believe that the structure of Mingxing as a studio is the key to understanding the uniqueness of its distribution system.

Six out of the seven films released from January to May 1933 were distributed in this 'clearancefree' manner. For instance, *Adventures in the Battlefield* (戰地歷險記, dir. Zhang Shichuan, 1933) premiered at the Palace on 14 January 1933. As shown in Table 3.7, it started a second-run showing at the South-East Theatre without any 'clearance' period in Shanghai. The third-run round began from 25 January, only three days after the second round. Meanwhile, on 30 January, the fourth-round showing began. Similarly, without any 'clearance,' the fifth round started immediately after the fourth round. Before its seventh-round showing, the interval between screenings of *Adventures in the Battlefield* was less than four days. An exception to the rule was *The Flower of Liberty* (自由之花, dir. Zheng Zhengqiu, 1933). This film did have 'clearance' periods between first-run and second-run showings. After the first showing at the Peking Theatre on 2 February, it was put into a 21-day 'clearance' period, before the Peking and the Palace carried the second-run show on 23 February.

Although Mingxing did not use the 'clearance' system, it employed the rule of 'zones' in distribution, that is, the productions of Mingxing would show in cinemas one after the other. Table 3.8 shows the distribution schedule for *Torrent* (狂流, dir. Cheng Bugao, 1933) in Shanghai. It indicates that *Torrent* was screened at 12 houses in Shanghai from March to May. Apart from four days (24 March, 25 March, 8 April, and 28 April), there was only one theatre showing *Torrent* on any given day in these two months. *Torrent* was not alone in having zone restrictions. Screenings of the other six films produced by Mingxing had more or less conformed to the 'zone' system in Shanghai. As Table 3.7 shows, apart from 30 and 31 January, the showing of *Adventures in the Battlefield* in Shanghai conformed to the 'zone' restriction as well.

An explanation of the engagement of the 'zone without clearance' distribution system can be traced to the corporate structure of the Mingxing Company in the 1930s. In 1933, all Mingxing productions were shown at cinemas that belonged to the Central Motion Picture Corporation (中央影戲公司). The Central Motion Picture Corporation was a theatre chain in charge of five cinemas, including the Palace, Victoria, Empire, Carter, and Universal. The relationship between Mingxing and the Central Motion Picture Corporation could be described as that of 'twin brothers'

Table 3.7 The Distribution Schedule of *Adventures in the Battlefield* (1933) in Shanghai

Cinemas	Run	Time
Palace	1	14–17 January
South-East	2	18–22 January
Star	2	25–31 January
Carter	2	30 January–3 February
Victoria	2	4–7 February
Universal	3	11–14 February
China	3	4 April

Source: Xinwen Bao (Shanghai), 1933.

Table 3.8 The Distribution Schedule of *Torrent* (1933) in China

Cinema	Run	Time
Isis	1	5–8 March
Palace	1	5–11 March
South-East	2	12–16 March
Star	2	21–25 March
Victoria	2	24–28 March
Eastern	2	1–5 April
Western	2	6–10 April
Empire	3	8–12 April
China	3	20–22 April
Paradise	3	25–26 April
Carter	3	27 April
Universal	3	28 April–1 May

Source: Xinwen Bao (Shanghai), 1933.

in ownership. Most members of the Board of Directors in the Central Motion Picture Corporation were also the owners of Mingxing, including Yao Yuyuan 姚豫元, Zhang Shichuan, Zhang Juchuan 張巨川, Zheng Zhengqiu, and Bian Yuying 卞毓英.[40] The Central Motion Picture Corporation commenced its operation in April 1925. In 1926, by obtaining the lease rights to the Victoria, Empire, Carter, and Universal theatres, the Central Motion Picture Corporation became the first theatre chain for Chinese films. Unlike its American counterpart, this theatre chain covered three runs, rather than just focussing on the first run. In addition, it had its own orderly sequence for screening Chinese films: namely the Palace, Victoria, Empire, Carter, and then Universal Theater. The Star Theatre, a cinema fully owned by Mingxing itself, was designated to screen Chinese films after the Victoria and before the Empire.

A major concern for Mingxing in conducting the 'zone' system was how to guarantee the sales of the Central Motion Picture Corporation. If it allowed the simultaneous screening of a film in two cinemas, it would certainly be a threat for either cinema's box office sales. Similarly, there was a consideration for extending the showing time and avoiding local competition within nominated 'zones' in the theatre chain. From the viewpoint of the Mingxing stockholders, all box office sales would be their own income, no matter how the revenue was shared. Therefore, in order to optimise revenue income, it would be rational to take advantage of the chain houses of the Central Motion Picture Corporation.

The 'without clearance' system can be regarded as a sacrifice for cost-recovery for Mingxing. Like other corporations, Mingxing also had financial problems in the 1930s. According to its annual report, their average annual profit, for this, the largest studio in China, was only around 20,000 yuan until the early 1930s. In 1934, however, Mingxing had a dramatic deficit of 600,000 yuan, due to the importation of sound machines and to mismanagement.[41] Therefore, Mingxing had to sacrifice its setting of 'clearance' periods, in order to achieve cost-recovery as soon as possible.

Power relations in China's response

This section looks at power relations as a rationale for understanding the process of response to the American film industry in the Chinese industry. The analysis of power relations is one of the central concerns in the theory of political economy.[42] In the case of the Chinese film industry, I suggest that the analysis of power relations is a key to identifying different patterns, stages, and types of mixing in the process of China's response to the American film industry.

In explaining the process of the indigenisation of foreign culture, Paul Lee suggests that a particular pattern of indigenisation, such as the 'parrot' or 'butterfly' mentioned earlier, is configured by the interplay of a series of factors.[43] Lee notes seven factors that contribute to the emergence of various patterns: three direct, two indirect, and two contextual factors.[44] The three direct factors are consumer power, strength of indigenous production, and strength of exogenous production. Indirect factors include competition and stimulation from other forms of culture. Demographic changes and government policies are the two contextual factors.[45] In the case of the Chinese film industry, the response to the American film industry in the distribution system is attributed to the interplay of a great variety of factors, including the strength of the Chinese film industry, the strength of the American film industry, and governmental policy on licence application. The strength of the two industries were the two direct factors. Government policy was an indirect factor in the process of responding to the American film industry in 1930s China.

The correlation of power between the strength of the Chinese film industry and that of America is crucial for the pattern of response to the latter within the distribution system. Generally speaking, the extent of the growth of the distribution system is positively correlated with the strength of the Chinese film industry. The weaker the Chinese film industry, the greater the likelihood of the 'parrot' pattern in its distribution systems. The Chinese film industry in 1925 remained at a nascent stage compared with the American film industry. The number of production studios had a significant boost in this period, although the production quality remained at a low level. The first integrated theatre chain for Chinese cinema did not appear until 1926 with the Central Motion Picture Corporation. Prior to that, studios suffered from frustration with respect to distribution channels.[46] Another issue that needs to be considered is that in the 1920s the distribution system of China had just emerged, and references to systems other than that of America could seldom be made, considering the weakness of the European film business in China. At the same time, the American film industry, on the contrary, was enjoying a period of stability after a decade of exploration in China's film market. One source shows that 125 of the 215 films shown in Tianjin in 1925 were of American origin.[47] Professional corporations for the distribution of Hollywood films had emerged, such as the Peacock Motion Pictures Corporation. Theatres which were showing Hollywood films were visible, and runs were fixed. With little doubt, at that time the balance of power was significantly held by the American film industry. Therefore, there were few options for the Chinese film industry in the 1920s except to mimic America in its distribution system.

The stronger the Chinese film industry became, the greater the likelihood of the 'butterfly' pattern emerging. The strength of the Chinese film industry had increased significantly from the 1920s to the 1930s. However, the American film industry had changed little in terms of its strength in the field of distribution. Therefore, power relations between the Chinese film industry and that of America had changed and the dominance of Hollywood had been challenged. The production quality of the Chinese film industry had improved both in silent and sound film-making. Professional distribution corporations had grown in maturity after a decade of development. The income of distribution corporations such as Huawei, the largest distribution corporation in China at that time, had increased up to 700,000 yuan, and the net profit was around 30,000 yuan in 1934.[48] In addition, the number of cinemas in 1930 had doubled from the figure in 1927, as mentioned earlier. This increase in the number of houses suggests an upsurge in audiences. Theatre chains for showing Chinese film had been established in big cities like Shanghai, Tianjin, and Hankou. By contrast, in 1933 Hollywood seldom carried out improvements to its distribution system compared with those of the Chinese film industry. Although major Hollywood studios had established branches in Shanghai in 1933, distribution had not progressed significantly and the exhibition of Hollywood films was still limited to no more than ten major cities in China.[49] As one source indicates, the barriers to expansion for the American industry included "the lack of communication facilities, the disturbed political situation and the low purchasing power of the largest part of inhabitants."[50] The American film industry's distribution work is well indicated by the imports of motion picture films. In 1925, the positive film reels imported into China amounted to 2,738,222 feet, while increasing to 3,484,265 feet in 1929. This figure declined to 927,461 feet in 1930, largely due to China's indifference to Hollywood sound pictures.[51] In addition, after 1929, Hollywood had suffered much with the Great Depression in the early 1930s. This initiated a decline of the film industry, and the national economy of the United States would not recover until 1934. Therefore, it is fair to say that American dominance in distribution was challenged by the Chinese film industry in the 1930s, despite its dominance in other fields such as film technology and exhibition.

Apart from the efforts of the Chinese film industry itself, the power of the Nationalist Government penetrated into the field of film distribution and facilitated China's challenge to the American film industry's dominance. Government involvement was dissimilar to other issues faced by the Chinese film market as the Nationalist Government became deeply involved in film distribution through its licence application and tax policy. This Government set up a national committee to deal with film censorship and licence application issues in 1931. It held a discriminative policy on licence applications. Initially, the censorship committee issued licence permits for no charge to Chinese films. The policy was then changed so that 15 yuan was charged for Chinese films, due to financial difficulties in operating the censorship committee. By contrast, the application fee for Hollywood films was 100 yuan, and one needed to pay another 100 yuan for re-registration when the permit expired. Apart from licence fees, taxation was another heavy burden for the American film industry. One source shows that the Chinese Nationalist Government levied a charge of around 800 yuan for censorship and tariff on every foreign film imported into China.[52] In addition to the central government, three other censorship committees existed in Shanghai in the 1930s. One direct influence of the licence application policy was that it greatly limited the number of Hollywood prints in China. In the 1930s, most Hollywood films had only one print circulated in China, with the exception of several highly popular films like *All Quiet on the Western Front* (dir. Lewis Milestone, 1930) and *The Love Parade* (dir. Ernst Lubitsch, 1929). Therefore, the American film industry could do little except to employ the 'run-clearance-zone' system with one print in order to guarantee sales from the first-run theatres in major cities. On the other hand, with Chinese films, studios usually applied for more than one print due to the low application fee. Mingxing, for example, regularly applied for eight permits for exhibition. Another big studio, Lianhua, applied for seven permits when releasing a new film in the 1930s. The multiple prints strategy then provided the possibility of employing different distribution systems. This strategy of multiple prints had a direct influence on the circuits of distribution for Chinese films. In the 1920s, these circuits had been similar to those of Hollywood films. Both Chinese and Hollywood films alike followed a 'broken line' route. A print of a Hollywood film usually started its journey from Shanghai or Hong

Kong and then went on to the big cities one by one. It travelled back to Shanghai or Hong Kong and was shipped to another location in Asia, such as Nanyang.[53] However, the strategy of multiple prints changed the route for distribution of Chinese films, which now went out simultaneously from Shanghai to other major centres. For example, a usual circuit for Mingxing's distribution in the 1920s was Shanghai, Nanjing, Hankou, Tianjin, and Fuzhou. After the exhibition in Fuzhou, audiences in Xiamen then had the opportunity to watch a new film.[54] However, in the 1930s, Mingxing divided the country into several districts, including the Shanghai district, the Zhejiang district, the West China district, the North China district, the South China district, the Shandong district, the Fujian District, and the Sichuan district.[55] Mingxing usually employed eight prints for a new film and then sent these prints simultaneously to the districts. Therefore, audiences in Fuzhou could watch the film simultaneously with those in Tianjin or Hankou. The time for a film to reach a place like Qingdao was greatly shortened as well due to the multiple prints being circulated.

The power relations between the strength of the Chinese and American film industries affected the patterns of systematic response to the American film industry in distribution. However, it is a mistake to regard it as a necessary condition. In an imbalanced structure, the pattern of response could also potentially take an advanced form, such as the 'butterfly' pattern. As shown in the field of the distribution system, a lack of capital was one of the major handicaps for the Chinese film industry. However, it was this difficulty that contributed to innovation in the distribution system. Due to a lack of capital, Chinese film practitioners had to spare efforts for cost-recovery, which forced Chinese distributors to abandon the 'clearance' system after the second-run theatres. The pressure of cost-recovery led Chinese distributors to employ a 'same-run-multipoint-exhibition' system in Shanghai to avoid losing their audience. Similarly, Mingxing had to give up 'clearance' periods between the first- and second-run theatres for the sake of cost-recovery. Another factor, which could sometimes result in a 'butterfly' pattern in imbalanced power relations, was the structure of the corporation. In 1930s Shanghai, no studios except Mingxing owned an integrated theatre chain (Lianhua only owned one cinema in Shanghai, the Guanghua). Therefore, apart from Mingxing, studios had little desire to set 'zones' in Shanghai to protect the interests of theatres. This may have served as a reason for employing the system of 'same-run-multipoint-exhibition.' With respect to the corporate structure of Mingxing, the theatre chain it owned was different from that of major Hollywood studios as well. In the American film industry, most theatre chains owned by major Hollywood studios concentrated on first-run theatres.[56] However, Mingxing's theatres belonged to the first, second, and third run separately. Therefore, it was rational for Mingxing to employ the technique of 'continuous exhibition' rather than a 'clearance' system that would protect the interests of the first-run theatres.

Conclusion

The relations between the American and the Chinese film industries is one of the most significant topics in Chinese film studies, considering the paramount function of Hollywood's influence on Chinese films. How China responded to the American film industry is becoming a hot topic in Chinese film studies, since scholarship regards the attitude of the Chinese film industry towards its American counterpart as being crucial for the future of the former. Scholars have noticed that China learned film language, film institutions, and film technology from Hollywood. Imitation, adaption, and sinification are three major terms used in explaining the attitudes towards the American film industry.[57] This chapter has analysed China's response to the American film industry in its distribution systems during the 1920s and 1930s. My analysis suggests that China's response to the American film industry involved different stages of response including duplication, imitation, integration, sinification, and even rejection. This chapter calls for an analysis of power relations to explain the rationale involved in configuring different stages.

I have tried to demonstrate that the process of responding to the American film industry can be explained through the analysis of power relations in the context of the political economy. The relative strength of the Chinese and American film industries in China were two direct factors impacting the pattern of China's response to the American industry. A common logic is that the pattern of response is positively correlated to the strength of the Chinese film industry, while negatively correlated to the strength of the American film industry in China. In the field of distribution systems, American dominance was challenged with the growth of the Chinese industry. However, the 'butterfly' pattern does not exist in a power structure in which the Chinese film industry is stronger than that of America. Some negative conditions for the Chinese distribution market could also contribute to the configuration of the 'butterfly' pattern in an imbalanced power structure. As I have established, in its innovation of distribution systems, the Chinese industry benefited from both the lack of capital and the uniqueness of its corporate structure.

This chapter has examined the process of the Chinese cinema industry's response to the American film industry in the field of distribution in China during the 1920s and 1930s. It has shown that China's distribution system started from a 'parrot' pattern, with the Chinese film industry naively mimicking the American film industry in the 1920s. After a decade, the distribution system of China had grown into maturity and its uniqueness emerged. The 'parrot' finally became a 'butterfly.' However, this is not to say that the Chinese response to the American film industry was a linear process. In any given domain in the film market of China, the response to the American film industry would be quite different and the patterns of response would vary according to the interplay of power involved. Therefore, it is fair to say that China's response to the American film industry was far more complex, and the analysis of power relations may serve as a method to explain the dynamic of this response.

Notes

1. Zhen Zhang, *An Amorous History of the Silver Screen: Shanghai Cinema* (Chicago: The University of Chicago Press, 2005), 44.
2. Paul Lee, "The Absorption and Indigenization of Foreign Media Cultures: A Study on a Cultural Meeting Point of the East and West: Hong Kong," *Journal of Asian Communication* (1991), 64.
3. Ibid., 64.
4. "China," *Moving Picture World*, 9 September 1911, 703.
5. "A Chat from China," *Moving Picture World* 15, no. 2 (1913): 150.
6. Kar Law and Frank Bren, *Hong Kong Cinema: A Cross-Cultural View* (Lanham: Scarecrow, 2005), 121.
7. "Fox Closes Orient Deal," *The Film Daily*, 2 June 1922.
8. Qian Zhang, *From Hollywood to Shanghai: American Silent Films in China* (University of Pittsburgh, 2009), 33.
9. Zhiwei Xiao, "Hollywood in China, 1897–1950: A Preliminary Survey," *Chinese Historical Review* 12, no. 1 (2005): 77.
10. Richard P Butrick, The Motion Picture Industry in China, 893.4061, Motion Pictures/69." (4 October 1932), 52.
11. Ibid.
12. Ibid., 53.
13. Xu Chihen, "The Organization of the Central Motion Picture Corporation/中央影戲公司組織之經過," in *A Grand Sight of Chinese Cinema* (1927).
14. C. J. North, "The Chinese Motion-Picture Market," *Trade Information Bulletin* 1927, 9.
15. China Film Archive, entry for 14 March 1925 and for 25 April 19 in Lu Jie's diary.
16. "Advertisement of the Wha Wei Trading Co. Ltd/華威貿易公司廣告," *Shen Bao*, 15 March 1931.
17. Butrick, "The Motion Picture Industry in China, 893.4061, Motion Pictures/69," 56.
18. Ibid., 57.
19. Shanghai Municipal Archives, "The Industry of Film Production, a Survey Conducted by the Shanghai Commercial and Saving Bank/上海商業儲蓄銀行有關影片業調查資料, Q275-1-1949."
20. North, "The Chinese Motion-Picture Market," 8.
21. Eugene Irving Way, "Motion Pictures in China," (Washington United States Government Printing Office, 1930), 4.
22. Ibid.
23. "Advertisement of the Opening Ceremony of the United Film Exchange/六合影片公司開幕廣告," *Special Issue of Shenzhou Studio/神州特刊* 4 (1926).
24. Richard Abel, *Encyclopedia of Early Cinema* (London: Routledge, 2005), 270.
25. Alexandra Gil, "Breaking the Studios: Antitrust and the Motion Picture Industry," *New York University Journal of Law & Liberty* 3, no. 83 (2008): 86.
26. Ibid., 84.
27. Tino Balio, *Grand Design: Hollywood as a Modern Business Enterprise, 1930–1939* (New York: Macmillan, 1993), 7.
28. Michael Conant, *Antitrust in the Motion Picture Industry* (Berkeley: University of California Press, 1960), 58.

29 The other 170 foreign films were invalid data in terms of 'clearance' because they had been shown in only one cinema in Shanghai.
30 Another ten films had been shown in only one cinema and did not show the characteristic of 'clearance.'
31 North, "The Chinese Motion-Picture Market," 13.
32 Way, "Motion Pictures in China," 5.
33 Shen Hong, "Chinese Film in 1933/1933年的中國電影," Literature/文學 2, no. 1 (1934).
34 "Excerpt from General Report of 2 December 1935," in *United Artists Corporation Records: Series 1F: Black Books: Foreign Statistics* (Madison: Wisconsin Historical Society, 1935).
35 The Film of Trade (China)-Regulations as of March 15th, 1939, United Artists Corporation Records: Series 1F: Black Books, Foreign Statistics.
36 Shanghai Municipal Archives, "Market Survey of the Central Unit of Film Service/中央電影服務處調查報告, Q78-2-15."
37 Ibid.
38 North, "The Chinese Motion-Picture Market," 4.
39 Way, "Motion Pictures in China," 4.
40 Shanghai Municipal Archives, "The Industry of Film Production, a Survey Conducted by the Shanghai Commercial and Saving Bank/上海商業儲蓄銀行有關影片業調查資料, Q275-1-1949."
41 Yanqiao Fan, "A Chronological Table of the Star Motion Picture Corporation/明星影片公司年表," *Star*/明星 7, no. 1 (1936), no page number.
42 Peter Golding and Graham Murdock, "Culture, Communications and Political Economy," in *Mass Media and Society*, eds. James Curran and Michael Gurevitch (London: Arnold, 2000), 71.
43 Lee, "The Absorption and Indigenization of Foreign Media Cultures: Astudy on Acultural Meeting Point of the East and West: Hong Kong," 66.
44 Ibid.
45 Ibid.
46 Chihen Xu, *A Grand Sight of Chinese Cinema*/中國影戲大觀 (Shanghai: Cooperation Publishing House, 1927).
47 North, "The Chinese Motion-Picture Market," 2.
48 Shanghai Municipal Archives, "The Industry of Film Production, a Survey Conducted by the Shanghai Commercial and Saving Bank/上海商業儲蓄銀行有關影片業調查資料, Q275-1-1949."
49 Zhiwei Xiao, "American Films in China Prior to 1950," in *Art, Politics, and Commerce in Chinese Cinema*, ed. Ying Zhu and Stanley Rosen (Hong Kong: Hong Kong University Press, 2010), 25.
50 Way, "Motion Pictures in China," 4.
51 Ibid., 3.
52 "Report to Ministry of Interior Affairs and Ministry of Education," *Bulletin of Film Censorship Committee* 2, no. 29 (1933).
53 Xiao, "American Films in China Prior to 1950," 25.
54 North, "The Chinese Motion-Picture Market," 9.
55 Butrick, "The Motion Picture Industry in China, 893.4061, Motion Pictures/69," 57.
56 Mae Huettig, "Economic Control of the Motion Picture Industry," in *The American Film Industry*, ed. Tino Balio (Madison: The University of Wisconsin Press, 1985), 300.
57 Ying Zhu and Nakajima Seio, "The Evolution of Chinese Cinema as Industry," in *Art, Politics, and Commerce in Chinese Cinema*, ed. Ying Zhu and Stanley Rosen (Hong Kong: Hong Kong University Press, 2010), 17–34; Yuehyu Yeh, "Historiography and Sinification: Music in Chinese Cinema of the 1930s," *Cinema Journal* 41, no. 3 (Spring 2002): 78–97; Zhen Zhang, "Cosmopolitan

Projections: World Literature on Chinese Screens," in *A Companion to Literature and Film*, ed. Robert Stam and Alessandra Raengo (New York: Blackwell, 2004), 144–163.

References

Abel, Richard. *Encyclopedia of Early Cinema*. London: Routledge, 2005.
"Advertisement of the Opening Ceremony of the United Film Exchange/六合影片公司開幕廣告." *Special Issue of Shenzhou Studio*/神州特刊 4, 1926.
"Advertisement of the Wha Wei Trading Co. Ltd/華威貿易公司廣告." *Shen Bao*, 15 March 1931.
Balio, Tino. *Grand Design: Hollywood as a Modern Business Enterprise, 1930–1939*. New York: Macmillan, 1993.
Butrick, Richard P. "The Motion Picture Industry in China, 893.4061, Motion Pictures/69." (4 October 1932), 74–75.
"A Chat from China." *Moving Picture World* 15, no. 2 (11 January 1913): 150.
Chihen, Xu. "The Organization of the Central Motion Picture Corporation/中央影戲公司組織之經過." In *A Grand Sight of Chinese Cinema*/中國影戲大觀, edited by Chihen Xu, 1-2. Shanghai: Shanghai Cooperation Press, 1927.
"China." *Moving Picture World*, 9 September 1911.
China Film Archive, Entry for 14 March 1925 and for 25 April 19 in Lu Jie's Diary.
Conant, Michael. *Antitrust in the Motion Picture Industry*. Berkeley: University of California Press, 1960.
Escudero, Juan. "España Y Los Españoles En El Shanghai De Entreguerras (1918–1939)/Spain and Spanish in Interwar Shanghai (1918–1939)." Master Book, Pompeu Fabra University, 2012.
"Excerpt from General Report of 2 December 1935." In *United Artists Corporation Records: Series 1F: Black Books: Foreign Statistics*. Madison: Wisconsin Historical Society, 1935.
Fan, Yanqiao. "A Chronological Table of the Star Motion Picture Corporation/明星影片公司年表." *Star*/明星 7, no. 1 (October 1936).
"Fox Closes Orient Deal." *The Film Daily*, 2 June 1922.
Gil, Alexandra. "Breaking the Studios: Antitrust and the Motion Picture Industry." *New York University Journal of Law & Liberty* 3, no. 83 (2008): 83–123.
Golding, Peter, and Graham Murdock. "Culture, Communications and Political Economy." In *Mass Media and Society*, edited by James Curran and Michael Gurevitch, 71. London: Arnold, 2000.
Hong, Shen. "Chinese Film in 1933/1933年的中國電影." *Literature*/文學 2, no. 1 (1934).
Huettig, Mae. "Economic Control of the Motion Picture Industry." In *The American Film Industry*, edited by Tino Balio, 300. Madison: The University of Wisconsin Press, 1985.
Law, Kar, and Frank Bren. *Hong Kong Cinema: A Cross-Cultural View*. Lanham: Scarecrow, 2005.
Lee, Paul. "The Absorption and Indigenization of Foreign Media Cultures: A Study on a Cultural Meeting Point of the East and West: Hong Kong." *Journal of Asian Communication* 1, no. 2 (1991): 52–72.
North, C. J. "The Chinese Motion-Picture Market." *Trade Information Bulletin* 467 (1927): 9.

"Report to Ministry of Interior Affairs and Ministry of Education." *Bulletin of Film Censorship Committee* 2, no. 29 (21 November 1933).

Shanghai Municipal Archives. "The Evolution of Shanghai Cinema Theatres/上海電影院商業歷史沿革, S319-1."

———. "The Industry of Film Production, a Survey Conducted by the Shanghai Commercial and Saving Bank/上海商業儲蓄銀行有關影片業調查資料, Q275-1-1949."

———. "Market Survey of the Central Unit of Film Service/中央電影服務處調查報告, Q78-2-15."

"The Film of Trade (China)-Regulations as of March 15th, 1939," United Artists Corporation Records: Series 1F: Black Books, Foreign Statistics.

Way, Eugene Irving. "Motion Pictures in China." Washington United States Government Printing Office, 1930.

Xiao, Zhiwei. "American Films in China Prior to 1950." In *Art, Politics, and Commerce in Chinese Cinema*, edited by Ying Zhu and Stanley Rosen, 55–69. Hong Kong: Hong Kong University Press, 2010.

———. "Hollywood in China, 1897–1950: A Preliminary Survey." *Chinese Historical Review* 12, no. 1 (2005): 72–100.

Xu, Chihen. *A Grand Sight of Chinese Cinema*/中國影戲大觀. Shanghai: Cooperation Publishing House, 1927.

Yeh, Yuehyu. "Historiography and Sinification: Music in Chinese Cinema of the 1930s." *Cinema Journal* 41, no. 3, (Spring 2002): 78–97.

Zhang, Qian. *From Hollywood to Shanghai: American Silent Films in China*. University of Pittsburgh, 2009.

Zhang, Zhen. *An Amorous History of the Silver Screen: Shanghai Cinema*. Chicago: The University of Chicago Press, 2005.

———. "Cosmopolitan Projections: World Literature on Chinese Screens." In *A Companion to Literature and Film*, edited by Robert Stam and Alessandra Raengo, 144–163. New York: Blackwell, 2004.

Zhu, Ying, and Nakajima Seio. "The Evolution of Chinese Cinema as Industry." In *Art, Politics, and Commerce in Chinese Cinema*, edited by Ying Zhu and Stanley Rosen. Hong Kong: Hong Kong University Press, 2010.

4 Capitalism with Chinese characteristics
The mode of production in Chinese cinema

It is not an exaggeration to say that in the first half of the twentieth century, Hollywood stood as the most significant source of inspiration for the nascent Chinese film industry. Scholars have found abundant evidence of how Chinese film practitioners learned from Hollywood in such areas as camera movement, montage, and film production and exhibition.[1] The mode of production in Chinese studios was no exception. This chapter will show that in the early twentieth century, China's mode of production, on one hand, progressed in stages similar to those of Hollywood, from the cameraman system to the central producer system. On the other hand, however, Chinese production maintained its own characteristics, some of which would negatively impact the film industry. One particular characteristic – the strong position of the directors in the central producer system – significantly contributed to the vulnerability and the lack of enduring success of the Chinese film industry in the 1930s. A key primary source that reveals these characteristics and their impact is the unpublished diary of Lu Jie 陸潔, which provides an almost-daily insider's record of the Chinese film industry from the 1920s to the 1940s. Most importantly, it offers invaluable first-hand material on Lianhua's daily operation as Lu served as a producer/executive there.[2]

This chapter starts with a description of the concept of the mode of production and a brief introduction of the evolution of China's specific mode of production, from the cameraman system to the director system, the director-unit system, and finally to the central producer system. Drawing also on unpublished primary materials including producers' diaries and studio records, I examine the management structure of Lianhua as a case study on the central producer system in the Chinese film industry. I address two major characteristics of Lianhua: its unstable corporate structure and the weak position of the producers, in contrast to that of the directors, who retained powerful positions in Lianhua's mode of production. The chapter concludes with an analysis of the lessons of China's production practices in the 1920s and 1930s for the present-day Chinese film-making business.

The mode of production: perception, practice, and its evolution in Chinese cinema

Janet Staiger's study on the mode of production offers a model of how to analyse a film-making system. The mode of production, as a concept that originated with Karl Marx, refers to "the wider social character of production," and is used as a synonym for "the relations in which productive forces are developed."[3] The mode of production is composed of three elements that are involved in these relations: namely, "the labour force, the means of production, and the financing of production."[4] Marxism regards developing productive forces, a determining feature of historical development, as the impetus for the transition of the mode of production from primitive communism to ancient civilisation, feudalism, capitalism, and lastly to communism. Efficiency stands as one major gauge for the growth of productive forces, and a detailed division of labour is introduced as a type of work arrangement to pursue it. Hollywood's mode of production is classified as mass production, a specific method of the capitalist system. In Braverman's words, "No society before capitalism systematically subdivided the work of each productive specialty into limited operations."[5] In a detailed division of labour, "the process of making a product is broken down into discrete segments, and each worker is assigned to repeat a constituent element of that process."[6] As in the general sector, the detailed division of labour in Hollywood's mode of production "allowed faster and more predictable product output."[7] *The Classical Hollywood Cinema* splits the detailed division mode into five specific systems and describes how Hollywood experienced four modes of production, from its beginning to the late 1920s, "in a sequential order," consisting of "the cameraman system, the director system, the director-unit system and the central producer system."[8]

The evolution of China's methods for making films is akin to that of Hollywood, as the process can be characterised as moving from the cameraman system, to the director system, to the director-unit system, and finally to the central producer system. The Chinese film industry, in a broad sense or from a transnational perspective, emerged from foreign cameraman's film activities in the early twentieth century. Amerigo Enrico Lauro (1879–1937), an Italian cinematographer and an agent for Cines Co., was a pioneer producer of cinema in China dating back to 1902.[9] Among his productions, Lauro filmed some activities of Sun Yat-sen in Shanghai, taking pictures of the "cutting of the queues [that had been imposed on the Chinese by the Manchus] when everyone in Shanghai underwent the operation."[10] As with other film-makers who travelled China to make films at that time, Lauro produced films himself: he selected the subject, operated the camera, and developed and edited the film project. To improve production, in 1912 Lauro erected a studio that included a wooden stage and a machine room at 1001 Whangpoo (Huangpu) Road in Shanghai.[11] The cameraman system was inherited by Chinese production companies, such as the Commercial Press, which set up a film department in 1920 and invited Liao Enshou 廖恩壽 to serve as cinematographer. The productions of the Commercial Press focussed on scenes from Peking operas performed by Mei Lanfang, on natural scenes in China's cities from Shanghai to Beijing, and on newsreels. Although a director named Chen Chusheng 陳楚生 was assigned to production, most of the work, including filming, developing, and printing, was done by Liao himself. This situation did not change significantly after the Commercial Press shifted to fictional narratives. Like its American counterpart, the cameraman system phase was short in China because it relied mostly on the ability of a cameraman who had to know "the entire work process, and conception and execution of the product."[12] In the case of China, such talents were rare in the early 1910s. This can be attributed to the fact that film as a whole was still new there, in spite of the work of some foreign cinematographers. Few people watched films, let alone knew how to produce them.

The emergence of the director system is the result of the division of labour. Under the director system, a director is responsible for staging the action and the cameraman for filming it. Sino-foreign collaboration (usually a Chinese national was responsible for directing, while foreigners served as cinematographers) was particularly popular in the initial stages of the director system. Such a division of labour occurred when the subject of the films shifted from natural scenes to cultural topics, such as indigenous customs and dramas. On one hand, foreign cameramen in China may have understood how to produce a film, but probably they did not have sufficient knowledge of China's culture. Conversely, the Chinese gradually became interested in making films, but often lacked the necessary know-how and equipment. Therefore, a division of labour seemed necessary.

The director system continued to be the dominant method of production even after China started to set up its own production ventures. In 1922, Zhang Shichuan and Zheng Zhengqiu, the two directors in the Asiatic Film Company, set up Mingxing in Shanghai. Mingxing still employed the director system. Zhang Shichuan supervised the first short films and nine features it produced up to 1925, most of which were written by Zheng Zhengqiu. A considerable difference between Mingxing and the Asiatic Film Company was the position of directors. In the Asiatic, the directors and the cameramen were employed by the investors, Israel and Suffert. In Mingxing, Zhang Shichuan retained exclusive control over the entire production. As the sole director, owner, and executive of Mingxing, Zhang selected the cast, made decisions about cinematography, and edited films. Zhang Weitao 張偉濤, as the cinematographer, merely became a worker under the supervision of Zhang Shichuan. It is necessary to point out that, except for the role of director and cameraman, a detailed division of labour was fairly clear in Mingxing's production practice. The published plan for organising Mingxing claimed that one of its major merits was that it had talents, including film scriptwriters who had ten years' experience in studying literature and art (probably referring to Zheng Zhengqiu), film developers from the United States, film directors with extensive drama experience (referring to Zhang Shichuan), and set design professionals with abundant experience in oil painting.[13]

In the wake of the rapid progress of the film business, Chinese film studios moved into a period of director-unit system production in the late 1920s. Through releasing the box office hit *The Orphan Rescues Grandfather*, Mingxing had not only emerged from bankruptcy, but also moved into a period of prosperity and increased activity. After releasing *Orphan*, Mingxing's film-making crew, including Zhang Shichuan (director), Zheng Zhengqiu (scriptwriter), and Dong Keyi 董克毅 (cameraman), produced another eight features. With the expansion of its business, Mingxing organised a second film crew and released *Why Divorce* (新人的家庭, dir. Ren Jinping) in 1925, which signified the shift to a director-unit system in the company. The crew consisted of co-founder Ren Jinping 任矜萍, assistant director Chen Shouyin, and cameraman Bu Wancang 卜萬蒼. After Ren Jinping left Mingxing, Zhang Shichuan signed Hong Shen, a returned student from the United States who majored in drama studies, as director. The hierarchy of the directors was apparent in Mingxing's director-unit system. As the director/producer and the executive of Mingxing, Zhang retained more power than Hong Shen. At its peak in the 1920s, Mingxing maintained four production teams "under the direction of Zhang Shichuan, Zheng Zhengqiu, Hong Shen and Bu Wancang respectively."[14] After leaving Mingxing, Ren Jinping set up Xinren Company and employed the director-unit system as well. A news report from *Shen Bao* indicated that five directorial groups were working simultaneously in Xinren Company in 1927.[15]

A considerable feature of the director-unit system is a departmentalised organisation. Departmentalisation in the film industry developed following the "standard assembly system in mass production."[16] Different departments are organised to achieve "harmonious co-operation" and secure "the highest average of efficiency."[17] The date or name of the first studio employing departmentalisation in China's system cannot be precisely determined, but as early as 1925, Moonlight (月光) Company, a small studio, was reported to have set up a story consultant department in his studio.[18] An instance of departmentalisation is provided by Guoguang (國光) Company, a film company that originated from the Commercial Press. In 1926, Guoguang Company published its corporate structure: four departments under a Board of Directors. A studio department, headed by Yang Xiaozhong 楊小仲, undertook film scripting and directing. Two film scriptwriters and two film directors worked under Yang. A film production department was in charge of writing the scenario and shooting and developing film. The general business department was led by Chen Chunsheng, whose role was probably the provision of electrical, mechanical, and publicity services. The

76 Capitalism with Chinese characteristics

sales department, headed by Zhou Yongnian 周永年, was in charge of distributing films.[19] The division of these four departments clearly constituted an assembly line and aimed to increase efficiency.

China's film-makers experimented with independent production under the director-unit system in the late 1920s. Due to the financial losses of the studio and the lack of capital, in 1929 the executive of Great China Lilium enacted a method of independent production, or *baoxizhi* (包戲制, which literally means a system in which the director/producer is responsible for his own product, including the financing and producing of films). Under this system, the staff and equipment of Great China Lilium were divided into two groups, which were placed under the charge of Zhu Shouju 朱瘦菊 and Wang Yuanlong 王元龍 respectively.[20] These two groups were responsible for producing films separately. They used the studio facilities of Great China Lilium and distributed their products under that name. Each production group maintained personnel autonomy. For instance, Zhu Shouju employed Yang Xiaozhong in Zhu's group in April 1929.[21] It seems that at the beginning, Great China Lilium continued to invest in the film production of each group, but later it became each group's responsibility to find its own financing. Employing this independent production method enhanced the speed of production but sacrificed quality in a significant way. As Lu Jie, the head of the production department in Great China Lilium, pointed out, "each group could complete a film within twenty days, but the final product was short and the story was plain, therefore, the reputation of Great China Lilium significantly declined with the audience."[22] The independent production method was abandoned after Great China Lilium suspended its business and was amalgamated into Lianhua in 1930. Lianhu employed a different mode of production, termed the central producer system, which will be analysed in the following section.

The central producer system in Lianhua

A similar route of evolution does not mean that China's mode of production was merely a duplication of its Hollywood model. This and the following section will show the particular traits of China's mode of production by exploring China's central producer system in the 1930s. As a case study, I examine how the film production method functioned in Lianhua. There are two major reasons why Lianhua employed the central producer system: help in coordinating personnel relations and relieving the pressure caused by the shortage of capital. Nevertheless, no matter how it restructured, Lianhua did not change the weak position of the producer in its film-making system.

Lianhua is one of the most important film ventures in Chinese film history. It was established in 1930 by Luo Mingyou, incorporating several mid-size studios and soon became one of the "Big Three" in the Chinese film industry (along with Mingxing and Tianyi). Luo Mingyou became involved in the film business in 1919 by opening a film theatre in Beijing. Later, his business expanded into a film venture named North China Amusements Ltd, which controlled a dozen cinemas at its peak. Attracted by the thriving film business, Luo started to become involved in film production. Signing Sun Yu 孫瑜 as a director, by way of experiment he produced *Reminiscence of Peking*. The success of the film at the box office strengthened Luo's ambition to move into film production. In August 1930, Luo set up Lianhua by taking over Li Minwei's 黎民偉 China Sun Motion Picture Co. Ltd and Wu Xingzai's 吳性栽 Great China Lilium Film Company.[23] China Sun became Lianhua's first studio, and Great China Lilium was its second. After incorporating others studios in Shanghai, Beijing, Hong Kong, and Singapore, Lianhua became the largest film production venture in China at that time. Apart from film production, Lianhua was a vertically integrated firm that included film distribution, exhibition, and film journal publishing. Lianhua's headquarters was located in Hong Kong, with a management branch in Shanghai.

The general structure of Lianhua can be seen as that of a central producer system, under which, the producer, instead of the director, takes over "the management of the pre- and post-shooting work for *all* the films in the studio."[24] The producer 'superseded' the director and therefore, in terms of organisational structure, this system can be seen as a type of pyramid.[25] In the case of Lianhua, Luo Mingyou was the general manager and was therefore only answerable to the Board of Directors. He took care of all the general business of Lianhua. Under Luo Mingyou, there were four offices located in Hong Kong, Shanghai, North China (Beijing), and Singapore. The general management office was located in Hong Kong, in addition to a studio. Shanghai was the major base for Lianhua's production business with three studios. Each studio had a producer in charge of its day-to-day operations in the making of films, such as fundraising, discussion of scripts, and so forth. The producer in the first studio was Li Minwei, the producer in the second studio was Lu Jie, and the producer in the third studio was Zhu Shilin 朱石麟 (Zhu's third studio was incorporated into the first two studios in 1934). These three studios were under the direction of the Shanghai management office.

In Lianhua's producer system, one could see a detailed division of labour and departmentalisation. Each studio had its own directors and professional departments, including a general affairs department, art design department, production department, cinematography department, and printing department. A more detailed division of labour was also visible within these departments. For instance, the art design department included an art design unit (responsible for drawing and decorating) and a scene set unit (including a carpenter, painter, and blacksmith). In addition, each studio signed its own cast, and these actors/actresses served the studio exclusively. In contrast to Hollywood, there were few substantial differences in genres between films produced by each of Lianhua's studios, although some might have their own distinct production styles.

78 *Capitalism with Chinese characteristics*

The organisation of Lianhua, 1934

As a general manager, Luo Mingyou was responsible for adjusting the structure of Lianhua's production units. From 1930 to 1936, Lianhua had at least four major and six minor changes in its corporate structure. The two major concerns for structuring Lianhua were the coordination of personnel and the resolution of financing problems. In the following, I will explore several restructurings of Lianhua that were intended to solve these two kinds of problems. However, despite the efforts of restructuring, neither had a satisfactory resolution in the end.

The major production forces of Lianhua were organised by amalgamating Great China Lilium and China Sun. In his initial plan, Luo suggests that the organisation of Lianhua could at first implement the "branch system", which maintained the original production units including personnel, studios, and equipment. The production branches could be concentrated gradually into one general production factory which would become a 'film city.'[26] As a matter of fact, the separation of studios was a consideration in the coordination of the personal relationships between members of each studio, in particular between the first and second studio.[27] Partly due to their different personalities and partly due to competition with each other, the leaders of the two studios did not get along well together. A case in point concerns the 'borrowing' of actors from each other. Cai Chusheng 蔡楚生, a director of the second studio, once intended to invite Chen Yanyan 陳燕燕, an actress affiliated with Li Minwei's studio, as a cast member of *Volcano, Love, and Blood* (火山情血, dir. Cai Chusheng, 1932). Lu Jie recalled that Li requested 'an unacceptable condition' for 'borrowing' Chen Yanyan.[28] In the meantime, separate studios meant higher overheads as each one had its own equipment and personnel. In order to reduce overheads, Luo Mingyou finally incorporated these two studios into one in April 1935. Under the new structure, Lu Jie (the producer of the second studio) was in charge of general affairs while Li Minwei (the producer of the first studio) was in charge of

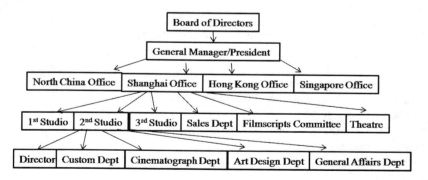

Figure 4.1 The Corporation Structure of Lianhua.
Source: Lianhua, "Four years' evolution of Lianhua," 970–971.

film technology, including film printing. However, the relationship problems among the personnel could still not be solved. Three months later, the production business had to be returned to the original structure – a separation of the two units, which were headed by Lu Jie and Li Minwei, respectively.[29] The problem of personnel relationships could not be solved until the ownership of Lianhua was shifted to a new company in 1936. Unable to resolve the economic crisis of Lianhua, Luo Mingyou decided to resign as general manager. These personnel difficulties were finally solved with the departure of Li Minwei and Luo Mingyou.

The lack of working funds was another reason for restructuring Lianhua. Apart from the original studios and capital, Luo Mingyou had invested little into Lianhua's film production business. In 1931, Luo Mingyou intended to increase investment by calling for capital but failed to raise the needed money. Lianhua therefore faced a serious lack of the working funds needed to maintain its studio operations. In 1932, after having rejected a proposal to sell Lianhua to Lu Gen, one film exhibition magnate at that time, Luo Mingyou transferred Lianhua's second studio to Wu Xingzai, a member of the Board of Directors. Wu restructured the second studio and renamed it Lian'an (聯安) after investing 50,000 yuan.[30] After releasing four productions, Luo Mingyou restored the operating rights of the second studio by investing in Lian'an in early 1933. However, Lianhua still suffered from a lack of working funds. In 1933 and 1936, Luo Mingyou and Zhu Shilin twice promoted the idea of employing independent production systems, with the intention of solving these financial problems. Under the system of independent production, it was the producers and directors who had the responsibility for raising funds for film production, instead of Lianhua's management branch. Lianhua was merely in charge of providing studios and distributing the product. However, the suggestion of an independent production system was rejected due to strong objections from producers and directors.[31] The shortage of capital resulted in the final restructuring of Lianhua in 1936 and the transfer of ownership of Lianhua to Wu Xingzai.

Another significant trait of Lianhua's corporate structure was that the position of the producer was highly restricted. Lu Jie, as a producer in the second studio, acted as the liaison between Luo Mingyou and the directors. Lu was well known in film circles due to his involvement as an editor of *Movie Magazine* (影戲雜誌), the first professional film publication in China. In 1924, Lu, together with other merchants, organised the Great China Film Company, with Lu acting as scriptwriter. In 1925, Lu became the head of the production department and a film director after Great China merged with the Lilium Film Company. Lu Jie took charge of the second studio after Great China Lilium Company was amalgamated into Lianhua in 1930, serving as the executive producer, answerable only to Luo Mingyou, the studio head. Lu Jie supervised directors including Sun Yu, Cai Chusheng, Shi Dongshan 史東山, and Tan Youliu 譚友六. As the executive producer,

Lu made budgets for every production, supervised the production process, coordinated personnel relationships, and signed contracts with studio staff in the second studio of Lianhua. Under Lianhua's system, however, Lu Jie did not have financial and personnel autonomy since financial rights were vested in the management branch, a department directly controlled by Luo Mingyou. As a producer, Lu was responsible for drawing up production budgets with directors. The budget plans were submitted to the management branch, but due to the lack of capital, it was common for the management branch to not provide money to the production unit. Therefore, much of Lu Jie's energy was wasted in applying for funds from the management branch. For instance, from 1931 to 1936, Lu Jie's diary is full of complaints concerning these problems: at least once every month. In June 1931, Lu spent four days applying for money from the management branch without any success. Similarly, Lu could sign contracts with film staff, but the dis/approval of the management branch and Luo Mingyou superseded Lu's authority.

The relative lack of finance and control over personnel limited Lu's control over the production process. Lianhua employed story and script committees to make decisions on scripts, although Lu did participate in the committees. In addition, it seems that Lianhua had no effective punitive regulations to control the pace of production. Supervising the speed of production was one of Lu's jobs, but in fact it was quite common for directors not to finish production on time. However, Lu seemed to have few solutions to control production pace except for 'trying to persuade directors,' partly due to the lack of punitive measures. For instance, Lu wrote in his diary on 26 January 1934:

> The production of *Wind* (風, dir. Wu Cun, 1934) has been suspended several times due to the personal affairs or sick leave of the director Wu Cun 吳村. This afternoon, I visited Wu and tried to persuade him to complete the production as soon as possible.[32]

Even the directors of Lianhua, such as Sun Yu, admitted that it was they who were responsible for the slow speed of production, rather than the producers.[33]

The powerful position of directors in Lianhua's producer system

In this section, I explore the role of directors in Lianhua's producer system. The weak position of the producer resulted in enhanced power of the director in Lianhua's mode of production. Although Lianhua employed a central producer system, directors rather than producers stood at the top of the hierarchy. The directors in Lianhua not only had 'complete control' over every stage of film production (including pre- and post-shooting) but also served as unit heads.[34] Four characteristics of the powerful position of directors are suggested in this section.

First, an intriguing trait of the mode of production of Lianhua, and arguably of all Chinese film studios, is that the division of labour between the scriptwriter and director was not obvious in the 1930s. In her survey on the evolution of Chinese films, Zhang Zhen points out that Chinese films only had 'a lean outline' and "a shooting script was unheard of" in the 1910s.[35] "With the onset of the long story film, however, a synopsis was no longer adequate for a cinema that relied on a sustained plot and dramatic conflict."[36] Therefore, from the 1920s onwards, a number of fiction writers, such as Bao Tianxiao 包天笑, Zhu Shouju, and Zhou Shoujuan 周瘦鵑, were employed to write film scripts. In some cases, film studios would solicit scripts from outside, and use selected scripts for production. However, in the majority of cases, the writing of film scripts was still left to the director. Out of a total of 63 films produced by Lianhua from 1930 to 1936, there are 40 films with scripts written by directors. In addition, it is necessary to point out that the term 'scriptwriters' here denotes the people who wrote the original film story. The scriptwriters were not responsible for writing shooting scripts. In the case of China, it was the responsibility of directors to turn film scripts into shooting scripts, even though the director was not the scriptwriter.[37] Like its Hollywood counterpart, the shooting script was designed to be a "blueprint for the workers" in China's central producer system, and the published shooting scripts, such as that of *Song of China* (天倫, dir. Fei Mu, 1935), show that "each shot was numbered consecutively" and "the description of the *mise-en-scène* and action was very detailed."[38] However, the shooting scripts offered little control over the director, since the director could easily change the scripts during the shooting process.

Second, because they retained the rights to write shooting scripts, directors could easily exercise their influence on cast selection. In some cases, the director had already made his decision regarding the cast during the writing of the film script. In his memoirs, Sun Yu, the scriptwriter and director of *Big Road*, claimed that he selected the main cast of the film.[39] In another case, Sun selected Wang Renmei 王人美 as the protagonist of his production *Wild Rose* (野玫瑰, dir. Sun Yu, 1932) because the film script was deliberately written for that actress. Sometimes, the producer or president of Lianhua might be involved in the casting, but the director's decision was usually respected. A case in point is Shi Dongshan's film *Strive* (奮鬥, 1932). It seems that Shi Dongshan insisted on using Chen Yanyan as a protagonist. Lu Jie, the producer of the film, had to help Shi 'borrow' Chen from the first studio, though he had reservations about the casting arrangement, as mentioned earlier.[40]

Third, directors sometimes retained the final decision on issues such as selecting shooting locations and stage sets, although some technical work was done by department experts. It seems that the budget plan which had been drawn up by the producer was not strictly executed due to the ambiguity of the scripts. When Cai Chusheng prepared the shooting location of *The Lost Lamb* (迷途的羔羊, 1936) in Suzhou, he himself decided the number of extras and props to be used.[41] When conflicts occurred during film production, directors, particularly influential ones, could sometimes win in negotiations with the producers, or even with the studio president. During the production of *Return to Nature* (到自然去, 1936), the director Sun Yu insisted on adding a luxurious scene set in the Presidential Palace. Lu Jie wrote in his diary on 4 July 1936: "The stage set that is needed is quite grand, which will not only be too expensive, but also take a long time to put together."[42] Twenty-five days later, Luo Mingyou joined Lu Jie to negotiate with Sun over abandoning the scene, but Sun still insisted on his idea. It seems that both Luo Mingyou and Lu Jie yielded. On 1 September, Lu wrote that Sun had begun to shoot the Presidential Palace scene. To be sure, directors with less fame may not have enjoyed as much leeway as Sun did; however, his case still provides a glimpse of the powerful position of the director in Lianhua.

Fourth, the directors of Lianhua, and in China in general, had responsibility for editing. A close look at the crew listed in 1930s Chinese films reveals that no editors were credited, although in the corporate structure of Lianhua a position of film editor did exist in the printing department. As an article from the period points out,

> [the work of] the film editor is significant and should develop into a separate job in the film-making process. An inappropriate editor might destroy the integrity and sentiment of a film. In the case of China, however, the editing job is just done by directors.[43]

Lu Jie's diary records several times that he had cautioned directors about the slow pace of film editing.[44]

One consequence of the powerful position of the director in Lianhua's mode of production is its extremely slow speed. Because directors retained major control over production and because much of the energy of directors was spent on writing the shooting script and editing the film, the pace for releasing a film was fairly slow. Such delays were attributed to the selfishness of the directors. An article in Lianhua's own publication pointed out that

> Directors are the head of a production unit in the Chinese film industry. In a situation in which China's mode of production is not well organised, directors retain a great deal of responsibility. Greater responsibility has resulted in greater selfishness. For the sake of his own reputation, the director spends extra time on choosing a film script, selecting the film cast, and doing retakes again and again. It may benefit the quality of film, but throws cold water on the passion for the development of the Chinese film industry.[45]

The slow speed of Lianhua is evidenced by the number of films it released. Although Lianhua maintained several studios, there was no significant difference in production speed between Lianhua and other film companies with one sole studio. A director in Lianhua could only release one or two films a year. In his five years' service in Lianhua, Cai Chusheng only made six films. The worst case is Wu Cun. Based on his contract with Lianhua, Wu was required to shoot three films in one year. However, he only finished one film. In 1934, Lianhua released eighteen films. Other than Zhu Shilin, Jiang Qifeng 姜起鳳, and Zheng Jiduo 鄭基鐸, each of whom released two films, respectively, the other film directors only produced one film in a year. The situation in 1935 was even worse – only nine films were released. Other than Yang Xiaozhong, no directors released more than two films. Some directors, such as Cai Chusheng, could not even complete one production in an entire year.

The slow speed might improve the stylistic finesse of the film, but it could jeopardise the economic situation of the production studio. In Chinese film history, the films produced by Lianhua, such as *Big Road, Toys*, and *The Song of the Fishermen* (漁光曲, 1934) are seen as "classics" and made a great contribution to the "golden age of Chinese films" in the 1930s. However, their production did not bring a golden age to Lianhua in terms of financial success. The slow speed and the small number of products increased Lianhua's costs in a significant way and extended the cost-recovery period. Lianhua's own publication *Lianhua Pictorial* (聯華畫報) admitted, "Even if the sale of the product is profitable, such profit may be highly diminished by more overhead, not to mention that some products failed to make a profit."[46] *The Song of the Fishermen* was probably the most successful Chinese film of the 1930s, bringing Lianhua a gross return of 200,000 yuan. However, the net profit of the film was quite low due to its high expense and year-long production schedule. To make things worse, a slow speed of production was not a guarantee for good box office receipts. For instance, *Wind*, Wu Cun's first film at Lianhua, took eight months (from August 1933 to April 1934) to complete, but the result proved to be a failure both in terms of artistic quality and box office receipts.

Lianhua's managers clearly recognised the problem of high overheads caused by the powerful position of directors and made efforts to reduce them. A 1935 market survey indicated that the overhead expenses of Lianhua were over 15,000 yuan per month, which topped the figure for China's film studios.[47] For the sake of solving this problem, Lianhua executives employed several methods. Increasing the number of productions was the first. In 1932, Luo Mingyou set a target for Lu Jie and his second studio of releasing twelve films each year. However, the plan was aborted due to the strong resistance of Lu Jie, who argued that it would sacrifice quality. In 1935, during the strike of Lianhua's staff, one proposal initiated by Wu Bangfan, head of the Shanghai management branch, was to increase the number of products.[48] Wu argued that if Lianhua could increase the number of products to

27 each year (in 1935 Lianhua only released ten films), the crisis would be resolved.[49] The second method for reducing overhead was to merge Lianhua's studios into one. In a 1934 document titled *A Summary Statement Regarding Raising Capital for Lianhua*, Luo Mingyou claimed that "by means of merging two studios into one, there will be a savings in overhead of 6,000 yuan if Lianhua could produce three products every month rather than one."[50] Unfortunately, neither increasing the number of products nor merging the studios reduced overhead significantly.

Conclusion

Like its American counterpart, China's mode of production also experienced an evolution from the cameraman system to the central producer system. In addition, China developed its own characteristics in this domain. In China's production system, film directors retained a great deal of control over film production compared with their colleagues in Hollywood. However, financially speaking, this was not a positive characteristic.

The vulnerability and the lack of enduring success of the film industry was one major consequence of China's mode of production in the 1920s and 1930s. The powerful position of directors, as Kristin Thompson argues, generally results in the "industry's continued dependence on small production companies"[51] and, I would like to add, upon the personal performance of the directors. The case of China supports this argument. In the first half of the twentieth century, when unexpected bad luck struck directors, it could significantly shake the foundations of a studio. Take Mingxing for instance: after the death of Zheng Zhengqiu, the director of *Two Sisters* (1933), in 1935 the company was unable to return to prosperity. Generally speaking, China reached its peak in the film industry in the first half of the twentieth century in 1933 and 1934. In those two years, box office hits like *Two Sisters, The Song of the Fishermen*, and *Big Road* were all released. But China's film industry entered a chilly winter in the years that followed. Other than macroeconomic factors, such as China suffering from the world economic crisis and the threat of the war between China and Japan, the decline of the Chinese film industry could also be attributed to its mode of production.

Notes

1 Leo Ou-fan Lee, *Shanghai Modern: The Flowering of a New Urban Culture in China, 1930–1945* (Cambridge: Harvard University Press, 1999), 10.
2 The original version of Lu Jie's diary was donated to the China Film Archive, but it is not available to readers (it has possibly been lost). In 1962, China Film Archive edited and issued a mimeographed version of Lu Jie's diary, which was not made public. Despite its incomplete nature (it only spans 1920–1949), the years 1930–1937 were relatively well recorded in this abridged version. For this

book, I have used a digital copy of this mimeographed version kindly provided by Professor Shi Chuan at the Shanghai Theatre Academy.
3 S. H. Rigby, *Marxism and History: A Critical Introduction* (Vancouver: University of British Columbia, 1998), 24.
4 David Bordwell, Staiger Janet, and Thompson Kristin, *The Classical Hollywood Cinema, Film Style and Mode of Production to 1960* (New York: Columbia University Press, 1985), 89.
5 Harry Braverman, *Labor and Monopoly Capital: The Degradation of Work in the Twentieth Century* (New York: Monthly Review Press, 1973), 71.
6 Bordwell, Staiger, and Thompson, *The Classic Hollywood Cinema*, 91.
7 Ibid., 93.
8 Ibid., 93.
9 Anon, "The Isis Theatre," *The Shanghai Times*, 22 May 1917.
10 Anon, "Far East Pioneer Here," *The North-China Herald*, 15 May 1935.
11 Anon, "Plans of New Buildings Approved," *The Municipal Gazette*, 13 June 1912.
12 Bordwell, Staiger, and Thompson, *The Classic Hollywood Cinema*, 116.
13 Anon, "The Origin of the Star Motion Picture Producing Co. Ltd./明星影片股份有限公司組織緣起." *Movie Magazine*/影戲雜誌 1, no. 3 (1922): 40.
14 Xuelei Huang, "Commercializing Ideologies: Intellectuals and Cultural Production at the Mingxing (Star) Motion Picture Company, 1922–1938" (PhD diss., Heidelberg University, 2009), 41.
15 Anon, "The Development of Xinren Company/新人公司之發展." *Shen Bao*, 3 May 1927.
16 Bordwell, Staiger, and Thompson, *The Classic Hollywood Cinema*, 124.
17 Ibid.
18 Anon, "The Film Yang Guifei, Produced by Moonlight Company/記月光銳意進取中之楊貴妃." *Shen Bao*, 8 September 1925.
19 Dequan Huang, *A Textual Survey of Early Chinese Film History*/中國早期電影史事考證" (Beijing: China Film Press, 2012), 119.
20 China Film Archive 1962, entry for 30 December 1928 in Lu Jie's diary.
21 China Film Archive 1962, entry for 15 April 1929 in Lu Jie's diary.
22 China Film Archive 1962, entry for 30 June 1929 in Lu Jie's diary.
23 China Sun was amalgamated into Lianhua for a price of 40,000 yuan, while Great China Lilium was acquired for 45,000 yuan. Wu Xingzai, one owner of Great China Lilium, invested an extra 55,000 yuan in cash into Lianhua. See Mingyou Luo, "A public letter to colleagues concerning the organisation of Lianhua/為聯華組織報告同仁書." *Film Magazine*/影戲雜誌 1, no. 10 (1931): 46.
24 Bordwell, Staiger, and Thompson, *The Classic Hollywood Cinema*, 136; emphasis in original.
25 Ibid.
26 Sunlu Gong, "*An Unofficial History of Chinese Cinema*/中國電影史話." vol. 3 (Hong Kong: Tiannan Book Publishing House, 1961), 12–13.
27 It seems that the problem of relations between personnel was not confined to the Lianhua studios: a *Movietone* (電聲) report points out some conflicts between Luo Mingyou and Wu Bangfan 吳邦藩, the head of the sales department. A major reason was that the staff in the sales department, whose salary was paid by Lianhua, were also involved in distributing films produced by other corporations, but they did not share those profits with Lianhua. See Anon, "The Issue behind the Move of Lianhua/聯華影業佈置遷移問題" *Movietone*/電聲, 5, no. 25 (1936).
28 China Film Archive 1962, entry for 21 April 1932 in Lu Jie's diary.

29 China Film Archive 1962, entry for 29 June 1935 in Lu Jie's diary; Xi Li, ed. 2003. *Li Minwei's Diary*/黎民偉日記. Hong Kong: Hong Kong Film Archive, entry for 29 June 1935.
30 China Film Archive 1962, entry for 16 April 1932 in Lu Jie's diary.
31 China Film Archive 1962, entry for 29 June 1933 in Lu Jie's diary.
32 China Film Archive 1962, entry for 26 January 1934 in Lu Jie's diary. To be fair, the slow speed of production of *Wind* was not entirely attributable to the director. Lu Jie mentioned that the lack of punctuality of Tan Ying, the leading actress of the film, was also a major reason (China Film Archive 1962, entry for 26 October 1934 in Lu Jie's diary).
33 China Film Archive 1962, entry for 17 April 1934 in Lu Jie's diary.
34 Bordwell, Staiger, and Thompson, *The Classic Hollywood Cinema*, 136.
35 Zhen Zhang, *An Amorous History of the Silver Screen* (Chicago: Chicago University Press, 2005), 153.
36 Ibid.
37 Yuqian Ouyang, "Directing Method/導演法". *Film Monthly*/電影月報 1, no. 1.1 (1928).
38 Bordwell, Staiger, and Thompson, *The Hollywood Cinema*, 138.
39 Yu Sun, *Sailing in the Film Sea*/銀海泛舟 (Beijing: China Film Press, 1980), 179.
40 China Film Archive 1962, entry for 20 June 1932 in Lu Jie's diary; entry for 23 June 1932 in Lu Jie's diary.
41 Chusheng Cai, "The Location Shooting Log in Suzhou/蘇垣紀行". *Lianhua Pictorial*/8, no. 1 (13 July 1936): 13.
42 China Film Archive 1962, entry for 4 July 1936 in Lu Jie's diary.
43 Weiming, "Comments on Film/電影插話". *Lianhua Pictorial* 5, no. 12 (1936): 1.
44 China Film Archive 1962, entry for 2 February 1933 in Lu Jie's diary. On that day Lu wrote in his diary,

> [I] talked to Cai (Chusheng) and reminded him that it had been half a year since *Morning in the Metropolis* started. I hoped that he could complete the film editing as soon as possible.
> (China Film Archive 1962, entry for 2 February 1933 in Lu Jie's diary)

45 Ce Zhao, "The Reason Why Domestic Films Cannot be Mass Produced/何以國產片不能大量生產". *Lianhua Pictorial* 7, no. 12 (1936): 2.
46 Ibid.
47 Shanghai Municipal Archive, "A Summary Statement Regarding Raising Capital for Lianhua/聯華影業製片印刷公司增收資本節略". In The Industry of Film Production: A Survey Conducted by the Shanghai Commercial and Saving Bank, Q275-1-1949.
48 Anon, "A Riot Caused by Salary Cutting/發生減薪風潮". *Film News*/電影新聞1, no. 4 (1935): 4.
49 Ibid.
50 Shanghai Municipal Archive, *The Industry of Film Production: A Survey Conducted by the Shanghai Commercial and Saving Bank*, Q275-1-1949.
51 Kristin Thompson, "Early Alternatives to the Hollywood Mode of Production: Implications for Europe's Avant-Gardes," *Film History* 5, no. 4 (1993): 391.

References

Anon. "Plans of New Buildings Approved." *The Municipal Gazette*. 13 June 1912.
Anon. "The Isis Theatre." *The Shanghai Times*. 22 May 1917.

Anon. "The Origin of the Star Motion Picture Producing Co. Ltd/明星影片股份有限公司組織緣起". *Movie Magazine*/影戲雜誌 1, no. 3 (1922): 40.
Anon. "The Film Yang Guifei, Produced by Moonlight Company/記月光銳意進取中之楊貴妃". *Shen Bao*. 8 September 1925.
Anon. "The Development of Xinren Company/新人公司之發展". *Shen Bao*. 3 May 1927.
Anon. "Far East Pioneer Here." *The North-China Herald*. 15 May 1935.
Anon. "A Riot Caused by Salary Cutting/發生減薪風潮". *Film News*/電影新聞1, no. 4 (1935): 4.
Anon. "The Issues behind the Move of Lianhua/聯華影業佈置遷移問題". *Movietone*/電聲 5, no. 25 (1936): 605.
Bordwell, David, Janet Staiger, and Kristin Thompson. *The Classical Hollywood Cinema, Film Style and Mode of Production to 1960*. New York: Columbia University Press, 1985.
Braverman, Harry. *Labor and Monopoly Capital: The Degradation of Work in the Twentieth Century*. New York: Monthly Review Press, 1973.
Cai, Chusheng. "The Location Shooting Log in Suzhou/蘇垣紀行". *Lianhua Pictorial* 8, no. 1 (13 July 1936): 27–34.
China Film Archive ed. *An Abridgement of Lu Jie's Diary*/陸潔日記摘存. Unpublished version, 1962.
Gong, Sunlu. *An Unofficial History of Chinese Cinema*/中國電影史話. vol. 3. Hong Kong: Tiannan Book Publishing House, 1961.
Huang, Dequan. *A Textual Survey of Early Chinese Film History* 中國早期電影史事考證. Beijing: China Film Press, 2012.
Huang, Xuelei. "Commercializing Ideologies: Intellectuals and Cultural Production at the Mingxing (Star) Motion Picture Company, 1922–1938." PhD diss., Heidelberg University, 2009.
Huang, Yasheng. *Capitalism with Chinese Characteristics: Entrepreneurship and the State*. Cambridge: Cambridge University Press, 2008.
Lee, Leo Ou-fan. *Shanghai Modern: The Flowering of a New Urban Culture in China, 1930–1945*. Cambridge: Harvard University Press, 1999.
Li, Xi, ed. *Li Minwei's Diary*/黎民偉日記. Hong Kong: Hong Kong Film Archive, 2003.
Lianhua. "Four Years' Evolution of Lianhua/聯華影片公司四年經歷史". In *1934 Chinese Film Yearbook*/中國電影年鑒, edited by the China Educational Film Association. Beijing: China Radio and TV Press, [1934] 2008.
Luo, Mingyou. "A Public Letter to Colleagues Concerning the Organisation of Lianhua/為聯華組織報告同仁書". *Movie Magazine*/影戲雜誌 1, no. 10 (1931): 46.
Ouyang, Yuqian. "Directing Method/導演法". *Film Monthly*/電影月報 1, no. 1 (1928): 38–42.
Rigby, S. H. *Marxism and History: A Critical Introduction*. Vancouver: University of British Columbia, 1998.
Shanghai Municipal Archive. "A Summary Statement Regarding Raising Capital for Lianhua/聯華影業製片印刷有限公司增收資本節略". In The Industry of Film Production: A Survey Conducted by the Shanghai Commercial and Saving Bank, Q275-1-1949.
Sun, Yu. *Sailing in the Film Sea*/銀海泛舟. Beijing: China Film Press, 1980.

Thompson, Kristin. "Early Alternatives to the Hollywood Mode of Production: Implications for Europe's Avant-Gardes." *Film History* 5, no. 4 (1993): 391.

Weiming. "Comments on Film/電影插話. *Lianhua Pictorial* 5, no. 12 (1936): 1.

Zhao, Ce. "The Reason Why Domestic Films Cannot be Mass Produced/何以國產片不能大量生產." *Lianhua Pictorial* 7, no. 12 (1936): 2.

Zhang, Zhen. *An Amorous History of the Silver Screen*. Chicago: Chicago University Press, 2005.

5 Movie matchmakers

The intermediaries between the American and the Chinese film industries

It is a cliché to say that Chinese film-makers learned from the American film industry in the first half of the twentieth century. However, major executives and directors in the Chinese film industry, such as Zhang Shichuan, never visited Hollywood. Their perceptions of the American film industry were largely obtained through American film-makers who came to China, and through watching American movies, many of which were imported by Chinese distributors. Such an interesting phenomenon calls for light to be shed on a group of figures who have long since passed into oblivion, their place in the history of Chinese cinema misunderstood: the intermediaries. Who were they? To what extent were they responsible for the expansion of the American film industry business in China? What did they bring to the Chinese film industry?

In the literature on Chinese film history fuelled by nationalism, a number of intermediaries are either obscured or labelled as 'aggressors' or 'traitors' since they are regarded as having helped the expansion of the American industry and thus oppressed the domestic film industry. In my view, this nationalistic film historiography reduces the complex role that intermediary figures played in Chinese film history. Employing extensive research in Chinese and American archives, this chapter attempts to demonstrate that intermediaries served as 'matchmakers' between Hollywood and the Chinese film industry. I argue that intermediaries bridged the gap between the film industries of America and China, and made significant contributions to the evolution of the Chinese film industry.

By 'intermediary' I mean the figures and enterprises responsible for the intercommunication between the American and the Chinese film industries. Hao Yen-ping's seminal account on the compradors in modern China provides an excellent model for my study on the intermediaries between these two industries.[1] Hao articulates the significance of the comprador, as a middleman, to China's early industrialisation. In contrast to criticisms that compradors were the "spearheads of foreign colonialism and economic imperialism," Hao points out that the compradors to some extent "competed with foreign merchants in the management of modern enterprises, and thus in a way [prevented] the unchecked foreign incursion."[2] Xiao Zhiwei is one pioneer who notices the significance of the intermediaries in Chinese film studies. Xiao incisively introduces the notion of 'in-between production' into the history of how distributors appropriated Hollywood content in the Chinese cultural context.[3] In linguistic studies, 'in-between production' refers to a process of "repetitions, evocations, translations and reproductions" in areas such as the introduction of English words into the Chinese language.[4] In the vein of Hao and Xiao, I intend to address the functions of intermediaries between the American and the Chinese film industries in the early twentieth century. Two types of intermediaries are stressed here: (1) American citizens who came to China for the film business and (2) Chinese merchants who did business with American corporations, particularly film distributors. The former type is exemplified by William Henry Lynch, and the latter by Lo Kan. It should be noted that the intermediaries between the Chinese and American film industries are not limited to these two groups. Students such as Hong Shen, who returned from education in America, marked themselves as prominent intermediaries in Chinese film history by introducing American film knowledge to the Chinese film industry and importing sound film equipment. In addition, it is necessary to point out that the functions of intermediaries are reciprocal. Whilst this study focusses on the influence of America on China, the opposite deserves critical attention as well.

To provide some background, I turn now to a brief introduction on the nationalistic approach to Chinese film studies and the attitudes of its proponents towards intermediaries. The chapter then follows the contributions to the Chinese film industry of American practitioners, a group of intermediaries who are labelled as 'aggressors' in nationalistic writing. I identify William Lynch, the cinematographer of the Asiatic Film Company, as someone who played a crucial role in developing the skills and careers of the first-generation Chinese directors. The chapter then investigates another type of intermediary: Chinese merchants distributing Hollywood films in China. On the one hand, these intermediaries helped the exploration of China as a critical sector in the American industry's strategy of localisation, while on the other hand, they benefited the Chinese film industry in various ways. I conclude by suggesting in broader terms that patriotic sentiment should not be the only criterion in the study of Chinese film history.

Nationalism in Chinese film studies

A nationalistic approach dominates the study of Chinese film history. Nationalism is defined as a concept that emphasises "national identity as that aspect of individuals' self-image that is tied to their nation." [5] China's nationalism emerged along with the rise of the nation-state in modern China in the late nineteenth century and grew into a major ideology of the Chinese Nationalist Party in the first half of the twentieth century. A nationalistic approach in the history texts coincides with a broader social context. As early as the 1930s, Gu Jianchen, one of the first film historians, subscribed to nationalism in his research.[6] Gu's nationalistic sentiment is well expressed in his statement on the cinema department of the British American Tobacco Company, which produced films with Chinese casts and purchased small cinemas in 1920s China. The commercial expansion of the cinema department, from Gu's point of view, was an example of the 'economic oppression' of the Chinese film industry.[7]

Nationalistic sentiment went further in publications after the Communist Party takeover in 1949. According to Dirlik, Mao Zedong developed his ideas by "subsum[ing] Marxism with nationalism" and structured Chinese society with this theory in mind.[8] In *History of the Development of Chinese Film*, Cheng Jihua and his colleagues consciously employ Mao Zedong's thought in their study of Chinese film history. Cheng and his colleagues consider Chinese film history to be a struggle between "the progressive culture for socialism, national liberation and people's democracy" and "imperialist and other reactive cultures."[9] The contribution of the Chinese 'national capitalists' prior to 1949 is only acknowledged in this scholarship due to their patriotic sentiments and their efforts to build a national film industry, while American merchants, together with Hollywood films, are regarded as a force of economic and cultural aggression towards the national industry.

Recent literature within the theoretical framework of 'national cinema' avoids the over-ideologisation found in the previous literature; however, a focus on nation-building means that the role of foreigners still occupies a blind spot. In the wake of the focus on national cinema, Hu Jubin positions nationalism as a principal axis in Chinese films prior to 1949.[10] According to Hu, "what the Chinese cinema, as a national cinema, participated in and reflected, was a nationalism about politics."[11] Hu divides the pre-1949 history of Chinese cinema into five periods and characterises each period with a different type of nationalism. For instance, the 1920s saw the upsurge of industrial nationalism, which prioritised "the establishment of the film industry as the Chinese nation's domestic industry."[12] However, an exaggerated emphasis on nationalism in the Chinese film industry is liable to neglect the contribution of those figures who had few connections with nation-building. For instance, American film merchants, in Hu's account, are merely the Chinese national industry's rivals, whose intention it was to monopolise the film industry.[13] Other than noting that their presence stimulated the "advocacy of a national cinema" in China, Hu remains silent on the contributions of American merchants to the domestic film industry.[14]

American film practitioners in China

In Chinese film history, Zhang Shichuan is known as the co-founder of Mingxing and was from its inception the main investor and head executive. In addition, Zhang, together with Zheng Zhengqiu, is regarded as a 'Father of Chinese Cinema.' During his 40-year film career, Zhang

Shichuan directed over 150 silent and sound films. However, Zhang confessed that, prior to becoming involved in the film business, he seldom watched movies.[15] It was his experience as director of the Asiatic Film Company that inspired his interest in film-making and educated him in the field. The Asiatic Film Company was the first professional company in Chinese film history, but it was staffed from both the United States and China. The following passage examines the contributions of the American film practitioners to the Chinese film industry, with special attention given to William H. Lynch, the cinematographer and an executive of the Asiatic Film Company.

Oddly enough, the Asiatic Film Company has received little attention in Chinese film studies. The name of the corporation is misspelled as 'China Cinema Company' or 'Asia Film Company' in the existing literature.[16] Early historical writings identified Benjamin Brodsky, the owner of China Cinema Company and the Variety Film Exchange, as the organiser of the Asiatic Film Company.[17] However, recent research suggests that Brodsky did not involve in himself the film business in China until the 1910s and his business had little connection with the Asiatic Film Company.[18] At this stage, it is safe to say that the Asiatic was in the hand of two American merchants in 1910s Shanghai: Thomas Henry Suffert (薩弗, 1869–1941) and Arthur Julius Israel (依什爾, 1875–1948). As with the mangling of its corporate name, these two names are mistakenly referred to as 'Yashell' or 'Elsser' and 'Lehrmann.'[19] The Asiatic Film Company perhaps commenced its business in 1913 and was defunct after 1915.[20]

Thomas H. Suffert's contribution to the Asiatic and to Zhang Shichuan is very likely to have been limited to the financial and executive realms. Suffert was born in Cleveland, Ohio. He moved to Shanghai in 1895 for commercial exploration. The historical record shows that Suffert mainly served as a speculator in Shanghai.[21] In a 1916 passport application, he is referred to as "the owner and manager of an American registered firm which engaged in the import and export trade with the United States and other countries," the Central Trading Company (坤和) in Shanghai.[22] With respect to the operation of the Asiatic, Suffert seems to have been its executive. For instance, a 1913 source shows that Suffert, representing the Asiatic Film Company, applied for permission to show films at the Little Street Theatre (*de la Rue Petit*) in Shanghai.[23] In addition, Suffert attended the Annual Meeting of Ratepayers under the name of the Asiatic Film Company in 1918.[24] As a friend of Zhang Shichuan, Suffert continued to participate in Zhang's later film business, after the dissolution of the Asiatic. In 1921, when Zhang Shichuan was organising Mingxing's predecessor, the Mutual Stock & Produce Company (大同日夜物權交易所), Suffert served as a consultant.[25] It was he who introduced his friend, Carl Louis Gregory, to Zhang Shichuan. As a leading cinematographer and professor from Columbia University, Gregory favoured Zhang Shichuan and Mingxing in various ways, including film shooting, film printing, and script writing.[26] Suffert was also involved in the management of the Mingxing Shadow-play School in 1921.

In addition, Mingxing's affiliated cinema, the Star, was registered under the name of Suffert in the United States for the sake of avoiding taxation.[27]

In comparison with Suffert, Arthur J. Israel appears to have played a lesser role. The existing literature identifies Israel as the Asiatic's cameraman.[28] However, no certain evidence has come to light so far to support this identification. Israel was born in San Francisco in 1875. In his 20s, he became a cigar dealer in California. His passport application records showed that he travelled to China as early as 1902.[29] In his 30 years in Shanghai, Israel mainly focussed on the business of the Shanghai Life Insurance Company, a British Company with mostly American capital.[30] During the period from 1913 to 1915, Israel served as a director, the third highest position, in the company. In addition, he was occupied as the director of the Consolidated Rubber Estates Limited, a member of the board of directors of the Laou Kung Mow Cotton Spinning & Weaving Company, and served on the executive committee of the Shanghai Amateur Baseball League.[31] Moreover, during the period 1913–1915 when the Asiatic was active, Israel spent several months on a business trip to Vancouver and Hong Kong from November 1913 to March 1914.[32] Therefore, even if he did operate a camera, Israel could not have had enough time to produce more than a dozen films during this period. It seems that he was merely an investor in the Asiatic Film Company, given his abundant experience in finance and investment.[33] The credit for projecting films and the daily operation of the Asiatic should go to other figures in that field.

Figure 5.1 Arthur Israel.
Source: US Passport Application of Arthur Israel, 1918. Photo courtesy of National Archives and Records Administration and www.ancestry.com

Figure 5.2 Thomas Suffert.
Source: US Passport Application of Thomas Suffert, 1916. Photo courtesy of National Archives and Records Administration and www.ancestry.com

I believe that an American citizen named William H. Lynch is owed the credit for this enterprise. Along with several English sources, one Chinese source supports my speculation.[34] Prior to his involvement in the film business, William Lynch operated a photographic studio named the North Beach Studio in Santa Monica, Los Angeles (a city close to Hollywood) from 1905.[35] His experience in the photo studio facilitated his job in the motion picture industry as a cinematographer. In 1912, Lynch was hired as a film cameraman by the Globe Motion Picture Company. Lynch, together with Rochefort Johns, initiated a three-month trip to Asia to film in locations including China.[36] This trip probably generated Lynch's interest in the Orient. Therefore, he agreed to join the Asiatic Film Company in Shanghai as early as 27 January 1913.[37]

The date when Lynch joined the Asiatic must have been no later than March 1913. The reason is that at that time, he wrote back from China to *The Daily Outlook*, a local newspaper issued in Santa Monica.[38] Lynch first described his experience in the Asiatic Film Company:

> We have located a moving picture studio and complete plant for making and finishing moving pictures here. We are starting in a new field and pictures made with Chinese actors are to be shown to the Chinese

people. It is something that has not been done to this date and from reports we believe it will be a big success. We will also operate in connection with the production of the films, several theatres throughout China for the purpose of creating a greater demand and later on will put our entire time and efforts to the production of film only.[39]

According to this letter, it is clear that using Chinese actors was a deliberate production and marketing strategy for the Asiatic with the purpose of satisfying its target consumers: Chinese audiences. In addition, the letter demonstrates that even if the Asiatic Film Company was not originally organised by Israel and Suffert, their alleged predecessor, Benjamin Brodsky, might not have produced substantial movies at Shanghai as is suggested in the existing literature.[40] To Lynch, a film producing career seemed promising and therefore he "decided to make [his] permanent home abroad (in China)" in 1913.[41]

A 1914 report of *The Moving Picture World* provides a detailed illustration of the operation of the Asiatic.[42] The report is fairly reliable since the author, Clarke Irvine, based it on his meeting with William Lynch in China in 1913.[43] According to this report, William Lynch, the "Shanghai manager of the Asiatic Film Company," was making films for the Asiatic, "which ha[d] many releases each month."[44] In addition, it states that

> The Asiatic Film Company maintains a large studio in Shanghai, where sixteen star actors are daily posing before the camera. These men—no women are allowed to do this kind of work—are the first, and so far, the only Chinese to act before the camera. There are two directors and two interpreters who work under the supervision of Mr. Lynch. These stars are supported by a well-organized company of twenty-five actors. The laboratory and finishing plant is equipped to turn out 10,000 feet of finished film a day. The supply is for the entire country, and the releases are made just as in America and Europe. There are a number of theaters in Shanghai, two of which are operated by this company.[45]

This passage clearly shows the significance of William Lynch to the Asiatic Film Company and by extension to the Chinese film industry in its initial stage. According to this passage, Lynch was in charge not only of projecting films, but also of supervising all Asiatic Film Company productions. This would have been the most prominent position in the Asiatic, given that none of the other staff, foreigners or Chinese, had professional knowledge of how to produce motion pictures. Zhang Shichuan and Zheng Zhengqiu were arguably the two directors, under the supervision of William Lynch. With respect to the division of labour in the Company, Zhang Shichuan claimed that he was responsible for supervising camera movement while Zheng was in charge of guiding the actors' performance.[46] However, in the early 1910s, the perception of the director's role was not well developed within the Chinese film industry. In addition, the initial Chinese film productions were close to documentaries of the original *wenmingxi* (civilised drama文明戲).[47] There were few tasks left for directors once actors started to perform. Furthermore, as I mentioned earlier, Zhang's directorial knowledge was initially next to nothing.[48] Therefore, the position of Lynch in the productions of the Asiatic is likely to have been more significant than that of directors such as Zhang Shichuan and Zheng Zhengqiu.

William Lynch returned to the United States in June 1914. His initial plan was to return to China as long as "the revolution in China subside[d] enough for operations to continue."[49] However, why Lynch did not manage to travel back to China remains unclear. Lynch's departure is one major reason the Asiatic went into decline, apart from the shortage of film stock due to the outbreak of the First World War.

Apart from the presence of Lynch, the Asiatic Film Company deserves notice because it is one of the first Chinese concerns which distributed films in overseas markets. In September 1913, Arthur R. Oberle, representing the Asiatic Film Company, passed by Honolulu when travelling back to the United States; Oberle stated that he secured "many thousand feet of pictures depicting actual scenes in the series of battles" in China.[50] Arguably, this is the documentary titled *Shanghai Battles* (淞滬戰事, 1913) referred to in the Chinese records.[51] Unfortunately, I have been unable to identify any exhibition information in the United States regarding this documentary. Nevertheless, the Asiatic Film Company successfully circulated its productions in South-East Asia. A preview commercial shows that *Khoojin Whatchay/A Poor Man Won a Lottery* (苦力人發財, 1913), an Asiatic production, was exhibited at the Empire Theatre in Singapore in 1917.[52] Chinese film corporations followed the pathway of the Asiatic and turned South-East Asia into the largest overseas market for Chinese films in the first half of the twentieth century.

The contribution of the American intermediaries in many cases is not appreciated but instead attacked by nationalistic Chinese literature. For instance, foreign figures in the Asiatic Film Company are described as imperialists who conducted economic and cultural aggression against China.[53] If we put the validity of the denouncement aside, the contribution of foreign figures in the Asiatic such as Lynch is far greater than their potential threat to the Chinese film industry. As a matter of fact, the Asiatic can be seen as crucial to the emergence of the domestic film industry. In addition, this company's productions, as the first trials of cooperation between foreign practitioners and China, stimulated China's interests in producing films.[54] Therefore, it is not an exaggeration to say that William Lynch was a 'torchbearer' for Zhang Shichuan and Zheng Zhengqiu, the fathers of Chinese cinema, providing them with crucial film knowledge. It is also possible that Lynch enlightened and fostered the interests of Zhang and Zheng within the industry. As a result, Zhang and Zheng organised Mingxing in 1922 and thus contributed to the upsurge of the Chinese film industry in the 1920s and 1930s.

William Lynch and his Asiatic Film Company are merely one example of numerous American practitioners who were active in modern China. American film practitioners facilitated the Chinese film industry by systematically introducing performance practice and sophisticated film equipment and techniques. In evaluating such foreign intermediaries, Zheng Junli is balanced when he admits that much film knowledge of Chinese film-makers was obtained from their working experiences with American intermediaries, quite aside from any intention of 'colonial aggression' by these American merchants.[55]

Chinese merchants straddling the divide between Hollywood and China

We now turn to Zhang Shichuan. In addition to his early experience with the Asiatic, Zhang continuously updated his skills as a director through watching Hollywood films.[56] A large number of these Hollywood films were distributed by Chinese independent distributors, who constitute the second type of intermediary between the American and the Chinese film industries. In this section, I examine this type of intermediary and their contributions to the domestic film industry, with a focus on Lo Kan.

Chinese independent distributors were a prominent force in distributing Hollywood films in the first half of the twentieth century. In the 1910s, American films were mainly circulated into China through British and French film exchange corporations. The outbreak of the First World War resulted in an upsurge of requests for American films due to the fall in availability of French films. In 1921, Universal set up its subsidiary organisation in Shanghai to take care of its Chinese distribution business. Fox, Paramount, and Metro-Goldwyn-Mayer followed suit and opened their respective subsidiary distribution organisations in the 1930s. Nevertheless, direct representatives and independent distributors were prominent forces (comprising 14 of 18 distribution corporations in 1932).[57] The Peacock Motion Picture Corporation, for instance, a Sino-American corporation registered in the United States, was the direct representative of Radio-Keith-Orpheum in 1932. In addition, independent distributors, who were granted film screening rights in China from their American counterparts, circulated films nationwide. A case in point is Lo Kan. Born in Canton in 1888, Lo became involved in the distribution business by establishing the first distribution agent, Hong Kong Amusements Ltd, in 1921. In its heyday in 1922–1923, Hong Kong Amusements almost monopolised the distribution of Hollywood films in China.[58] Even in the 1930s when the key Hollywood studios operated through direct representatives or distribution agents in China, Hong Kong Amusements Ltd maintained a large business with studios including United Artists.[59]

In addition to Hong Kong Amusements, Lo became a film magnate, operating and owning several large film firms involving equipment, distribution, and exhibition. These firms included China Theatre Ltd, Yangtze Amusements Ltd, Eastern Amusements Ltd, Cathay Amusements Ltd, Puma Films Ltd, The Theatre Equipment Company Ltd, and North China Amusements Ltd.[60] Film exhibition was one of Lo's key businesses. In the 1930s, he directed and controlled "more than 30 of the leading cinema-theatres in China and Hong Kong, of several of which he [was] the owner."[61] The highlight in Lo's legendary life was that he rebuilt the Grand Cinema in Shanghai and updated it into the most superior first-run cinema in the Far East. In 1932, Lo set up the United Theatres Corporation and registered it in the United States with 5,000,000 Mexican dollars. This was probably the largest film business in China in the first half of the twentieth century in terms of registered capital. The United Theatres Corporation was designed to be a vertically integrated film enterprise, including production, distribution, and exhibition. One intention of the company was to organise a theatre chain that could monopolise the exhibition of Hollywood films in Shanghai. In its heyday, the member theatres of United Theatres encompassed nine theatres, including the Grand, Cathay, Carlton, Isis, Paris, Crystal Palace, Ritz, Ward, and Pearl Theatres.[62]

As intermediaries, domestic film distributors such as Lo Kan were beneficial to the American film industry's expansion into unfamiliar markets like China. To Hollywood executives, the political, economic, and cultural situation in China was quite different from that in the United States. Domestic distributors could help smooth the way for the business of the American film industry in China. For instance, the Isis served as the second-run theatre for United Artists in Shanghai. According to a resource in 1927, "the theatre [was] located in Chinese territory and suffered very much from the strict Chinese martial law regulations."[63] Under the management of Lo Kan, the Isis changed its entrance to open into the International Settlements territory. Thereby, it successfully bypassed the Chinese military troubles. In addition, Lo's expansion into the interior cities was beneficial for the exhibition of United Artists movies. In 1928, Lo contemplated opening cinemas in interior cities including Ningbo, Hangzhou, Nanjing, Yantai, Jinan, and Wuxi. Lo's plan brought opportunities for the expansion of United Artists' film business. The United Artists report for 1928 noted that "we [had] been able to negotiate for a number of our old pictures to play at these interior cities."[64]

One prominent feature of foreign film distributors was the position they straddled between America and China. Although the entire business of the distributors focussed on the Chinese film market, most of the corporations owned and operated by the distributors were registered in the United States. There were several advantages in being an American corporation, one of which I want to stress: as an American corporation, Lo's company could seek support from the American authorities if any conflict occurred. The

American government is known for protecting its citizens and their economic interests in China. An example is the events which surrounded the opening of a theatre in Changsha, an interior city. In 1923, Joseph Y. Tsau, an American citizen who opened the Lyceum theatre within the walls of the city in Changsha, filed a complaint with American consuls against the Chinese government. The Chinese authorities requested that Tsau move the theatre outside the walls since the inner city was not regarded as a commercial port. Such a move would jeopardise Tsau's business. With the help of the American vice consul and the Changsha Foreign Office, Tsau eventually obtained permission to continue operating his theatre within city walls.[65] It is certain that Tsau would not have enjoyed such treatment if his theatre had been registered in China. The kind of benefit Tsau obtained is one of the most important reasons for Chinese corporations being registered in the United States. Similarly, for the sake of seeking protection from the British government, Lo Kan became a British citizen.

The nationalistic scholarship is hostile to foreign film distributors such as Lo Kan. Radical nationalists have labelled Lo as a 'traitor' or 'imperialist' who invaded or betrayed China's economic rights by benefiting from the American industry's exploration in China. For instance, Cheng Jihua and his colleagues equate Lo's United Theatre Company with American imperialism and treat its appearance as "a further development of American intention to aggress the Chinese film industry," because it was registered in the United States.[66] However, it is necessary to point out that such attacks on Sino-American companies are highly selective. As I have mentioned previously, the Peacock Motion Pictures Company and the Star Theatre were both registered in the United States, but they were free from nationalistic attacks. However, recent historians who subscribe to a national cinema approach, such as Hu Jubin, choose to be silent on Lo's company. Due to the distribution of films from Hollywood, an economic rival of the national industry, Lo's company, from Hu's point of view, may be thought of as non-beneficial to the development of the national film industry, even if it did not hinder that industry.

The question here is the extent to which the distribution of Hollywood films threatened the development of the domestic film industry. The expansion of the American film industry and the development of the Chinese film industry are not necessarily mutually exclusive. In a rapid growth market such as China in the 1920s, the output of the Chinese film industry and Hollywood were able to increase simultaneously. One gauge of this is the footage of film stock imported from the United States to China. The linear feet of exposed film stock for exhibition purposes in 1929 was more than 20 times larger than that in 1913. The inflation of the figure for unexposed film (i.e. for producing Chinese films) was more striking: in 1925 this figure was 220 times larger than in 1920.[67] Even if there may be some truth to the idea that the American industry was a threat, the other side of the coin should not be neglected. In some cases, competition from Hollywood became an inspiration for the Chinese film industry. Additionally, Hollywood films circulated by Chinese distributors provided one of the few channels for Chinese practitioners to learn from Hollywood. In the first half of the twentieth century, American films remained a vital resource for China to imitate in terms of camera movement, direction, performance, and industrial systems. The American film industry brought film equipment and production techniques to China during its transition to talkies. If nationalists intend to admit the positive contribution of Hollywood films to China, the function of Chinese distributors as intermediaries introducing Hollywood films into China should not be neglected.

In addition, nationalistic accounts subscribing to the national cinema approach and excluding foreign film distributors from national historiography ignore the multiple identifications of these distributors. In many cases, distributing Hollywood films was merely one part of the complex business enterprises operated by these intermediaries. Intermediaries usually participated in other sectors of the film industry, and therefore blurred the boundary between national capitalists and intermediaries. Lo Kan, for instance, in addition to distributing and exhibiting Hollywood films, was responsible for distributing domestic films in Hong Kong. In the 1920s, Lo's Hong Kong Amusements scored in circulating *The Burning of Red Lotus Temple* (火燒紅蓮寺, dir. Zhang Shichuan 1928) in Hong Kong.[68] In addition, Lo was one of the key shareholders of Lianhua, a prominent force in the Chinese film industry in the 1930s.[69] In 1932 there was even a possibility that the ownership of Lianhua would shift to Lo Kan.[70] Sometimes, intermediaries even competed directly with their Hollywood counterparts through involvement in domestic film productions. Due to their abundant capital, they turned out to be the most effective rivals to foreign merchants in China. At the moment of China's sound conversion, Lo's United Theatres had "a definite project of establishing a modern sound studio and leasing it to Chinese producing companies."[71] An advertisement for the United Theatres from this era mentions that Lo had purchased modern sound equipment in advance and invited an expert from the Radio Corporation of America to supervise the erection of studios and the installation of the equipment.[72] If the plan were to eventuate, through leasing the studios to Chinese film-makers, United Theatres would not only "obtain a handsome return on its capital," but also "obtain a first refusal on all pictures produced at the studios."[73] In the Chinese film industry in general, the number of local sound pictures would increase from 15 per annum to at least 40 per annum. As analysts for the American consul pointed out, such a substantial increase in the number of Chinese talkies would "curtail the demand for foreign pictures."[74] Unfortunately, Lo's plan was aborted due to unexpected economic circumstances. However, he did not terminate his investment in film production. In 1933, employing the sound equipment purchased for the United Theatres, Lo released a box office hit *The Fool Pays Respect* (呆佬拜壽, dir. Hou Yao 1933), and in 1935, he finally erected a sound studio in Hong Kong.[75] Here, what I want to stress is the multi-functional role of distributing merchants like Lo Kan. It is true that they were beneficial to the expansion of the American film industry's business in China, serving as so-called 'traitors.' Nevertheless, the multi-functional role these intermediaries played in the relationship between America and China should not be ignored. Some of them may have benefited the Chinese film industry in a way.

Conclusion

When one discusses China's response to the American film industry, the implied discourse is that China had already built relations with the latter. However, 'building relations' is not an abstract notion. Figures and enterprises are necessary to connect the relations between the American and the Chinese film industries. As this chapter has shown, these intermediary figures, standing between America and China, bridged the communication gap between Hollywood and Chinese cinema.

The study of intermediaries between Hollywood and the Chinese film industry is linked to transnational Chinese cinemas studies. In the past two decades, transnationalism became a keyword in Chinese cinemas studies. Apart from very few exceptions, most of the academic discussion has centred on the post-1978 period, when Mainland China started to employ an open policy to encourage transnational capital and cooperation in the film industry.[76] However, inviting transnationalism into film history could not only fill the intellectual void, but also makes space for the blind spots like "the phenomena that not only cross but straddle and defy borders."[77] Under the national cinema paradigm, the contributions of border-crossing figures such as the intermediaries between Hollywood and China have been neglected. Yet, as this chapter tries to demonstrate, in the early twentieth century these intermediaries bridged relations between the American and the Chinese film industry. The making and development of the domestic film industry would have been much slower without their contributions. The complexity of history risks simplification in the shadow of nationalism.

Notes

1 Yenping Hao, *The Comprador in the Nineteenth Century China: Bridge between East And West* (Cambridge: Harvard University Press, 1970); Shuren Cheng, *China Cinema Year Book*/中華影業年鑑 (Shanghai: China Film Society, 1927), 10.
2 Hao, *The Comprador in the Nineteenth Century China*, 5.
3 Zhiwei Xiao, "Translating American Films into Chinese Audiences," in *Transnational Asian Identities in Pan-Pacific Cinemas*, ed. Philippa Gates and Lisa Funnell (New York: Routledge, 2012), 88–100.
4 Leyda Liu, *Translingual Practice: Literature, National Culture, and Translated Modernity-China, 1900–1937* (Stanford: Stanford University Press, 1995), xvii.
5 P. Greis, *China's New Nationalism: Pride, Politics, and Diplomacy* (Berkeley: University of California Press, 2004), 9.

6 Jianchen Gu, "The Development of Chinese Film/中國電影發達史," in *1934 Chinese Film Yearbook*/中國電影年鑒*1934*, ed. China Educational Film Association (Nanjing: China Education Association, 1934).
7 Ibid.
8 Arif Dirlik, *Marxism in the Chinese Revolution* (Lanham: Rowan & Littlefield Publishers, 2005), 129.
9 Jihua Cheng, Shaobai Li, and Zuwen Xing, *History of the Development of Chinese Cinema*/中國電影發展史, vol. 1 (Beijing: China Film Press, 1980), 3.
10 Jubin Hu, *Projecting a Nation* (Hong Kong: Hong Kong University Press, 2003), 25–27.
11 Ibid., 19.
12 Ibid., 48.
13 Ibid., 20.
14 Ibid.
15 Shichuan Zhang, "Since My Director Career Commenced/自我導演以來," *Star*/明星 3 (1935): 11.
16 Yingjin Zhang and Zhiwei Xiao, *Encyclopaedia of Chinese Cinema* (London: Routledge, 1998); Zhen Zhang, *An Amorous History of the Silver Screen* (Chicago: Chicago University Press, 2005); Kar Law and Frank Bren, *Hong Kong Cinema: A Cross-Cultural View* (Lanham: Scarecrow, 2004). I identify the English name of this company based on an English Yellow Pages book published in Shanghai named *1915 North China Desk Hong List* (*North China Daily News & Herald, 1915 North China Desk-Hong List* (Shanghai: North China Daily News Publishing House, 1915).
17 Cheng, *China Cinema Year Book*/中華影業年鑑; Cheng, Li, and Xing, *History of the Development of Chinese Cinema*/中國電影發展史, 1; Jay Leyda, *Dianying/Electric Shadow: An Account of Films and the Film Audience in China* (Cambridge: MIT Press, 1972).
18 Kar Law, "The Doubts and Suspicions of Hong Kong Movie's Origin/解開香港電影起源的謎團," *Contemporary Cinema*/當代電影 4 (2010); Dequan Huang, *A Textual Critical on Early Chinese Film History*/中國早期電影史事考證 (Beijing: China Film Press, 2012). The relationship between Benjamin Brodsky and the Asiatic Film Company is still open to study. I note that one still picture that Brodsky provided to the *New York Tribune* [G Kaufman, "Bret Harte Said It: The Heathen Chinese Is Peculiar," *New York Tribune*, 27 August 1916] is the same as the still picture (named *La Ha Naung Middong*) which appeared in a report about the Asiatic Film Company in *The Moving Picture World*. See C. Irvine, "Chinese Photoplays," *The Moving Picture World* 19, no. 8 (1914). Second, another still picture in the report on Brodsky is labelled as *The Three Thieves*/三賊案, which is believed to be a production of the Asiatic Film Company. See Huang, *A Textual Critical*, 73. Third, William H. Lynch, the cinematographer of the Asiatic Film Company, claimed that he was a cinematographer of *A Trip Through China*, one documentary of Brodsky's China Cinema Company. See *The Daily Outlook*, 27 October 1916. Fourth, the office and sales room of Brodsky's China Cinema Company was located at # 2 Hongkong Road, and appeared in *1916 North China Desk Hong List*, while the same address appeared as the Asiatic Film Company in *Shanghai Street Directory*, another part of the same publication. See *North China Daily News & Herald, 1916 North China Desk-Hong List* (Shanghai: North China Daily News Publishing House, 1916), 47, 200.
19 Yingjin Zhang, *Chinese National Cinema* (London: Routledge, 2004), 19; Leyda, *Dianying/Electric Shadow: An Account of Films and the Film Audience in China*, 15.

20 Huang, *A Textual Critical on Early Chinese Film History*/中國早期電影史事考證, 62.
21 Anonymous, "Toeg & Read V. Suffert, Septmber 3, 1907," in *Extraterritorial Cases*, ed. Charles Lobingier (Manila: Bureau of Printing, 1920), 112–120.
22 "U.S. Passport Application of Thomas Suffert, Passport Applications for Travel to China, 1906–1925" (1916).
23 Municipal Administrative, *Account Management of 1913/Compte Rendu De La Gestion Pour L'exercice 1913* (Shanghai: Imprimerie Muncipale, 1913), 65.
24 "The Municipal Gazette," *The North-China Herald*, 14 March 1918.
25 "Minutes of the Establishment of the Mutual Stock & Produce Company/大同交易所創立會記," *Shen Bao*, 28 November 1921.
26 Bo Lu, "Miss Anna May Yang/耐梅女士," *Movie Magazines*/電影雜誌 1, no. 1 (1924).
27 Yoshino Suguwana, "Film Theatres in Shanghai in Republic of China: A Research on the Business Operation of Theatres Showing Chinese Films/民国期上海の映画館について—国産映画上映館と映画館の経営状況を中心に," *Wild Grass*/野草 (2008).
28 Cheng, *China Cinema Year Book*/中華影業年鑑 Cheng, Li, and Xing, *History of the Development of Chinese Cinema*/中國電影發展史, 1, 18; Zhang, *An Amorous History of the Silver Screen*, 431–439. My identification of Arthur Israel as the mysterious 依什爾 in Chinese literature is based on three reasons. The first is Israel's employee record: he worked in the Shanghai Life Insurance Company [U.S. Passport Application of Arthur Israel, "Emergency Passport Application, Argentina Thru Venezuela, 1906–1925," in *General Records of the Department of State, 1763–2002* (Washington, DC: 1917)], a fact which is supported by a Chinese source [Gongsu, "A Record of New Play's Degradation/新劇蛻變記," *New Play Magazine*/新劇雜誌 1 (1922), 2]. The second is Israel's visa application records, in which he identified his own Chinese name as 依思爾 ["U.S. Passport Application of Arthur Israel, Passport Applications, January 2, 1906-March 31, 1925," (1918)] and 依碩而 ["U.S. Consular Registration Certificates of Arthur Israel, U.S. Consular Registration Certificates, 1907–1918," in *General Records of the Department of State, 1763–2002* (Washington, DC: The National Archives and Records Administration, 1914)], a name which is phonetically similar to the word 依什爾 in Chinese. The third is the close relationship between Israel and Suffert. In Suffert's visa application record in 1916, Israel wrote the identification letter and claimed that Israel had known Suffert since 1902 ["U.S. Passport Application of Thomas Suffert, Passport Applications for Travel to China, 1906–1925."]. I take this opportunity to thank Professor Ramona Curry at the University of Illinois, whose seminar account on Brodsky enlightened me to search these passport application records.
29 U.S. Passport Application of Arthur Israel, "Emergency Passport Application, Argentina Thru Venezuela, 1906–1925."
30 The Chinese name of the corporation is 華洋人壽保險公司, not 上海南洋人壽保險公司, as suggested in the existing literature [Junli Zheng, *Modern Chinese Film History*/現代中國電影史 (Shanghai: Liangyou Book Store, 1936), 12; Cheng, Li, and Xing, *History of the Development of Chinese Cinema*/中國電影發展史, 1, 16]. As a matter of fact, a company named 上海南洋人壽保險公司 did not exist in 1910s China. In addition, I am unable to find evidence regarding Israel and the Asiatic attending the Panama Pacific International Exposition as suggested in the existing literature. See Jianyun Zhou et al., *Syllabus on Introduction to Shadow Play*/影戲講義 (Shanghai: Dadong Book Store, 1924); Cheng, *China Cinema Year Book*/中華影業年鑑. Israel stayed in Shanghai at least up to 1922, while Suffert died in Shanghai in 1941.

31 "Consolidated Rubber Estates Limited," *The North-China Herald*, 13 December 1913; "Sport, Baseball," *The North-China Herald*, 21 March 1914. "Meeting, Shanghai Life Insurance Co.," *The North-China Herald*, 13 June 1914; "Laou Kung Mow Cotton S. & W. Co.," *The North-China Herald*, 19 February 1915.

32 "Passengers," *The North-China Herald*, 15 November 1913. *"Passengers," The North-China Herald*, 28 March 1914.

33 The claimed studio manager of the Asiatic Film Company was E. M. Gross, according to *1915 North China Desk-Hong List* [*North China Daily News& Herald, 1915 North China Desk-Hong List*, no page]. The details on E.M. Gross are open to study.

34 Irvine, "Chinese Photoplays"; Zhou, "An Introduction to Film Magazine," (1922).

35 "Advertisement," *The Daily Outlook*, 20 August 1905.

36 *"Start on Trip," The Daily Outlook*, 5 September 1912. Another report showed that Lynch would "stop first at Honolulu, then to Guam, Manila, and the countries of the Orient." See "Moving Pictures of the Fire," *The Daily Outlook* (5 September 1912). The "countries of the Orient" here would include China. The passenger list shows that William Lynch departed Shanghai to Kobe on 26 October 1912. See "Women's World," *The Daily Outlook*, 27 January 1913.

37 "Women's World."

38 I have found that Lynch's name appeared in the published hotel register of Kalee Hotel in Shanghai from 23 June 1913 to 14 March 1914. See *North China Daily News*.

39 "Lynch Writes to the Outlook," *The Daily Outlook*, 9 April 1913.

40 Some scholars argued that before Israel and Suffert took over the Asiatic, Benjamin Brodsky had produced at least two films. See Cheng Cheng, *China Cinema Year Book*/中華影業年鑑 and Cheng, Li, and Xing, *History of the Development of Chinese Cinema*/中國電影發展史, 1.

41 *The Daily Outlook*, 27 October 1913.

42 Clarke Irvine, "Chinese Photoplays," *The Moving Picture World*, 21 Februrary 1914.

43 Ibid.

44 Ibid.

45 Ibid.

46 Zhang, "Since My Director Career Commenced/自我導演以來," 11.

47 Law, "The Doubts and Suspicions of Hong Kong Movie's Origin/解開香港電影起源的謎團," 81.

48 Zhang, "Since My Director Career Commenced/自我導演以來," 11.

49 "Home from Orient," *The Daily Outlook*, 29 June 1914; Clarke Irvine, "Doings at Los Angeles," *The Moving Picture World* 21, no. 10 (1914). Lynch quit from the film industry after returning to the United States and became an agent in a real estate company ["10 Lots Sold in Topanga," *The Daily Outlook*, 19 July 1915] and later a farmer. It seems that Lynch has no descendants.

50 *Honolulu Star-Bulletin*, 15 September 1913.

51 Huang, *A Textual Critical on Early Chinese Film History*/中國早期電影史事考證, 56.

52 "Advertisement," *The Singapore Free Press and Mercantile Advertiser*, 11 July 1917.

53 Cheng, Li, and Xing, *History of the Development of Chinese Cinema*/中國電影發展史, 1.

54 Law, "The Doubts and Suspicions of Hong Kong Movie's Origin/解開香港電影起源的謎團," 84.

55 Zheng, *Modern Chinese Film History*/現代中國電影史, 18.

56 Xiujun He, *Zhang Shichuan and His Star Motion Picture Corporation/* 張石川和他的明星影片公司, The Anthology of Literature and History Materials/ 文史資料選輯 (Beijing: China Literature and History Press, 1980), 194.
57 Richard P Butrick, "The Motion Picture Industry in China, 893.4061, Motion Pictures/69." (4 October 1932), 156–157.
58 Law and Bren, *Hong Kong Cinema: A Cross-Cultural View*, 121.
59 Anonymous, "General Ledgers and Producers Account," in *Series 5C: Foreign General Ledgers and Journals*, ed. United Artists Corporation (Madison: Wisconsin Historical Society, 1934).
60 "On the Theatre Houses Industries, a Survey Conducted by the Shanghai Commercial & Saving Bank/上海商業儲蓄銀行有關影戲院的調查報告, Q275-1-2041," (Shanghai Municipal Archive).
61 Ibid.
62 Ibid.
63 Qian Zhang, "From Hollywood to Shanghai: American Silent Films in China" (University of Pittsburgh, 2009), 48.
64 Anonymous, "General Report for Two Months Ending 20 June 1928," in *Series 2A: O'Brien Legal File, 1919–1951*, ed. United Artists Corporation Archive (Madison: Wisconsin Historical Society, 1928).
65 "Motion Picture Theatre Permitted within the Walls of Changsha, Letter from C.D. Meinhardt to American Consulate, January 30, 1923," in *Record of the Department of State Relating to Internal Affairs of China, 1910–1929* (Washington: National Archives and Records Service, 1923).
66 Cheng, Li, and Xing, *History of the Development of Chinese Cinema/*中國電影發展史, 1, 188.
67 Richard P. Butrick, "The Motion Picture Industry in China," in *Confidential U.S. State Department Central Files, China, Internal Affairs* (Washington: National Archives and Records Administration, 1932), 101.
68 Muyun Yu, *Story of Hong Kong Cinema/*香港電影史話 (Hong Kong: Sub-Culture Press, 1996), 102.
69 "The Survey of Our Country's Talkie Picture Business/我國有聲電影事業之調查," *Commerical and Industrial Semimonthly/*工商半月刊 7 (1931).
70 Anonymous, "The Dairy of Lu Jie/陸潔日記," (Beijing: China Film Academy, 28 March 1932).
71 Butrick, "The Motion Picture Industry in China," 49.
72 "On the Theatre Houses Industries, a Survey Conducted by the Shanghai Commercial & Saving Bank/上海商業儲蓄銀行有關影戲院的調查報告, Q275-1-2041."
73 Ibid.
74 Ibid.
75 Law and Bren, *Hong Kong Cinema: A Cross-Cultural View*, 121.
76 cf. Chris Berry, "Sino-Korean Screen Connections: Towards a History of Fragments," *Journal of Chinese Cinemas* 10, no. 3 (2016): 247–264; Jeremy Taylor, *Rethinking Transnational Chinese Cinemas: The Amoy-Dialect Film Industry in Cold War Asia* (New York: Routledge, 2011).
77 Chris Berry, "Transnational Chinese Cinema Studies," in *Chinese Cinema Book*, eds. Song Hwee Lim and Julian Ward (London: BFI, 2010), 11.

References

"10 Lots Sold in Topanga." *The Daily Outlook*, 19 July 1915.
Administrative, Municipal. Account Management of 1913/Compte Rendu De La Gestion Pour L'exercice 1913. Shanghai: Imprimerie Muncipale, 1913.

"Advertisement." *The Daily Outlook*, 20 August 1905.
"Advertisement." The Singapore Free Press and Mercantile Advertiser, 11 July 1917.
Anonymous. *The Dairy of Lu Jie*/陸潔日記. Beijing: China Film Academy, 28 March 1932.
———. "General Ledgers and Producers Account." In *Series 5C: Foreign General Ledgers and Journals*, edited by United Artists Corporation. Madison: Wisconsin Historical Society, 1934.
———. "General Report for Two Months Ending 20 June 1928." In *Series 2A: O'Brien Legal File, 1919–1951*, edited by United Artists Corporation Archive. Madison: Wisconsin Historical Society, 1928.
———. "Motion Picture Theatre Permitted within the Walls of Changsha, Letter from C.D. Meinhardt to American Consulate, January 30, 1923." In *Record of the Department of State Relating to Internal Affairs of China, 1910–1929*. Washington: National Archives and Records Service, 1923.
———. "Toeg & Read V. Suffert, September 3, 1907." In *Extraterritorial Cases*, edited by Charles Lobingier, 112–120. Manila: Bureau of Printing, 1920.
Berry, Chris. "Sino-Korean Screen Connections: Towards a History of Fragments." *Journal of Chinese Cinemas* 10, no. 3 (2016): 247–264.
———. "Transnational Chinese Cinema Studies." In *Chinese Cinema Book*, edited by Song Hwee Lim and Julian Ward, 11. London: BFI, 2010.
Butrick, Richard P. "The Motion Picture Industry in China, 893.4061, Motion Pictures/69." (4 October 1932), 74–75.
———. "The Motion Picture Industry in China." In *Confidential U.S. State Department Central Files, China, Internal Affairs*. Washington, DC: National Archives and Records Administration, 1932.
Cheng, Jihua, Shaobai Li, and Zuwen Xing. *History of the Development of Chinese Cinema*/中國電影發展史. Vol. 1, Beijing: China Film Press, 1980.
Cheng, Shuren. *China Cinema Year Book*/中華影業年鑑. Shanghai: China Film Society, 1927.
"Consolidated Rubber Estates Limited." *The North-China Herald*, 13 December 1913.
Dirlik, Arif. *Marxism in the Chinese Revolution*. Lanham: Rowan & Littlefield Publishers, 2005.
Gongsu. "A Record of New Play's Degradation/新劇蛻變記." *New Play Magazine*/新劇雜誌 1 (1922): 9.
Greis, P. *China's New Nationalism: Pride, Politics, and Diplomacy*. Berkeley: University of California Press, 2004.
Gu, Jianchen. "The Development of Chinese Film/中國電影發達史." In *1934 Chinese Film Yearbook*/中國電影年鑑1934, edited by China Educational Film Association. Nanjing: China Education Association, 1934.
Hao, Yenping. *The Comprador in the Nineteenth Century China: Bridge between East and West*. Cambridge: Harvard University Press, 1970.
He, Xiujun. *Zhang Shichuan and His Star Motion Picture Corporation*/張石川和他的明星影片公司. The Anthology of Literature and History Materials/文史資料選輯. Beijing: China Literature and History Press, 1980.
"Home from Orient." *The Daily Outlook*, 29 June 1914.
Hu, Jubin. *Projecting a Nation*. Hong Kong: Hong Kong University Press, 2003.
Huang, Dequan. *A Textual Critical on Early Chinese Film History*/中國早期電影史事考證. Beijing: China Film Press, 2012.

Irvine, Clarke. "Chinese Photoplays." *The Moving Picture World* 19, no. 8 (21 February 1914).

———. "Doings at Los Angeles." *The Moving Picture World* 21, no. 10 (7 September 1914).

———. "Chinese Photoplays." *The Moving Picture World*, 21 Februrary 1914.

Kaufman, G. "Bret Harte Said It: The Heathen Chinese Is Peculiar." *New York Tribune*, 27 August 1916.

"Laou Kung Mow Cotton S. & W. Co." *The North-China Herald*, 19 February 1915.

Law, Kar. "The Doubts and Suspicions of Hong Kong Movie's Origin/解開香港電影起源的謎團." *Contemporary Cinema*/當代電影 4 (2010): 78–85.

Law, Kar, and Frank Bren. *Hong Kong Cinema: A Cross-Cultural View*. Lanham: Scarecrow, 2004.

Leyda, Jay. *Dianying/Electric Shadow: An Account of Films and the Film Audience in China*. Cambridge: MIT Press, 1972.

Liu, Leyda. *Translingual Practice: Literature, National Culture, and Translated Modernity-China, 1900–1937*. Stanford: Stanford University Press, 1995.

Lu, Bo. "Miss Anna May Yang/耐梅女士." *Movie Magazines*/電影雜誌 1, no. 1 (1924): 46.

"Lynch Writes to the Outlook." *The Daily Outlook*, 9 April 1913.

"Meeting, Shanghai Life Insurance Co." *The North-China Herald*, 13 June 1914.

"Minutes of the Establishment of the Mutual Stock & Produce Company/大同交易所創立會記." *Shen Bao*, 28 November 1921.

"Moving Pictures of the Fire." *The Daily Outlook*, 5 September 1912.

"The Municipal Gazette." *The North-China Herald*, 14 March 1918.

"No Title." *Honolulu Star-Bulletin*, 15 September 1913.

"No Title." *The Daily Outlook*, 27 October 1916.

North China Daily News & Herald, 1915 North China Desk-Hong List. Shanghai: North China Daily News Publishing House, 1915.

North China Daily News & Herald, 1916 North China Desk-Hong List. Shanghai: North China Daily News Publishing House, 1916.

"On the Theatre Houses Industries, a Survey Conducted by the Shanghai Commercial & Saving Bank/上海商業儲蓄銀行有關影戲院的調查報告, Q275-1-2041." Shanghai Municipal Archive.

"Passengers." *The North-China Herald*, 15 November 1913.

"Passengers." *The North-China Herald*, 28 March 1914.

"Sport, Baseball." *The North-China Herald*, 21 March 1914.

"Start on Trip." *The Daily Outlook*, 5 September 1912.

"The Survey of Our Country's Talkie Picture Business/我國有聲電影事業之調查." *Commerical and Industrial Semimonthly*/工商半月刊 7 (1931): 29–32.

Taylor, Jeremy. *Rethinking Transnational Chinese Cinemas: The Amoy-Dialect Film Industry in Cold War Asia*. New York: Routledge, 2011.

"U.S. Consular Registration Certificates of Arthur Israel, U.S. Consular Registration Certificates, 1907–1918." In *General Records of the Department of State, 1763–2002*. Washington, DC: The National Archives and Records Administration, 1914.

U.S. Passport Application of Arthur Israel. "Emergency Passport Application, Argentina Thru Venezuela, 1906–1925." In *General Records of the Department of State, 1763–2002*. Washington, DC, 1917.

"U.S. Passport Application of Arthur Israel, Passport Applications, January 2, 1906-March 31, 1925." 1918.

"U.S. Passport Application of Thomas Suffert, Passport Applications for Travel to China, 1906–1925." 1916.

"Women's World." *The Daily Outlook*, 27 January 1913.

Xiao, Zhiwei. "Translating American Films into Chinese Audiences." In *Transnational Asian Identities in Pan-Pacific Cinemas*, edited by Philippa Gates and Lisa Funnell, 88–100. New York: Routledge, 2012. 88–100.

Yoshino Suguwana, "Film Theatres in Shanghai in Republic of China: A Research on the Business Operation of Theatres Showing Chinese Films"/民国期上海の映画館について—国産映画上映館と映画館の経営状況を中心に. *Wild Grass*/野草 (2008): 96.

Yu, Muyun. *Story of Hong Kong Cinema*/香港電影史話. Hong Kong: Sub-Culture Press, 1996.

Zhang, Qian. *From Hollywood to Shanghai: American Silent Films in China*. Pittsburgh: University of Pittsburgh, 2009.

Zhang, Shichuan. "Since My Director Career Commenced/自我導演以來." *Star*/明星 3 (1935): 10–14.

Zhang, Yingjin. *Chinese National Cinema*. London: Routledge, 2004.

Zhang, Yingjin, and Zhiwei Xiao. *Encyclopaedia of Chinese Cinema*. London: Routledge, 1998.

Zhang, Zhen. *An Amorous History of the Silver Screen*. Chicago: Chicago University Press, 2005.

Zheng, Junli. *Modern Chinese Film History*/現代中國電影史. Shanghai: Liangyou Book Store, 1936.

Zhou. "An Introduction to Film Magazine." (1922).

Zhou, Jianyun, et al. *Syllabus on Introduction to Shadow Play*/影戲講義. Shanghai: Dadong Book Store, 1924.

6 Measuring the outcome of China's response through statistics

An investigation of China's industrial approach to its American counterpart in the early twentieth century naturally leads to questions such as, what are the results, and how can one evaluate China's response? Film directors and critics will evaluate a film from artistic perspectives, while film business practitioners look at market indicators, such as box office receipts. However, due to the extreme scarcity of box office records for both domestic films and foreign films in China, scholars have had to turn to expedient measures to demonstrate theses such as the centrality of U.S. cultural imperialism to the Chinese film market. In this chapter, I use a method named POPSTAT (*popularity statistics*) to probe film popularity in the early Chinese film industry. POPSTAT is a methodology introduced by film economist John Sedgwick, which has proved to be "a reliable method for estimating general patterns of film popularity for audiences."[1] In this chapter, I analyse the exhibition records from 38 cinemas which advertised in the daily newspapers *Xinwen Bao, North China Daily News*, and *Shen Bao* in Shanghai in the year of 1934. The chapter demonstrates that the American industry's dominance was not monolithic, and that from some perspectives it was outranked by the Chinese domestic film industry.

The film market in Shanghai: background

Shanghai was the home of film production, distribution, and exhibition in China in the first of half of the twentieth century. In 1931, as the largest city in China, Shanghai had three million people and 49 theatres. Nationwide, that year, the total number of theatres was 264 and the population amounted to 202,692,000 people.[2] The ratio of cinemas to population in Shanghai was then one cinema for every 61,224 persons, compared to 1:767,772 for China. By contrast, the ratio for Britain in 1934 was one cinema for every 10,600 persons. This explains the weak position of China in the world film market. As one American distributor claimed, "Shanghai is not a big city from the standpoint of revenue (for American film distributors worldwide). Yet pictures are released here much sooner than in many American cities."[3] Shanghai was recognised as the most prominent city in China, both for domestic and foreign films distributors. For an American film distributor, income in Shanghai constituted roughly one-third of its total receipts in China (excluding Hong Kong). It was also a flagship endeavour because of its nationwide performance.

Shanghai adopted run systems for film exhibition, like other cities that were popular for cinemas. Chapter 3 has demonstrated how the run system operated in 1920s and 1930s Shanghai. Each major Hollywood distribution company signed several theatres and separated them as first, second, and subsequent-run theatres. Metro-Goldwyn-Mayer chose the Grand and the Cathay as their first-run theatres, the Metropolis for the second run, and the Paris Theatre and the Crystal Palace for subsequent runs. The first-run theatre for Warner Bros was the Cathay. Fox, RKO, and First National chose the Nanking as their first-run theatre, and the Embassy and the Willies for their second runs. In some cases, however, subsequent runs were not fixed, due to low profit for Hollywood distributors. A similar run system was adopted for domestic films. Mingxing's first-run venue was the Strand, while Lianhua's was the Lyric theatre 金城. Mingxing's subsequent runs were in theatres from its own theatre chain, including the Palace, Victoria, Empire, Cater, and Universal Theatres. Other Chinese production corporations adopted the Peking, Eastern, Western, and Republic Theatres as entry points. Apart from several theatres which showed foreign films exclusively, a large number of theatres in Shanghai exhibited both domestic and foreign films. Theatres such as the Peking were the second or third run for foreign films, while also acting as first-run theatres for domestic films.

Different runs employed different distribution rental pricing strategies. Runs with good market potential engaged in a revenue-sharing system, while subsequent runs usually used a flat fee system, in which distributors charged a set amount of picture rental to theatres. With American films, the revenue-sharing system applied to first-, second-, and occasionally third- and fourth-run theatres, while the subsequent runs employed the flat fee system. The revenue-sharing terms were much more complicated than one may have expected. For instance, the distribution rental fee for *Modern Times* (dir. Charles Chaplin, 1936) was either 60% of the box office gross or else a guaranteed minimum of 25,000 Shanghai dollars, whichever was greater. In addition, the film was guaranteed a run of nine days and would remain in release at the Nanking and the Metropole cinema as long as it brought in 1,500 Shanghai dollars per day.[4] Therefore, the theatre gross of *Modern Times* at the Nanking and the Metropole was 50,011 Shanghai dollars, while the picture rentals accounted for 28,364 Shanghai dollars. The flat fee system was relatively simple. United Artists charged 500 Shanghai dollars for showing *Monte Cristo* (dir. Rowland V. Lee, 1934) at the Ritz, a fourth-run theatre in Shanghai. Similar distribution terms were employed in Hong Kong. In cities like Nanjing, Hankou, and Beijing, the revenue-sharing system was employed only at certain fine cinemas, while the majority were all subject to the flat fee system. Despite the lack of statistical evidence, Chinese distributors also adopted similar revenue-sharing terms.[5]

Three ways to measure popularity

Finding a way to measure film popularity is fairly necessary in the absence of box office records. Film scholarship needs to use economic indicators to test the reception of a film genre, to examine the comparison between the domestic film industry and its American counterparts, to inspect the effectiveness of a distribution channel, to probe the impact of film policy on film economy, and to survey the reception of an ideology in the film domain. There's little doubt that box office receipts are the most powerful indicator in film economy. However, it is next to impossible to secure primary box office records from China's film market in the first half of the twentieth century. Substantial materials have been destroyed by years of war, political campaigns, and lack of preservation.

Chinese film literature, therefore, has employed two indirect methods with which to measure the popularity of a film in the absence of box office records. The first is to measure the length of its exhibition at the first-run cinema. The oft-cited examples are *Two Sisters*, which was shown at the Strand for 57 days, and *The Song of the Fishermen*, which had a record of 83 days at the Capitol. It is true that the picture rental from the first-run cinema was a considerable component of a film's income. The total income of a film, however, came from all runs. *The Song of the Fishermen* ran longer than *Two Sisters* at its first run. The latter, however, outranked it in terms of screening time in Shanghai's theatres. Taking advantage of its chain theatres, Mingxing showed *Two Sisters* in Shanghai a total of 256 times, as opposed to *The Song of the Fisherman* which was shown 204 times. In addition, the calculation of the popularity of a film should take into account the seating capacity and admission price of the cinema in which it is exhibited.

The second method is to compare the number of films imported with domestic ones when demonstrating notions like that of cultural imperialism. For instance, in the 1930s, American film distributors exported more than 300 films to China; however, the number of domestic films released each year was around 50. The problem with such comparisons is that distributing a large number of films does not automatically translate into a fine market performance. In addition, such calculations cannot identify the performance of individual films. More importantly, these numbers only refer to films which were newly imported and released each year. However, numerous old films, both domestic and foreign, also circulated in China's film market. This method, therefore, fails to present a clear picture of a film's popularity.

Unlike the two methods mentioned earlier, POPSTAT, developed by John Sedgwick, is an effective proxy measure to examine film popularity and to investigate quantitatively China's response to the American film industry. Four variables are considered when calculating a POPSTAT score, namely: seating capacity, admission price, exhibition status (single-bill or double-bill programme), and duration of exhibition. Each film thus generates a figure which expresses its popularity. Therefore, one may compare the market performance of films in a quantitative way. In this study, I have not taken exhibition status into consideration. The reason for this is that cinemas in Shanghai screened three times per day and presented single-bill programmes in most cases. In addition, the length of run variable is calculated in days, instead of weeks (as in Sedgwick method). The assumption of the POPSTAT measure is that the longer a film is shown, the more expensive its admission price, and the larger the seating capacity, the higher the revenue potential. Attendance is a neglected variable due to the difficulty of investigation. The formula for calculating a POPSTAT score, therefore, is as follows:

$$POPSTAT_{it} = \sum_{j=1}^{n_i} cinema\ weight_j * length\ of\ run_{ij}$$

$$cinema\ weight_j = \frac{s_j * p_j}{r}$$

where

i is a given film.
t is the duration investigated, in this case the year 1934.
j is a given cinema.
n_i is the number of cinemas in the defined population of cinemas.

Cinema weight_j is a weighting factor for cinema j, reflecting its relative revenue-generating potential. The revenue-generating potential of a cinema j is given by its seating capacity (s_j) multiplied by its mid-range price (p_j) and then divided by the average revenue-generating potential of all cinemas (r). For instance, the *cinema weight* of the Grand Theatre (5.9) is established by its seating capacity (1986) multiplied by its mid-range admission price (1.71 yuan) and then divided by the average revenue potential (578).

Length of run_{ij} is the duration of exhibition of film i at cinema j. *Length of run* is measured in days.

This study collected the screening records for 38 cinemas in Shanghai in the year 1934. The admission prices for these cinemas ranged from 0.1 to 2 yuan. Therefore, the midrange ticket price varied from 0.15 (the Paradise Theatre) to 1.71 yuan (the Grand Theatre 大光明). The datasets of the seating capacity are derived from the *Municipal Gazette*, a publication of the Council for the Foreign Settlements of Shanghai, and the Confidential Report from the American Consul of Shanghai.⁶ The seating capacity ranged from 468 (the New Palace) to 2,000 (the Metropolis). Therefore, the highest weight for Shanghai's cinemas was given to the Grand Theatre with 5.9, and the lowest to the Universal Theatre with 0.1. That is to say, given the same duration of exhibition, according to the POPSTAT equation, the revenue generated for a film showing at the Grand Theatre would be 5.9 times greater than for the one at the Universal Theatre.

In addition, it should be mentioned that these 38 cinemas were not the only screening venues in Shanghai. All 38 cinemas were standard theatres, showing films exclusively. However, Shanghai at that time had several vaudeville-like venues. These venues presented various types of entertainment, including local opera, magic shows, and song and dance. Such venues included the Foh On Theatre, Little World 小世界, Great World 大世界, New World 新世界, Sun Sun Roof Garden 新新花園, Chapei 閘北大戲院, Wong On Roof Garden 永安天韻樓, and Sincere Roof Garden 先施樂園. These vaudeville-like places screened movies as well. Most of the films shown were Chinese films. Foreign films shown were out of date, and it is hard to trace their original film titles. Therefore, I did not include these venues in my investigation.

In 1934, 1,010 feature films were shown in Shanghai 11,635 times, in addition to 14 unidentified films. These features came from eight countries: China, the United States, the United Kingdom, France, Germany, the Soviet Union, Italy, and Mexico. Of these, 264 were domestic pictures and 666 were American films. Forty British films (aside from 14 films distributed by United Artists) were circulated in 1934. Germany had 24 films screened, half of which were distributed by Universum-Film A G. In addition, eight French films, eight Soviet Union films, four Italian films, and one Mexican film were shown on Shanghai's screens. The distribution of POPSTAT scores ranges from the value of 0.1 for *Moral Treasures* (道德寶鑒, dir. Wang Xianzhai, 1933) to 201.7 for *Two Sisters*. Ironically, both features were released by the Mingxing company.

Some initial findings may be drawn from these statistics. First, Shanghai had a much larger volume of films in circulation than is imagined in current literature. As mentioned earlier, until now, film scholarship has merely taken newly released films into consideration. However, thanks to effectively run management, cinemas in 1930s Shanghai could screen more than 1,000 pictures per year. Second, in this large-volume market, what domestic films faced was not only 300 newly released foreign films, but 751 pictures in total. This situation should be borne in mind when one evaluates China's response to its American counterparts. Third, the POPSTAT calculation has further confirmed my earlier argument for the dual monopoly structure of the Chinese film market, as discussed in Chapter 1. Domestic and American films maintained absolute dominance in terms of both the number of films circulated and POPSTAT scores.

Measuring the outcome of response through POPSTAT

Using the POPSTAT method, I have calculated the POPSTAT score for all 1,010 films. Appendix 1 lists the first 100 films based on their POPSTAT scores. In the following sections, I will analyse the outcome of China's response to the American film industry using three perspectives, namely: a microeconomic perspective, examining the top ten list; a studio-based perspective; and an overall or macroeconomic perspective. My analysis will show that domestic films were at an advantage with respect to bestsellers. The sales of big Chinese studios like Mingxing and Lianhua surpassed those of several of the Hollywood majors. The market share for the domestic film industry reached 26.1 per cent in comparison with 68.7 per cent of its American counterparts.

Microeconomic perspective: the top ten list

Chinese films led the way in competing with American films in terms of bestsellers, as can be seen in Appendix 1, which lists the top 100 films by POPSTAT score. Domestic films dominate the top ten list, occupying seven of ten seats. In addition, the top three are exclusively domestic films. *Two Sisters* and *The Song of the Fishermen* were two phenomenal features in 1934 and by extension the first half of the twentieth century; they were the two most popular features in Shanghai. The POPSTAT scores of *Two Sisters* and *The Song of the Fishermen* reached 201.7 and 196.3 respectively, outranking the third film by 90 per cent. As mentioned earlier, *The Song of the Fishermen* holds the record for the longest continuous run at a first-run cinema. However, *Two Sisters* outranks *The Song of the Fishermen* in the POPSTAT index because *Two Sisters* had more showing times arranged in total. In addition, the success of *Two Sisters* appears to have been larger than that of *Song of the Fishermen*, since the latter was also one of the most expensive films made at that time. It was reported that *Song of the Fishermen* took more than one year and cost at least 20,000 U.S. dollars (an equivalent of around 60,000 yuan) to make.[7]

It is intriguing to notice that four of the seven Chinese bestsellers directly contain the word "female" or "sisters" in their titles. Apart from *Two Sisters*, the bronze medal of popularity was granted to *Bible for Females* (女兒經, dir. Shen Xiling, 1934), a Mingxing film, reaching 105.9. In addition, *Female* (女人, dir. Shi Dongshan, 1934) was ranked seventh, with a POPSTAT score of 64.4. *Three Sisters* (三姊妹, dir. Li Pingqian, 1934) ranked eighth with 60.9. Mingxing is clearly the biggest winner, producing four out of seven best domestic sellers, that is, *Two Sisters, Female Bible, Three Sisters*, and *Wayside Willow* (路柳墻花, dir. Xu Xinfu, 1934). The variety in genres propelled Mingxing's market success: *Bible for Females* is an anthology film, *Wayside Willow* has an all-star cast, while *Three Sisters* is a follow-up to the sensational *Two Sisters*. This can also be seen as a triumph of leftist film since, in the most extensive definition of that term, the top three, *Two Sisters, The Song of the Fishermen,* and *Bible for Females*, are all considered leftist films. One exceptional domestic film in the top ten list is *Mr. Wang* (王先生, dir. Shao Zuiweng, 1934). This is a comedy adapted from a popular Chinese cartoon strip. Following the success of *Mr. Wang*, the protagonist Tang Jie 湯杰 produced seven further films from the strip, making it a popular comedy brand.

Only three foreign films appear in the top ten list, and all of them are Hollywood films. The triumph of a Warner Bros production, *I am a Fugitive from a Chain Gang* (dir. Mervyn LeRoy, 1932) (ranking four) was exceptional. The feature was banned from the International Settlements and French Concession but passed for exhibition in Chinese territory. The Isis Theatre was located at the boundary between Chinese territory and the International Settlements. Therefore, it could escape from prohibitions of either side. Using its geographical advantage, the Isis Theatre screened a considerable number of sensitive films, including Soviet Union propaganda features. On 13 May 1934, *I am a Fugitive from a Chain Gang* commenced a 22-day run at the Isis Theatre. The advertisement claims that this was the "longest that any foreign picture ever showed in China and [it has] returned in answer to hundreds of requests from patrons who wish to see it again and again." It eventually showed for 43 days at the Isis, and the Boon Lai screened it for another 13 days, putting *I am a Fugitive* on the bestseller list for foreign films.

Tarzan and His Mate (dir. Cedric Gibbons, 1934), an MGM production, was first shown at the Nanking Theatre for 15 days. The advertisement claimed that it had broken the screening record in the first-run cinema for the past three years.[8] The POPSTAT value of *Tarzan and His Mate* is 59.8. This is not the first Tarzan film shown in China. In 1934 alone, Shanghai had shown *Tarzan the Fearless* (dir. Robert F. Hill, 1933), (ranking 45 with a 37.3 POPSTAT score), and *Tarzan the Ape Man* (dir. W.S. Van Dyke, 1932) (ranking 271, with a 15.0 POPSTAT score). Encouraged by the success of Tarzan films, the Paris cinema even picked up a 1921 Tarzan production, *The Adventures of Tarzan* (dir. Robert F. Hill, 1921) and screened it for four days in November 1934.

The reason another MGM production, *Queen Christina* (dir. Rouben Mamoulian, 1934), is listed in the top ten must be attributed to the attraction of its protagonist Greta Garbo. Garbo enjoyed great popularity in China's screenland. The local newspaper described Garbo as "the great, the glorious, [and] the glamorous."[9] This film can be seen as a "come-back" production after "rumors had it that her retirement—in Europe—was a retirement in fact."[10] A Chinese newspaper even employed more a sensational notion, exclaiming: "All stars wither before Garbo, All films wither before *Queen Christina*."[11]

The studio perspective

Table 6.1 shows the POPSTAT scores of American films from the perspective of release companies. In 1934, there were 666 American films in circulation on Shanghai's screens. Films distributed by Hollywood majors accounted for 612, capturing 91.9 per cent. The POPSTAT for American films totalled 8,027.8, or 68.7 per cent of the market. The median POPSTAT figure for American films reached 12.0. The distribution and income structure of Hollywood majors reflected each studio's relative position worldwide. Paramount, Metro-Goldwyn-Metro, Warner Bros (including First National), Fox, and RKO Radio were named the Big Five, or the majors, while Universal, United Artists, and Columbia were titled the Little Three, or the minors, in the American film market.[12] On China's distribution map, Paramount, MGM, Warner Bros, and Fox maintained their advantages, comprising the first four studios in terms of number of films released and POPSTAT scores. Each studio reached over 11 per cent in number of films released, and over 10 per cent in POPSTAT. RKO's position in China did not match its position in the United States with regard to the number of films released. The reason is probably due to the method of POPSTAT calculation. As a new company established in 1928, RKO Radio Corporation could not compete with other studios in terms of total films released. However, RKO demonstrated its popularity in film receipts through the median index of POPSTAT. Its median POPSTAT figure reached 11.3, similar to that of the other majors and better than those of the Little Three. In contrast to the majors, the Little Three – that is, Universal, United Artists, and Columbia – had a smaller number of films released (no more than 72) and lower total POPSTAT figure (no more than 1,000). However, it should be noted that the average POPSTAT score of the Little Three had no major discrepancy from those of the Majors. The worst record median POPSTAT score for a Hollywood studio was for Universal, at 9.3. By contrast, the best figure was Warner Bros' 17.7, with just an 8.4 point difference. The even distribution in median POPSTAT suggests that the market performance for Hollywood studios was relatively homogenous on average.

Paramount maintained its leading position among Hollywood majors by distributing 108 films and achieving 1,480.2 in POPSTAT. MGM ranked second in terms of its quantity of films circulated and total POPSTAT figures, which were 101 and 1,331.5, respectively. MGM had nine features scoring in the top 50 in POPSTAT figures, suggesting its popularity in the Chinese film market. Warner Bros, which distributed 43 films in Shanghai, obtained the best median POPSTAT figure, scoring 17.7. Despite continuing to use the First National logo, First National had belonged outright to Warner Bros since 1929.[13] Including the films of First National, Warner Bros circulated 74 films and ranked third among Hollywood majors. Although only three of its features scored in the top 50 POPSTAT, the POPSTAT champion for American films was Warner Bros. Columbia ranked as the last among Hollywood majors, circulating 51 films and gaining a score of 493.2 in POPSTAT. Small American companies or so-called independent companies did not lag far behind the Hollywood majors. The independent companies circulated 53 films, and their POPSTAT scores reached 449.1. The mean POPSTAT score for independent studios amounts to 8.5, slightly less than Universal's 9.3.

The market structure of Chinese films was considerably different to that of its American counterparts. Like the latter, the Chinese film market was also, in economic terminology, an oligopoly. The difference was that the concentration of Chinese film companies was even greater. Mingxing, Lianhua, and Tianyi were the largest film companies in China, the so-called "Big Three," whether in terms of the number of films circulated or the films' POPSTAT scores. Out of 259 films, 141 or 54.4 per cent of films circulated in Shanghai were produced by these three companies. These 141 films generated 76.4 per cent of total POPSTAT. By contrast, in terms of the number of films circulated, the largest three companies only totalled 45.8 per cent. The market share of the Big Five Hollywood majors combined amounted to 70.4 per cent, still 6 per cent less than that of the Big Three Chinese films. In other words, the Chinese film market was heavily dominated by Mingxing, Lianhua, and Tianyi.

Table 6.1 American Film Company Performance in Shanghai

Production Company	Films	Aggregate POPSTAT	Mean POPSTAT
Paramount	108(16.2%)	1480.2(18.4%)	13.7
Metro-Goldwyn-Mayer	101(15.2%)	1331.5(16.6%)	13.2
Warner Bros	43(6.5%)	763(9.5%)	17.7
First National	31(4.7%)	464.2(5.8%)	15
Fox Film	96(14.4%)	1014.3(12.6%)	10.6
Universal	72(10.8%)	667.3(8.3%)	9.3
United Artists	56(8.4%)	745.7(9.3%)	13.3
RKO Radio	55(8.3%)	619.3(7.7%)	11.3
Columbia	51(7.7%)	493.2(6.1%)	9.7
Other Small Companies	53(8.0%)	449.1(5.6%)	8.5
Total	666	8027.7	12.0

Source: Author's own calculation.

Table 6.2 Chinese Film Company Performance in Shanghai

Production Company	Films	Aggregate POPSTAT	Mean POPSTAT
Mingxing	62(23.9%)	1040.5(34.1%)	16.8
Lianhua	45(17.4%)	823(27.0%)	18.3
Tianyi	34(13.1%)	466.6(15.3%)	13.7
Kuaihuolin	13(5.0%)	70.9(2.3%)	5.5
Youlian	11(4.2%)	39.5(1.3%)	3.6
Yihua	7(2.3%)	196.9(6.5%)	32.8
Other Small Companies	86(34.2%)	411.7(13.5%)	4.7
Total	259	3049.1	11.8

Source: Author's own calculation.

Mingxing was the leading company in the Chinese film industry as Table 6.2 shows. No other film company could compete with Mingxing in terms of market share and the number of films shown. In 1934, Mingxing exhibited 62 films in Shanghai's market, taking 23.9 per cent of the market share. The total POPSTAT score for Mingxing that year amounted to 1,040.5, or 34.1 per cent. That is to say, Mingxing occupied more than a one-third market share of domestic films in 1934. Apart from its film quality, the success of Mingxing in market performance can also be attributed to its theatre chain system. In 1930s Shanghai, Mingxing was the only film company which had substantial theatre chains in Shanghai. Mingxing's theatre chains ascertained the screening times of its features, a privilege which other companies lacked.

The polarisation in POPSTAT scores for Mingxing pictures deserves special notice. *Two Sisters* scored as high as 201.7. It was more than 200 times greater than the worst seller *Moral Treasures*, which scored 0.1. In 1934, among nine features whose POPSTAT was over 60, Mingxing had four, demonstrating its great popularity. However, 34 out of 62 (over 55 per cent) Mingxing features scored under ten in POPSTAT in 1934. Two reasons can explain this low figure in POPSTAT. First is the long screening life of a film, if it is an old film. The second is that of poor market performance, as a close look at those films under ten in POPSTAT reveals. Some films were released in 1928 and earlier, and their scores can be ascribed to the former reason, but major films were newly released, suggesting their poor market performance. These films include several so-called classic leftist films such as *Torrent* and *Spring Silkworm* (春蚕, dir. Cheng Bugao), both released in 1933. In contrast to *Two Sisters* and *The Song of the Fishermen*, the poor market performance of *Torrent* and *Spring Silkworm* suggest that the reception of leftist films is not monolithic. Polarisation in POPSTAT scores also suggests that Mingxing was highly reliant on a few fine and popular films, making its economic performance risky.

Lianhua, as the largest film production company by size, had shown 45 films and scored 823 in POPSTAT in 1934 Shanghai. The median POPSTAT for a Lianhua production was 18.3, which was better than Mingxing. That is to say, Lianhua's features were better received that Mingxing's on average. As a new company established in September 1933, Yihua only had seven features circulating in Shanghai. That is to say, the Yihua films were all new releases. Thanks to this, its median POPSTAT figure was 32.8, better than that of any other film company. This also reveals Yihua's market potential. Unlike American independent companies, small Chinese companies had very poor market performance. In addition to Yihua, the total POPSTAT score for 110 films from small companies was 522.1. The average POPSTAT score for features from small Chinese companies was 5.0. By contrast, that of Tianyi was 13.7, more than two times that of small companies. The absence of sufficient funds, attractive stars, and exhibition channels led to the poor film quality of small Chinese companies, contributing to their low median POPSTAT figure.

Taking a comparative perspective between Tables 6.1 and 6.2, one will find that Mingxing's POPSTAT score achieved fourth place in the total share of the Shanghai market, less than that of Paramount, MGM, and Warner Bros (including First National), but better than that of Fox, Universal, RKO, and United Artists. Lianhua ranked sixth, next to Fox. This can be seen as a significant achievement of the Chinese studios over their American counterparts, considering the vast financial advantages of American studios.

Macroeconomic perspectives – an overall picture

Domestic films gradually lose their quantitative edge when one expands scope. Only 17 films in the top 50 list are domestic features, while American films account for 33 spots. Still, there is no British film in the top 50 list. In the top 100, there are 31 domestic films versus 68 American films, and two British films are finally listed. The most popular British film seen through the lens of POPSTAT was *The Merry Monarch* (dir. Alexis Granowsky, 1933), ranked 70th by virtue of showing 20 times in five decent cinemas. From the perspective of POPSTAT scores, 31 domestic pictures reached 1,631.9, while 68 American films amounted to 2,558.6, around 1.6 times greater than their Chinese counterparts.

Table 6.3 provides overall information on the POPSTAT scores of films circulated in Shanghai. China released 259 films, against America's 666 films. No films from other countries could constitute any substantial threat to the dominant positions of Chinese and American pictures. In total, Chinese and American pictures occupied 91.8 per cent. The POPSTAT scores which indicate market share also show the absolute dominance of domestic and American pictures. The total share of Chinese and American films reached 94.8 per cent. Chinese films scored 3,049.1 in POPSTAT, compared with 8,027.7 for American films. The market share for Chinese films reached 26.1 per cent, and American films accounted for 68.7 per cent. Other countries shared the remaining 5.2 per cent. The United Kingdom constituted 2.6 per cent, and Germany constituted 1.5 per cent.

The total median POPSTAT score for a film in circulation in 1934 was 11.6. The median figure for domestic pictures reached 11.8. By contrast, the median score for American films was 12.0, slightly better than that of domestic pictures. No other features from foreign countries had a median POPSTAT over 10.0. The performance of pictures from the U.K. was similar to those from Germany and Italy, garnering median POPSTAT scores of around 7.5. Features from France and The Soviet Union performed almost identically in the Shanghai market, with POPSTAT scores of around 5.0.

An explanation is necessary, to account for the median POPSTAT scores. The figure for domestic pictures is slightly lower than that of American pictures, suggesting that the reception of American films was better than that of Chinese films on average. However, a close analysis of the data behind this figure will find that the median POPSTAT scores for American studios are relatively evenly distributed, ranging from 8.5 to 18.0. The median POPSTAT for large domestic studios was not in an inferior position. As a matter of fact, the mean POPSTAT for major Chinese companies surpassed that of almost every Hollywood counterpart. Yihua came first, with a median POPSTAT of 32.8. Apart from Yihua's exceptional success, Lianhua outranked all Hollywood companies with 18.3. Mingxing was only slightly behind Warner Bros (excluding First National) with a 16.8 median POPSTAT score. Tianyi's median score was 13.7, the same as that of Paramount. The higher median POPSTAT score suggests that Chinese audiences preferred more features from big Chinese studios than from American ones. Large domestic studios should not be held responsible for a lower median POPSTAT figure. Small domestic companies, as I mentioned earlier, dragged the median index down.

The distribution of POPSTAT figures reflects the difference between the domestic film industry's income structure and the American one. Previous studies of British and North American film markets in the 1930s by film historians have found that "the distribution of film revenues is highly skewed, implying that filmgoers were attracted in great numbers to relatively few films in the distribution."[14] The Chinese film industry, surprisingly, had a higher concentration ratio. The top 20 Chinese films have a cumulative score of 1,296.9, taking 42.5 per cent of the market share for domestic pictures. In other words, 42.5 per cent of market share for Chinese films was contributed by the top 20 films. By contrast, the top 20 American films had a cumulative score of 1,001.1, taking only 12.5 per cent of market share. In addition, another characteristic is the high proportion of low-scoring films in the domestic film market. Of the Chinese films, 157 scored under 7.0, accounting for 60.1 per cent of the total number of Chinese films. By contrast, America had 262 films with scores under 7.0, comprising just 29.3 per cent. Some old Chinese films which circulated in 1934 may have obtained low scores, but a major reason for a low POPSTAT score was poor market performance.

Table 6.3 The Overall Performance in Shanghai in 1934

Country of Origin	Number of Films	POPSTAT	Median POPSTAT
China	259(25.7%)	3049.1(26.1%)	11.8
U.S.	666(66.1%)	8027.7(68.7%)	12.0
U.K.	40(4.0%)	303.6(2.6%)	7.6
Germany	24(2.4%)	179.7(1.5%)	7.5
France	8(0.8%)	45.8(0.4%)	5.7
Soviet Union	8(0.8%)	41.6(0.4%)	5.2
Italy	4(0.4%)	31(0.3%)	7.8
Mexico	1(0.1%)	1.5(0.01%)	1.5
Total	1010	11680	11.6

Source: Author's own calculation.

To judge by a first impression of the total market share, it is not convincing to say that Chinese cinema performed well or attained success with 26.1 per cent in the early twentieth century. However, one must bear in mind that Chinese films in the 1930s were in a nascent stage. The history of the Chinese film industry can be traced back to as early as 1905, but its real, effective beginnings were in the early 1920s.[15] The first Chinese film allegedly appeared in 1905. A photographic studio in Beijing produced several short clips but went into bankruptcy soon after. The first professional Chinese film corporation did not commence until 1913, and the real development of the Chinese film industry had to wait until 1923, which was when Mingxing released *Orphan Rescuing Grandfather*. The release of *Orphan* later became a symbol of the Chinese film industry getting on track.[16] Therefore, the Chinese film industry in the 1930s can be seen as a teenager in terms of real development. Compared with its American counterpart, its performance was drastically lower in terms of the scale of productions, technology, and finance. This can be demonstrated by a comparison of the wages of film actors. In the 1930s, "expenditures for salaries range[d] from 25 yuan a month for featured players to 350 for a few stars."[17] Butterfly Wu, as the leading Chinese star, was the best-paid actress in China, receiving 500 yuan a month. It was reported that the salaries earned in China would "probably cause a Hollywood 'star' to faint, though not with envy."[18] In Hollywood, Mae West, the leading Paramount star in the 1930s, was able to earn 481,000 U.S. dollars a year, which was 240 times the salary of Butterfly Wu.

In addition, competition between the American and the Chinese film industries in the 1930s was probably fiercer than in any other period in Chinese film history. In the 1930s, Hollywood's studio system was in its golden age. More importantly, almost every American film was imported to China, due to the lack of import quotas. Considering the intense competition from the United States, the 26.1 per cent market share should be seen as a success for the domestic film industry, if not a triumph. One may gain a more accurate impression of the market performance of the Chinese film industry of the time by comparing it with that in the 1990s. The market share for Chinese films (including co-productions with Hong Kong) was 40 per cent in the 1990s, while Hollywood films had a 60 per cent share. However, only 20 Hollywood films per annum were allowed to screen in China at that time.

Going beyond POPSTAT: measure testing and a diachronic perspective

In the following section, I compare the POPSTAT figure with actual box office receipts from United Artists, to test the usefulness of the POPSTAT method. In addition, I extend my analysis of the outcome of China's response to the American film industry from Shanghai, 1934, to other periods and areas, and also approach it from a diachronic perspective.

The POPSTAT methodology for measuring film popularity can be tested by looking at fragmented box office receipts. Table 6.4 lists the box office receipts for 40 films distributed by United Artists and their POPSTAT index. It should be noted that the box office receipt figures for 1934 were collected from China nationwide. The POPSTAT index, however, was recorded from the Shanghai market alone. Therefore, some statistical errors should be allowed. To verify the POPSTAT method, I introduce the Pearson Product-Moment Correlation Coefficient. This is a very common statistical method used to "find the degree of the association of two sets of variables."[19] The coefficient figure ranges from 1 to −1. The value of 0 indicates no correlation. The closer the value to 1, the higher the positive correlation. In this case, the value obtained is 0.77, denoting a significantly high positive correlation. That is to say, the POPSTAT index's measurement of film popularity is largely supported by actual box office receipts. To use Sedgwick's words, the POPSTAT index is "clearly second best to actual historic data" to measure film popularity.[20]

The POPSTAT index was based on data collected in Shanghai cinemas in 1934. The following sections examine the scenario of China's response to the American films outside Shanghai and beyond the year 1934. It is believed that the situation outside Shanghai favoured the performance of the domestic film industry. In 1930s China, 33 cities had screen venues, from Amoy to Kunming. Apart from Shanghai and Hong Kong, the two largest film markets in China, it is very likely that domestic films dominated the film market.[21] In Jinan for instance, only one of seven theatres showed foreign films; the others showed Chinese pictures exclusively. As early as the 1920s, American film analysts realised that the dominance of Hollywood films in China varied "to a certain extent with different localities."[22] C. J. North revealed that American films controlled only about half the showings in cities such as Kunming.[23] In cities like Fuzhou, Chinese films occupied 90 per cent of Fuzhou's screenings while Hollywood films only accounted for 10 per cent. A general trend was that Chinese films had the greatest appeal in places where foreign influence was least felt.[24] One crucial reason for this is that foreign films could not cater to the tastes of people in interior areas. In addition, in these places the foreign populace was negligible, and the number of foreign-educated Chinese was also small. In treaty ports where there were a greater proportion of foreign residents, these two classes formed the bulk of first-run theatre audiences.

The year 1934 was the peak of the Chinese film industry, during which it received 26.1 per cent of total market share. The release of several successful films, including *Two Sisters* and *The Song of the Fishermen*, contributed to this market triumph. The top ten domestic films gained 914 POPSTAT scores, taking 30 per cent of the total Chinese market share. The revenue of *Two Sisters* was believed to exceed 200,000 yuan. It was circulated in 54 cities of China and six countries in South-East Asia.[25] The income of *Song of*

Table 6.4 The Box Office Receipt and POPSTAT Index for Films Distributed by United Artists in 1934

	Film Title	Release Date	Box Office (Shanghai Dollar)	POPSTAT
1	The Count of Monte Cristo	1934	20,940.97	51.5
2	The Affair of Cellini	1934	9,270.55	46.8
3	Bulldog Drummond Strikes Back	1934	9,877.65	39.8
4	Roman Scandals	1933	36,092.63	38.3
5	The House of Rothschild	1934	19,771.84	32.5
6	Broadway Through a Key Hole	1933	10,801.29	30.8
7	The Rise of Catherine the Great	1934	12,075.84	28.1
8	The Private Life of Henry VIII	1933	19,214.94	25.4
9	Nana	1934	14,367.54	25.1
10	Bowery	1933	9,000.07	22.9
11	Moulin Rouge	1934	10,626.64	19.3
12	Sky Devils	1932	370.47	18.2
13	Sorrell and Son	1933	2,380.54	17.6
14	Gallant Lady	1933	4,759.08	16.4
15	Palooka	1934	5,454.68	16.3
16	The Emperor Jones	1933	4,139.41	14.9
17	Devil to Pay	1930	89.06	14.9
18	Up to the Neck	1933	2,747.74	14.5
19	Scarface	1932	749.54	14.4
20	Advice to Lovelorn	1933	2,409.68	13.9
21	Blood Money	1933	2,535.49	13.6
22	Born to Be Bad	1934	2,606.75	12.6
23	That's a Good Girl	1933	4,784.33	12.2
24	Looking for Trouble	1934	3,921.26	12.2
25	Palmy Days	1931	711.76	11.7
26	Trouble	1933	3,039.04	11.4
27	City Lights	1931	2054.19	10.8
28	Kid from Spain	1932	5834.22	9.6
29	General John Regan	1933	516.07	9.2
30	Whoopee!	1930	1184.12	4.6
31	Around the World with Douglas Fairbanks	1931	270.25	3.8
32	Bad One	1930	255	2.5
33	Hell Harbor	1930	58.86	2.1
34	Hell's Angels	1930	997.89	2
35	Lottery Bride	1930	504.7	2
36	Reaching the Moon	1930	1230.81	1.4
37	Romantic Night One	1930	99.76	1.4
38	What a Widow	1930	42.99	1
39	Age for Love	1931	122.61	0.6
40	Street Scene	1931	843	0.6

Source: Income, *United Artists Corporations Records*. Series 5C: Foreign General Ledgers, 1929–1950. Madison: Wisconsin Historical Society Archives. United Artists Corporation Records.

the *Fishermen* was also reported to be around 200,000 yuan, similar to that of *Two Sisters*.[26] Without the emergence of outstanding films, the market share for the domestic film industry could drop dramatically. The reason is that China was more skewed to a few attractive films than its American counterparts, as I mentioned earlier. The 1930s market share of American films varied, depending on the performance of studios. Alexander Krisel, then President of the China Film Board, estimated that the gross income of MGM in 1934 showed a falling-off of approximately 200,000 Chinese yuan from the calendar year 1933. It was expected that a further decline of approximately 40 per cent would ensue for the calendar year 1935.[27] Fox's income, however, gradually increased in the early 1930s. In 1932, Fox's film rentals in China were 107,904.53 USD. The figure increased to 115,570 USD in 1932 and 119,309.14 USD in 1933. The rental income was trimmed slightly to 118,314.59 USD in 1935 and increased steeply to 145,358.03 USD in 1936.[28]

In the long term, as a more general trend, the output of both the Chinese film industry and the American industry increased continuously in the early twentieth century. Figure 6.1 lists the feet of motion-picture film shipped from the United States to China. Imported unexposed film stock was used for making Chinese films, while positive and negative exposed films were designed for exhibition purposes.[29] Figure 6.1 shows that the feet of exposed and unexposed film imported to China had increased notably in the 1920s when compared with that in the 1910s. In 1913, the linear feet of negative and positive film amounted to 170,740. By 1929 the figure had increased to 2,488,765, more than 20 times greater than that in 1913. The increase of unexposed film was more striking than that of exposed film. In 1925, the unexposed film imported to China totalled 2,165,005 feet. This was 220 times greater than the smallest number in 1920, which was just 9,800 feet.

The quantity of positive and negative film imported to China (seen in Figure 6.1) mirrors the development of the American film industry in China. Figure 6.1 shows that the rapid expansion of the American film business in China is likely to have started in 1919. Although Hollywood films dominated the Chinese market from 1916 onwards, the linear feet imported into China was merely 200,000 feet or around 10,000 U.S. dollars in value by 1918. In 1919, the linear feet of film intended for exhibition exceeded 150,000 for the first time. From 1919 onwards, the length of film for exhibition purposes remained between 350,000 and 170,000 feet. Despite the lack of data for the 1930s in Figure 6.1, it seems that the development of American business continued in the 1930s. A survey estimated "3,950,000 feet film imported into China during 1930 for exhibition purposes, and of this total 3,550,000 came from America."[30] This suggests a steadily increasing market in China for Hollywood films in the 1920s and early 1930s.

The unexposed film stock imported to China indicates the development of the Chinese film industry. Along with the development of Hollywood's market in China, the boom in the market for the local film industry was also visible. Because the Chinese were unable to produce film stock in the first

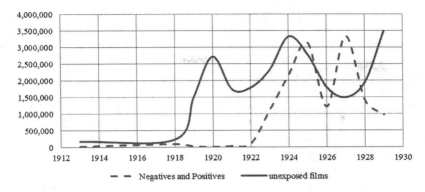

Figure 6.1 United States Exports of Motion-Picture Film to China (in feet).
Source: Richard P. Butrick, "The Motion Picture Industry in China, 893.4061, Motion Pictures/69." (4 October 1932), 101.

half of the twentieth century, importation was the only option for accessing motion-picture film for production. Roughly 90 per cent of imported film stock was from the United States.[31] As can be seen in Figure 6.1, the development of the Chinese film industry was continuous in general. Prior to 1923, no more than 120,000 feet of unexposed film stock was imported for film production. However, this figure increased to 1,000,000 feet from 1923, more than eight times greater than before. The performance of unexposed film imported into China confirms that the real development of the Chinese film industry started in 1923, the moment that Mingxing's benchmark film *Orphan Rescuing Grandfather* was released. The footage of motion-picture film echoes this argument. After 1923, the quantity of imported film stock remained above one million feet. This suggests the continuous development of the Chinese film industry in the 1920s. Notably, over three million feet of stock was imported to China for the purpose of film production in 1925 and 1927.

Clearly, the fluctuation of the development curve of unexposed films was greater than that of exposed films, which suggests instability in the development of the Chinese film industry. The first fluctuation occurred from 1918 to 1921. The reason is that this was a nascent period for the Chinese film industry when the opening or closure of a studio would have a strong effect on the total data. For instance, from 1919 to 1920, only nine short films were produced in China. In 1921, three feature films and six short films were released, and therefore the volume of imported film stock started to rally. Thanks to the establishment of Mingxing, the data for 1922 was greater than that of 1918 for the first time. A period of abnormal prosperity was responsible for the second fluctuation in 1924–1925. Inspired by the success of *Orphan*, capitalists rushed to invest in the Chinese film industry, lured by the vast potential profit. During the period from 1923 to

1926, about 100 film companies are supposed to have sprung up, and there was an ardent demand for unexposed film. However, a large number of the corporations organised during this period were so-called "mushroom" or "mosquito" companies. A typical "mushroom" company was likely to operate when "three or four optimists would scrape together a few thousand dollars, secure a play, rig up or hire studio and equipment of sorts, engage the necessary actors, and set to work."[32] By 1926, few of these "mushroom" companies survived. Alongside the waning of this "film fever," the demand for unexposed film as well as the development of the Chinese film industry returned to normality.

Studio income also confirms the growth of the Chinese film industry. Figure 6.2 indicates the income of Mingxing from 1926 to 1935. Mingxing was one of the leading production companies at the time. The figure indicates that the general trend of Mingxing's income increased in the 1920s and 1930s. As one of the earliest film studios in China, Mingxing had been set up in 1922 "with 10,000 yuan originally earmarked for stock speculations."[33] In 1926, the income of Mingxing amounted to 212,596.91 yuan thanks to the success of such releases as *Reconciliation* (空谷蘭, dir. Zhang Shichuan, 1925). Two years later, in 1928, Mingxing's revenue had increased to 431,144.62 yuan, more than double than that of 1926. The productions of *The Burning of Red Lotus Temple*, a series of martial arts pictures released in 1928, contributed much to the expansion of Mingxing's income. In 1933, the latter reached a peak with 829,149.74 yuan. However, the studio's outgoings in this year amounted to 914,827.15 yuan, resulting in a deficit of 85,867 yuan. Fortunately, Mingxing returned to a profitable status by reducing its expenses in 1935.

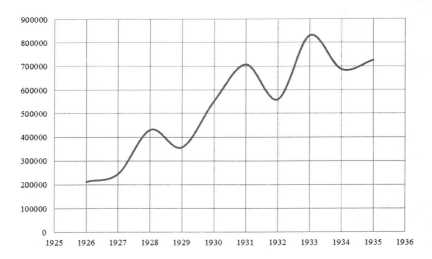

Figure 6.2 The Income of Mingxing, 1926–1935 (yuan).
Source: Yanqiao Fan, "A Chronological Table of the Star Motion Picture Corporation/明星影片公司年表," Star/明星 7, no. 1 (1936).

Conclusion

In the absence of box office receipts, this chapter introduces POPSTAT as a proxy and an empirical measure with which to examine the outcome of China's response to the American film industry. It has been shown in this chapter that the Chinese film industry achieved growth, along with its American counterpart in the early twentieth century. In terms of the total amount of market share, the American film industry still maintained its dominance in Shanghai in the year 1934, taking 68.7 per cent, versus China's 26.1 per cent. The Chinese film industry, however, did not lag far behind, and its achievements were even higher when we consider the performance of bestsellers, studio variation, and geographical location. This chapter has shown that dominance, like other terms in the film economy, is a monolithic concept. In order to reflect and grasp the actual issues of the film economy, one needs to consider not only the total amount of box office receipts or the number of films but also other detailed and multidimensional variations.

Appendix 1

Rank	Film Title	Country of Origin	Release Company	Director	POPSTAT
1	姊妹花/Two Sisters	China	Mingxing	Zheng Zhengqiu/鄭正秋	201.7
2	漁光曲/The Song of the Fisherman	China	Lianhua	Cai Chusheng/蔡楚生	196.3
3	女兒經/Bible for Females	China	Mingxing	Shen Xiling/沈西苓	105.9
4	亡命者/I Am a Fugitive from a Chain Gang	U.S.	Warner Bros	Mervyn LeRoy	93.7
5	王先生/Mr. Wang	China	Tianyi	Shao Zuiweng/邵醉翁	69.2
6	路柳墻花/Wayside Willow	China	Mingxing	Zheng Zhengqiu/鄭正秋	68.0
7	女人/Female	China	Yihua	Shi Dongshan/史東山	64.4
8	三姊妹/Three Sisters	China	Mingxing	Li Pingqian/李萍倩	60.9
9	泰山情侶/Tarzan and His Mate	U.S.	MGM	Cedric Gibbons, Jack Conway	59.8
10	瓊宮艷史/Queen Christina	U.S.	MGM	Rouben Mamoulian	58.0

(Continued)

Rank	Film Title	Country of Origin	Release Company	Director	POPSTAT
11	怕老婆/Sons of the Desert	U.S.	MGM	William A. Seiter	57.0
12	香雪海/Scented Snow Sea	China	Lianhua	Fei Mu/費穆	56.1
13	歌衫血痕/Murder at the Vanities	U.S.	Paramount	Mitchell Leisen	53.4
14	基督山恩仇記/The Count of Monte Cristo	U.S.	United Artists	Rowland V. Lee	51.5
15	仙侶情歌/The Cat and the Fiddle	U.S.	MGM	William K. Howard	51.0
16	華清春暖/Footlight Parade	U.S.	Warner Bros.	Lloyd Bacon	47.9
17	愛斯基摩/Eskimo	U.S.	MGM	W.S. Van Dyke	47.3
18	雲台春鎖/The Affairs of Cellini	U.S.	United Artists	Gregory La Cava	46.8
19	人間仙子/Mortal Fairy	China	Yihua	Dan Duyu/但杜宇	46.3
20	孤雛深恨/Now and Forever	U.S.	Paramount	Henry Hathaway	45.8
21	金剛/King Kong	U.S.	RKO	Merian C. Cooper	45.6
22	人生/Life	China	Lianhua	Fei Mu/費穆	45.2
23	彈性的女子/Bombshell	U.S.	MGM	Victor Fleming	44.3
24	歌后情痴/One Night of Love	U.S.	Columbia	Victor Schertzinger	44.1
25	健美運動/Search for Beauty	U.S.	Paramount	Erle C. Kenton	43.7
26	戀歌/The Song of Songs	U.S.	Paramount	Rouben Mamoulian	43.4
26	玉闕英雄/The Scarlet Empress	U.S.	Paramount	Josef von Sternberg	43.4
28	空谷蘭/Reconciliation	China	Mingxing	Zhang Shichuan/張石川	42.8
29	拉斯蒲丁逸事/Rasputin and the Empress	U.S.	MGM	Richard Boleslawski	41.8
30	飛燕驚鴻/Dancing Lady	U.S.	MGM	Robert Z. Leonard	41.6
31	歸來/Return	China	Lianhua	Zhu Shilin/朱石麟	40.6
32	紅樓春深/Spring in Red Chamber	China	Tianyi	Gao Lihen/高梨痕	40.4
33	麥夫人/Mrs. Mai	China	Mingxing	Zhang Shichuan/張石川	40.2
34	木偶寄情/I Am Suzanne!	U.S.	Fox	Rowland V. Lee	39.8

Rank	Film Title	Country of Origin	Release Company	Director	POPSTAT
34	霧夜飛尸夜/Bulldog Drummond Strikes Back	U.S.	United Artists	Roy Del Ruth	39.8
36	奇異酒店/Wonder Bar	U.S.	First National	Lloyd Bacon	39.5
37	一夜風流/It Happened One Night	U.S.	Columbia	Frank Capra	39.4
38	風流貴婦/Madame Du Barry	U.S.	Warner Bros.	William Dieterle	38.9
38	碧玉天香/Thirty Day Princess	U.S.	Paramount	Marion Gering	38.9
40	風流爵士/Meet the Baron	U.S.	MGM	Walter Lang	38.3
40	羅宮綺夢/Roman Scandals	U.S.	United Artists	Frank Tuttle	38.3
42	暴雨梨花/Pearl Flower in Storm	China	Lianhua	Maxu Weibang/馬徐維邦	38.2
43	黃金時代/Golden Age	China	Yihua	Bu Wancang/卜萬蒼	37.4
44	泰山之王/Tarzan the Fearless	U.S.	Sol Lesser Productions	Robert F. Hill	37.3
44	小娃娃/Baby Take a Bow	U.S.	Fox	Harry Lachman	37.3
46	虎魔王/The Devil Tiger	U.S.	Fox	Clyde E. Elliott	37.1
47	小安琪/Little Miss Marker	U.S.	Paramount	Alexander Hall	37.0
47	舊怨新愁/Only Yesterday	U.S.	Universal	John M. Stahl	37.0
49	戀愛成功/The Way to Love	U.S.	Paramount	Norman Taurog	36.7
50	再會吧上海/Farewell, Shanghai	China	Lianhua	Ki-tak Chung/鄭基鐸	36.6
51	小婦人/Little Women	U.S.	RKO	George Cukor	36.3
52	海京伯大馬戲/Hagenbeck-wallace Circus	China	Mingxing	Lin Zhusan/林祝三	36.2
52	花月爭輝/Dames	U.S.	Warner Bros.	Ray Enright, Busby Berkeley	36.2
54	春宵曲/Song of Spring	China	Tianyi	Wen Yimin/文逸民	35.8
55	影城艷史/Going Hollywood	U.S.	MGM	Raoul Walsh	35.7

(Continued)

Rank	Film Title	Country of Origin	Release Company	Director	POPSTAT
56	笛夫人的權威/Duck Soup	U.S.	Paramount	Leo McCarey	35.2
57	鐵鳥/Iron Bird	China	Lianhua	Yuan Yemei/袁業美	34.9
58	歡喜冤家/Happy Foe	China	Tianyi	Qiu Qixiang/裘芑香	34.8
59	啼笑因緣/Fate in Tears and Laughter	China	Mingxing	Zhang Shichuan/張石川	34.4
59	恩怨夫妻/Riptide	U.S.	MGM	Edmund Goulding	34.4
61	萬獸之王/King of the Jungle	U.S.	Paramount	H. Bruce Humberstone	34.3
62	骨肉之恩/Grace of Kindred	China	Lianhua	Jiang Qifeng/姜起鳳	34.2
63	愛的測驗/Death Takes a Holiday	U.S.	Paramount	Mitchell Leisen	33.6
64	回到自然/This Naked Age	U.S.	Crown Pictures	Michael Mindlin	33.3
65	又驚又愛/She Loves Me Not	U.S.	Paramount	Elliott Nugent	33.1
65	坐花醉月/Sitting Pretty	U.S.	Paramount	Harry Joe Brown	33.1
67	錦繡天/Flying Down to Rio	U.S.	RKO Radio	Thornton Freeland	32.8
68	大富之家/The House of Rothschild	U.S.	United Artists	Alfred L. Werker, Sidney Lanfield	32.5
69	白雲塔/White Cloud Pagoda	China	Mingxing	Zhang Shichuan/張石川	31.7
70	風流天子/The Merry Monarch	U.K.	Films Sonores Tobis	Alexis Granowsky	30.9
70	最新偵探術/From Headquarters	U.S.	Warner Bros.	William Dieterle	30.9
72	神秘的百老匯/Broadway Thru a Keyhole	U.S.	United Artists	Lowell Sherman	30.8
72	體育皇后/Sports Queen	China	Lianhua	Sun Yu/孫瑜	30.8
72	晚宴/Dinner at Eight	U.S.	MGM	George Cukor	30.8
75	多角戀愛/We're Not Dressing	U.S.	Paramount	Norman Taurog	30.3
75	華山艷史/Amorous History of Hua Mountain	China	Mingxing	Cheng Bugao/程步高	30.3
77	二對一/Two Versus One	China	Mingxing	Zhang Shichuan/張石川	29.9
78	牢獄二萬年/20,000 Years in Sing Sing	U.S.	First National	Michael Curtiz	29.5

Rank	Film Title	Country of Origin	Release Company	Director	POPSTAT
78	雲裳艷曲/Fashions of 1934	U.S.	First National	William Dieterle	29.5
80	碎花瓶/The Kennel Murder Case	U.S.	Warner Bros.	Michael Curtiz	29.2
81	神探尼萊/Hi, Nellie!	U.S.	Warner Bros.	Mervyn LeRoy	29.0
81	羅宮春色/The Sign of the Cross	U.S.	Paramount	Cecil B. DeMille	29.0
83	風/Wind	China	Lianhua	Wu Cun/吳村	28.8
84	時代的進展/The World Changes	U.S.	First National	Mervyn LeRoy	28.7
85	鴻運當頭/Happiness Ahead	U.S.	First National	Mervyn LeRoy	28.6
85	俠友/Manhattan Melodrama	U.S.	MGM	W.S. Van Dyke, George Cukor	28.6
85	終成眷屬/Belle of the Nineties	U.S.	Paramount	Leo McCarey	28.6
88	凱塞琳女皇/The Rise of Catherine the Great	U.S.	United Artists	Paul Czinner, Alexander Korda	28.1
89	情郎心香/Girl Without a Room	U.S.	Paramount	Ralph Murphy	27.9
90	青春之火/Fire of the Youth	China	Tianyi	Qiu Qixiang/裘芑香	27.5
90	蠻荒雙艷/Four Frightened People	U.S.	Paramount	Cecil B. DeMille	27.5
92	藝人韻事/His Double Life	U.S.	Eddie Dowling	Arthur Hopkins	27.4
93	俠士殲仇/Destry Rides Again	U.S.	Universal	Benjamin Stoloff	27.0
93	療情記/Men in White	U.S.	MGM	Richard Boleslawski	27.0
95	神女/The Goddess	China	Lianhua	Wu Yonggang/吳永剛	26.4
96	酒色財氣/Four Cardinal Vices	China	Lianhua	Tan Youliu/譚友六	26.3
96	氣壯山河/The Flag Lieutenant	U.K.	British & Dominions	Henry Edwards	26.3
98	藝海春光/Design for Living	U.S.	Paramount	Ernst Lubitsch	26.1
99	鐵窗艷侶/The Mayor of Hell	U.S.	Warner Bros.	Archie Mayo	25.9
99	浮生若夢/The House on 56th Street	U.S.	Warner Bros.	Robert Florey	25.9
99	鬥牛艷事/The Trumpet Blows	U.S.	Paramount	Stephen Roberts	25.9

Notes

1 John Sedgwick, "Cinemagoing in Portsmouth during the 1930s," *Cinema Journal* 46, no. 1 (autumn, 2006): 73.
2 Richard P. Butrick, "The Motion Picture Industry in China, 893.4061, Motion Pictures/69." (4 October 1932), 136.
3 American Film Distributor, "Shanghai Films A Vindication," *The North China Herald*, 17 May 1932.
4 I thank Professor Mike Walsh for explaining the distribution terms.
5 Chihen Xu, *A Grand Sight of Chinese Cinema*/中國影戲大觀 (Shanghai: Cooperation Publishing House, 1927).
6 Council for the Foreign Settlements of Shanghai, *Municipal Gazettes*, 1932, Shanghai Municipal Archives, U1-1-997. Richard P. Butrick, "The Motion Picture Industry in China, 893.4061, Motion Pictures/69." (4 October 1932), 147–150.
7 George Moorad, "Chinese Talkies," *Asia* 35, no. 10 (1935). Another estimate is that it cost 100,000 yuan. See "The Achilles'Heel of Lianhua/聯華公司的致命傷," *Movietone*/電聲 3, no. 24 (1934).
8 Advertisement, *Shen Bao*, 1 October 1934.
9 Garbo Superb in Picture Grand Theatre, *The China Press*, 19 April 1934.
10 Ibid.
11 *Shen Bao*, 14 April 1934.
12 Neale, Steve, "Introduction," in *The Classic Hollywood Reader*, ed. Steve Neale (London: Routledge, 2012), 2.
13 Steven Bingen, *Warner Bros.: Hollywood's Ultimate Backlot* (London: Taylor, 2014), 16.
14 John Sedgwick, Cinemagoing in Portsmouth during the 1930s, 62.
15 Lowenthal Rudolf. *The Present Status of the Film in China* (Peiping: The Collectanea Synodalis, 1936), 88.
16 Fan, "A Chronological Table of the Star Motion Picture Corporation/明星影片公司年表."
17 Rudolf, *The Present Status of the Film in China*, 90.
18 "The Kinema in China," *New York Times*, 17 June 1925.
19 Laurentina Paler-Calmorin and Melchor A. Calmorin, *Statistics in Education and the Sciences*, 125. Manila: Rex Book Store, 1997.
20 Sedgwick, Cinemagoing in Portsmouth during the 1930s, 71.
21 A study on the Hong Kong film market in the 1930s is beyond the ambition of this book. It is reported that "a number of pictures were exhibited in Hongkong before being screened in Shanghai, and this was solely due to the Sino-Japanese hostilities in Shanghai." In addition, "Hongkong has almost as big a cinema population as Shanghai" (American Film Distributor, "Shanghai Films A Vindication," *The North China Herald*, 17 May 1932).
22 North, "The Chinese Motion-Picture Market," 2.
23 Ibid.
24 "Motion Pictures in China," 29.
25 Ibid.
26 "A Survey of the Film Production Industry in Shanghai/滬市電影製片業近況調查," Economic Bulletin on Shanghai Economy/申時經濟情報, 1 May 1935.
27 Excerpt from A. Krisel's Letter of July 4, 1935. United Artists Corporation Records. Series 1F: Black Books, Foreign Statistics. Madison: Wisconsin Historical Society Archives.
28 Report on Examination of Accounts for the Period from 1 January to 30 December, 1933, 1934, 1935, 1936, Fox Film, Federal Inc. U.S.A., Shanghai, 20

Century-Fox, 1930–1949. Department of State. U.S. Consulate, Shanghai, China Commercial Section. College Park, Maryland: National Archives and Records Administration. Record Group 84, Series: China Trade Act Company Files, 1925–1949.
29 "Motion Pictures in China," 37–38.
30 Ibid., 58.
31 Ibid.
32 "The Chinese Film Industry," *People's Tribune* IX, no. 1 (1935): 26.
33 Yingjin Zhang, *Chinese National Cinema* (London: Routledge, 2004), 23.

References

"The Achilles' Heel of Lianhua/聯華公司的致命傷," *Movietone*/電聲 3, no. 24 (1934). 468.
Advertisement, *Shen Bao*, 1 October 1934.
American Film Distributor, "Shanghai Films A Vindication," *The North China Herald*, 17 May 1932.
Bingen, Steven. *Warner Bros.: Hollywood's Ultimate Backlot*. London: Taylor, 2014.
Butrick, Richard P. "The Motion Picture Industry in China, 893.4061, Motion Pictures/69." (4 October 1932).
"The Chinese Film Industry," *People's Tribune* IX, no. 1 (1935): 26.
Council for the Foreign Settlements of Shanghai, *Municipal Gazettes*, 1932, Shanghai Municipal Archives, U1-1-997.
Excerpt from A. Krisel's Letter of July 4, 1935. United Artists Corporation Records. Series 1F: Black Books, Foreign Statistics. Madison: Wisconsin Historical Society Archives.
Fan, Yanqiao. "A Chronological Table of the Star Motion Picture Corporation/明星影片公司年表." *Mingxing*/明星, 7, no.1, 1.
Garbo Superb in Picture Grand Theatre, *The China Press*, 19 April 1934.
George Moorad, "Chinese Talkies," *Asia* 35, no. 10 (1935).
"The Kinema in China," *New York Times*, 17 June 1925.
Neale, Steve. "Introduction." In *The Classic Hollywood Reader*, edited by Steve Neale. London: Routledge, 2012.1.
North, "The Chinese Motion-Picture Market," *Trade Information Bulletin*, 1927, no. 456, 2.
Paler-Calmorin, Laurentina, and Melchor A. Calmorin. *Statistics in Education and the Sciences*. Manila: Rex Book Store, 1997.
Report on Examination of Accounts for the Period from January 1 to December 30, 1933, 1934, 1935, 1936, Fox Film, Federal Inc. U.S.A., Shanghai, 20 Century-Fox, 1930–1949. Department of State. U.S. Consulate, Shanghai, China Commercial Section. College Park, Maryland: National Archives and Records Administration. Record Group 84, Series: China Trade Act Company Files, 1925–1949.
Rudolf, Lowenthal. *The Present Status of the Film in China*. Peiping: The Collectanea Synodalis, 1936, 88.
Sedgwick, John. "Cinemagoing in Portsmouth during the 1930s." *Cinema Journal* 46, no.1 (Autumn 2006): 52–84.
Shen Bao, 14 April 1934.

"A Survey of the Film Production Industry in Shanghai/滬市電影製片業近況調查." *Economic Bulletin on Shanghai Economy*/申時經濟情報, 1 May 1935.1-15

Way, E. I, "Motion Pictures in China," *Trade Information Bulletin,* 1930, no. 772, 29.

Xu, Chihen. *A Grand Sight of Chinese Cinema*/中國影戲大觀. Shanghai: Cooperation Publishing House, 1927.

Zhang, Yingjin. *Chinese National Cinema*. London: Routledge, 2004.

7 Conclusion

Conclusion

Few film industries can neglect the impact of the United States in the past 100 years, and the Chinese film industry is no exception. Other than some moment, American film always presented in China and influenced domestic Chinese films. Even during periods when the American films were swept out China, their influences were hardly in vain. With respect to America's impact on the domestic film industry, this book claims that the influence of the United States largely relied on how the domestic industry responded to it. In this study, I have attempted to explore how Chinese film practitioners in the 1920s and 1930s actively responded to the United States and forged its modern film industry by harnessing America. On the one hand, the expansion of American films would "operate to curtail the demands for domestic films as Hollywood diverted a large portion of Chinese patrons, in particular foreign residents and upper-class Chinese with a sufficient knowledge of English."[1] On the other hand, American films could benefit the development of the domestic film industry in its global expansion. Hollywood sets an example for domestic film enterprises to imitate but also continuously innovates the domestic film industry in technology and inspires and uplifts domestic film business through competition. What conclusions about the film industry maybe suggested by the response of China to the United States in the film industry during the early twentieth century then?

First, it is not certain that the domestic film industry would decline when competing with the American film industry. The case of the Chinese film industry in the early twentieth century demonstrated how the domestic film industry flourished along with the boom of Hollywood. In the 1920s and 1930s American films dominated the market in China with respect to film quantity and box office. However, the Chinese film industry still prospered in this period. It showed competitive advantages in the reception of individual films and studio incomes in comparison with American films in China. In addition, the growth of the Chinese film industry was continuous from the 1920s to 1930s in terms of scale. The Chinese film industry completed its sound conversion in five years, a relatively quick pace. The distribution system also became more sophisticated through imitating that of America. This evidence suggests there is no fixed relation between America's oppression and the shrinking of the domestic film industry.

Second, the boundary between the American and the Chinese film industry was blurred in the 1930s. As demonstrated in the history of the cinema's conversion to sound in China, the United States served as an active force in constructing the Chinese film industry. In the field of economy, American films inspired and stimulated its Chinese counterpart. In the field of technology, the United States supplied sound-on-film technology, trained domestic sound engineers, and served as the model that local cinemas aimed to imitate. This suggests that the transnational aspects of the Chinese film industry occurred not only in the 1990s, but also in the early twentieth century.

Third, "patriotism" should not be the first and foremost yardstick for domestic film practitioners. For a long time, historical literature about Chinese film has been dominated by nationalistic sentiment and the ideology of Marxism. Fuelled by nationalism, the merchants who assisted the business of the United States were condemned as "traitors," responsible for the incursion of the American film industry. The significance of the intermediaries as a bridge between China and the United States was greatly neglected. The intermediaries introduced the advanced film systems and modern equipment of the United States into China. In addition, the merchants also directly invested in all sectors of the domestic film business. Their contributions to the growth of the Chinese film industry should not be neglected under the light of nationalism.

It is necessary to note the potential threat and limitation of the Chinese film industry under the cover of its prosperity. China's mode of production is a case in point. Although it was devoted to learning from the Hollywood system, China's mode of production differed from its Hollywood counterpart by maintaining the powerful position of director within the producer system. As I mentioned in Chapter 4, the strong position of directors may contribute to the stylistic signature, but also make the Chinese film industry vulnerable. Due to largely relying on the performance of the directors, the Chinese film industry remained small-scale, and it was hard to achieve sustainable development.

Consequently, the prosperity of the Chinese film industry was not all pervasive. A great depression swept the Chinese film market in 1935. Even worse, the outbreak of the Sino-Japanese War in 1937 suspended the pace of the Chinese film industry. Nevertheless, a basic structure of response to the United States was inherited in the film market of China in the late 1930s and 1940s. China continued to import American equipment, maintain the Hollywood-style systems and compete with American films. From 1950 to the early 1990s, American films were expelled from the sight of Mainland Chinese ordinary audiences due to the outbreak of the Korean War and Chinese and American intervention.

Films from American major companies were re-introduced into China's market in an official way in 1994 when the Chinese film industry was facing a formidable crisis. To the Chinese film industry, Hollywood's re-entrance into China's markets in the 1990s raised once again the question which this study has asked: what did Hollywood bring to the domestic film industry? Due to different political and economic contexts, China's response to the United States film industry in the 1990s could not be simply seen as a repetition of history. However, China's film practitioners and policymakers may find lessons from history.

Note

1 Richard P. Butrick, "The Motion Picture Industry in China, 893.4061, Motion Pictures/69." (4 October 1932), 47–48.

Reference

Butrick, Richard P. "The Motion Picture Industry in China, 893.4061, Motion Pictures/69." (4 October 1932), 74–75.

Index

Adventures in the Battlefield, 戰地歷險記 61, 62
The Adventures of Tarzan 115
After Separation, 別後 53
All Quiet on the Western Front 65
Asiatic Film Company, 亞西亞製造影片公司 15, 74, 90, 92–7, 102
Awareness, 覺悟 53

Bao Tianxiao, 包天笑 81
baoxizhi, 包戲制 76
Bian Yuying, 卞毓英 62
Bible for Females, 女兒經 114, 115
Big Road, 大路 39, 81, 83, 84
Boon Lay Theatre, 蓬萊 56, 60, 115
British Theatre, 大英 53
Brodsky, Benjamin 92, 95, 102, 104
Bu Wancang, 卜萬蒼 75
The Burning of Red Lotus Temple, 火燒紅蓮寺 100, 126
Butterfly Wu, 胡蝶 34, 121

Cai Chusheng, 蔡楚生 78, 79, 82, 83
Capital Theatre, 首都 58
Carlton Theatre, 卡爾登 53, 55, 56, 98
Cater Theatre, 卡德 54, 56, 57, 61, 62
Cathay Theatre, 國泰 55, 56, 98, 110
The Central Motion Picture Corporation, 中央影戲公司 61, 62, 63, 64
The Central Trading Co., 坤和 92
Chapei Theatre, 閘北 53, 113
Chekiang Theatre, 浙江 56, 60
Chen Chusheng, 陳楚生 74
Chen Yanyan, 陳燕燕 78, 81
Children of the Clouds, 風雲兒女 39
China Star Theatre, 華星 57
The Commercial Press, 商務印書館 15, 51, 74, 75
Crystal Palace Theatre, 黃金 56, 98, 110

Ding Jun Mountain, 定軍山 15
Diantong, 電通 39
Dong Keyi, 董克毅 75

Eastern Theatre, 東海 32, 56, 57, 60, 62, 98, 110,
The Flower of Liberty, 自由之花 61
Embassy Theatre, 夏令配克 30, 31, 53, 110
Empire Theatre, 恩派亞 53, 54, 56, 57, 61, 62, 96, 110

Female, 女人 114
Foh On Theatre, 福安 60, 113
Folozu Theatre, 福祿壽 58
The Fool Pays Respect, 呆佬拜壽 100
Foundling, 棄兒 54
Freedom Theatre, 自由 53
French Concession Theatre, 法租界 53, 54

Garson, Harry 36–7, 40
Gong Jianong, 龔稼農 34
Gong Yuke, 龔玉珂 39
Grand Hotel 55, 56
Grand Theatre, 大光明 98, 110, 112, 113
Great China Lilium, 大中華百合 16, 51, 76, 77, 78, 79, 85,
Guanghua Theatre, 光華 56, 57, 60, 66
Guangming Theatre, 光明 59
Guoguang, 國光 75

Han Langen, 韓蘭根 23
Helen's Babies 53
Hong Shen, 洪深 34, 37, 45, 75, 90
Hongkew Theatre, 虹口 26, 53
Hopei Theatre, 河北 59

140   Index

Huaguang Sound-on-film Motion Picture Corporation, 華光 36
Huawei, 華威 21, 34, 38, 51, 64

I am a Fugitive from a Chain Gang 115
Isis Theatre, 上海 53, 57, 62, 79, 98, 115
Israel, Arthur, 依什爾 15, 74, 92–3, 95, 103, 104

Jiang Qifeng, 姜起鳳 83
Jinan, 暨南 45

Khoonjin Whatchay, 苦力人發財 96
Kuaihuolin, 快活林 45, 117

Lauro, Amerigo Enrico 73
The Legend of Taiping Heavenly Kingdom, 紅羊豪俠傳 39
Li Minghui, 黎明暉 34
Li Minwei, 黎民偉 77, 78, 79
Lian'an, 聯安 79
Lianhua, 聯華 16, 21, 25, 32, 34, 39, 42, 45, 51, 57, 59, 60, 65, 66, 72, 76–84, 100, 110, 114, 117, 118–19, 120,
Liao Enshou, 廖恩壽 74
Liu Jiqun, 劉繼群 24
Lo Kan, 盧根 10–11, 50, 90, 97–100
The Lost Lamb, 迷途的羔羊 82
Love and Duty, 戀愛與義務 32
The Love Parade 65
Lu Jie, 陸潔 72, 76–84
Luo Mingyou, 羅明佑 16, 32, 33, 76, 77, 78–9, 80, 82, 83, 84, 85,
Lynch, William 15, 50, 90, 92, 94–7, 102, 104

Ma Dejian, 馬德建 39
Mei Lanfang, 梅蘭芳 34, 74
Meihua, 梅花 45
The Merry Monarch 119
Metropol Theatre, 大上海 110, 113
Mingxing, 明星 15, 16, 17, 21, 32, 33, 34, 35, 36, 37, 38, 40, 51, 59, 61–3, 65–6, 74–5, 76, 84, 91–3, 96, 110, 111, 113, 114, 117–18, 120, 121, 125, 126,
Modern Times 110
Monte Cristo 110, 123
Moonlight, 月光 75
Moral Treasures, 道德寶鑑 113, 118
Morning in the Metropolis, 都會的早晨 57, 59, 60, 86
Mr. Wang, 王先生 115

The Mutual Stock & Produce Company, 大同日夜物權交易所 92

Nanking Theatre, 南京 34, 110, 115
New Allen Theatre, 新愛倫 53, 54
New Peach Blossom Fan, 新桃花扇 39
Night in the City, 城市之夜 55, 60

Orphan Rescuing Grandfather, 孤兒救祖記 15, 75, 121, 125,
Orpheum Theatre, 奧飛姆 60

Palace Theatre, 中央 53, 56, 57, 61, 62, 110
Pantheon Theatre, 百星 30
Paradise Theatre, 天堂 57, 60, 62, 112
Peace after Storm, 雨過天青 35–6
Peace Theatre, 平安 55
Peking Theatre, 北京 56, 57, 60, 61, 110
POPSTAT, 111–21
Pursuit, 追求 57

Queen Christina 115

Reconciliation, 空谷蘭 126
The Reminiscence of Peking, 故都春夢 32, 77
Ren Jinping, 任矜萍 75
Republic Theatre, 共和 53, 54, 56, 60, 110
Return to Nature, 到自然去 82
Ritz Theatre, 融光 55, 98, 110
Romance of Opera, 歌場春色 36

Sable Cicada, 貂蟬 39
Shao Zuiweng, 邵醉翁 38
Shanghai Battles, 淞滬戰事 96
Shanghai of Victory, 戰功 51
Shanse Theatre, 山西 57, 60
Shantung Theatre, 山東 58
Shi Dongshan, 史東山 79, 81
Shi Shipan, 石世磐 38, 39
The Singing Beauty, 虞美人 34, 36
The Singing Peony, 歌女紅牡丹 21, 34, 35, 37
Situ Huimin, 司徒慧敏 39
Situ Yimin, 司徒逸民 39
So, This is Paradise, 如此天堂 34
Song at Midnight, 夜半歌聲 39
Song of China, 天倫 81
The Song of the Fishermen, 漁光曲 39, 83–4, 111, 114–15, 118, 122, 124
South-east Theatre, 東南 56, 57, 60, 61, 62

The Spring Dream of the Lute,
 琵琶春怨 57
Spring Silkworm, 春蠶 118
The Stone of Life, 三生石 57
Strand Theatre, 新光 34, 36, 56
Strive, 奮鬥 81
Suffert, Thomas, 薩弗 15, 74, 92–4, 95, 103, 104
Sun Yu, 孫瑜 77, 79, 80, 81, 82

Tan Ying, 談瑛 23, 86
Tan Youliu, 譚友六 79
Tao Shengbai, 陶勝百 39
Tarzan and His Mate 115
Tarzan the Ape Man 115
Tarzan the Fearless 115
Three Sisters, 三姊妹 114
Tiangong Theatre, 天宮 59
Tianyi, 天一 16–17, 21, 36, 38, 39, 40, 44, 57, 58, 76, 117, 118, 120,
Tom Sawyer 15
Torrent, 狂流 61, 62, 118
Toys, 小玩意 55, 83
Two Sisters, 姊妹花 84, 111, 113, 114–15, 118, 122, 124
Two Stars, 銀漢雙星 34

Universal Theatre, 萬國 53, 56, 57, 61, 62

Venus Theatre, 榮金 56, 60
Victoria Theatre, 維多利亞 30, 53, 56, 57, 61, 62, 110
Volcano, Love and Blood, 火山情血 78

Wang Hanlun, 王漢倫 24
Wang Renmei, 王人美 81
Wang Yuanlong, 王元龍 76

Ward Theatre, 華德 56, 60, 98
Wayside Willow, 路柳牆花 114
wenmingxi, 文明戲 96
West of Shanghai 10
Western Theatre, 西海 56, 57, 60, 62, 110
When a Brother Sacrifices, 義雁情鴛 32
Why Divorce, 新人的家庭 75
Wild Rose, 野玫瑰 81
Wind, 風 80, 83, 86
World Theatre, 世界 58
Wu Bangfan, 吳邦藩 83, 85
Wu Cun, 吳村 80, 83
Wu Weiyun, 吳蔚雲 39
Wu Xingzai, 吳性栽 77, 79, 85

Xinhua, 新華 16, 17, 39, 45

Yan Heming, 顏鶴鳴 39
Yang Xiaozhong, 楊小仲 75, 76
Yao Yuyuan, 姚豫元 62
Yihua, 藝華 16, 17, 45, 117, 118, 120
Yin Mingzhu, 殷明珠 23
Youlian, 友聯 34, 35, 117

Zhang Juchuan, 張巨川 62
Zhang Shichuan, 張石川 15, 34, 40, 62, 74, 75, 89, 91–2, 95, 96, 97,
Zhang Zhiyun, 張織雲 24
Zhang Weitao, 張偉濤 74
Zheng Jiduo, 鄭基鐸 83
Zheng Zhengqiu, 鄭正秋 15, 62, 74, 75, 84, 91, 95, 96
Zhou Jianyun, 周劍雲 41
Zhou Shoujuan, 周瘦鵑 81
Zhou Yongnian, 周永年 76
Zhu Shilin, 朱石麟 77, 83
Zhu Shouju, 朱瘦菊 76, 81
Zi Luolan, 紫羅蘭 34